YOGA
to
Master the Mind

Yoga Philosophy- Through the Lens of Vedānta

Yoga-Sûtra of Patañjali, Bhagavad Gitā, Sanskrit, Mantra, Vedānta terms, Symbolism, Pronunciations

Anjani Gharpure

ISBN: 978-0-692-82236-4

Published by:

Anjani Gharpure
New Jersey, USA
www.yogatomasterthemind.com

Acknowledgement

First and foremost, I wish to pay my respects to and acknowledge Pujya Swāmi Dayānanda Saraswatī, a distinguished teacher and traditional scholar of Advaita Vedānta, and Pujya Swāmi Dayānanda's eminent disciples, whose masterful teachings of Vedānta have set me on a lifelong journey of spiritual growth. This book is a compilation of notes taken over the course of two decades while listening to innumerable lectures on spiritual teachings by these world renowned scholars of Vedānta.

I would like to thank Swāmi Tadātmānanda for his teachings and his encouragement to take the teachings of Yoga philosophy to Yoga teacher trainings. I am forever grateful to Swāmi Parmārthānanda for his invaluable teachings, and Swāmini Svātmavidyānanda for her encouraging words to compile the teachings on Yoga philosophy in book format.

I am grateful to my husband Vishwanath Gharpure for his constant support and guidance and for taking time to edit the manuscript. I am ever thankful to my children, Radhika and Anant, for inspiring me to strive for what I believe in. I would like to acknowledge my friends Bala and Geetha Narsimhamurthy, Hema Ramamurthy and Eileen Sinett for their valuable suggestions.

Any errors in this book are the author's sole responsibility and might be due to the author's inability to unravel profound Vedāntic concepts, and not because of any lack in the teachings.

“When the five senses and the mind are still, and the reasoning intellect rests in silence, then begins the highest path.

This calm steadiness of the senses is called Yoga.”

~ *Katha Upanishad*

Contents

Preface.. 1

Suggestions.. 7

Introduction – Why study Yoga philosophy............... 9

Chapter 1: Introduction to Sanskrit Language 25-36

Key to pronunciations...................... 26

Sanskrit Language.......................... 29

Learn to read Sanskrit characters.......... 36

Chapter 2: Mantra 39-56

Key to pronunciations....................... 40

Meaning and pronunciation of Mantras.... 41

Chapter 3: The Yoga-Sûtra of Patañjali 59-166

Key to pronunciations......................... 60

A Glimpse of Patañjali's Yoga-Sûtras........ 61

Sections 1 to 5................................. 68

Chapter 4: The Bhagavad Gitā 169-261

Key to pronunciations........................ 170

A Glimpse of the Bhagavad Gitā............ 171

Sections 1 to 10............................... 178

Chapter 5: Vedānta terms for Yoga 263-283

Key to pronunciations......................... 264

Vedānta terms................................... 265

Chapter 6: Symbolism 285-324

Key to pronunciations....................... 286

Commonly used symbols in Yoga........... 287

Chapter 7: Pronunciations of Hatha Yoga terms 327-340

Key to pronunciations......................... 328

Pronunciations.................................. 329

Online Resources.. 341

About the Author.. 342

Preface

"Yoga is not about bending the body;

Yoga is about straightening the mind".

Why straighten and master the mind? Because the mind is fickle, constantly influenced by desires and the outside world. A wandering mind is the cause of sorrow, misery and bondage. Straightening and mastering the mind leads to a regulated and disciplined mind which is pure, calm, serene and inward looking. Looking inwards, one finds a permanent source of security, peace, and happiness – source of liberation.

At present Yoga is predominantly practiced as a means to physical fitness, wellness and exercise. This physical practice of Hatha yoga is no doubt important and offers invaluable benefits, but how does this physical practice prepare one to deal with the mind? One needs a healthy body AND a mature and disciplined mind in order to live life intelligently. Yoga is much more than a mere physical exercise, fitness or wellness routine. In order to understand Yoga for what it is, it is crucial to understand the philosophy of Yoga.

Scriptures about Yoga philosophy from ancient India teach a person how to incorporate Yoga in daily life and how to live intelligently. Scriptures like Yoga Sutras and the Bhagavad Gitā teach a person to rein in and discipline the mind in order to live life to the fullest. Yoga philosophy teachings lead to a mature, pure and serene mind.

A mature, pure and mastered mind is essential to understand the truth of one's own self and the truth about the nature and meaning of life. This spiritual aspect and the philosophy of Yoga teachings are often sidelined in today's world.

The purpose of this book is to systematically explain the basic essence of the teachings of Yoga philosophy as presented in the Upanishad, or the ending part of the four Veda called Vedānta. Most Yoga practitioners, enthusiasts and Yoga teachers/ instructors are not able to study the essence of these teachings in a systematic and traditional way. It is essential to learn the basics of this philosophy in a systematic way, from a traditional guru through the teachings of an authentic *guru-shishya* (student) *paramparā* (lineage).

The structure of this book

This concise book helps a person interested in the complete system of Yoga, the mental and the spiritual aspect, to understand yogic wisdom as presented in the traditional teachings. The book deals with the following subjects:

An introduction to **Sanskrit**, the language for Yoga: It is critical to get the right understanding of the role of this divine language, the structure of Sanskrit language and the importance of correct pronunciations. The book offers an explanation of diacritical marks, how to read and pronounce sacred Sanskrit words using different types of marks and transliterations.

An introduction to **Mantra**: Mantras have to be chanted correctly in order to purify the mind. It is important to learn to chant these sacred sounds correctly with proper pitch, intonations and pronunciations to derive benefits of the *Mantra Shakti.*

A synopsis of the teachings of **Patañjali's Yoga Sutras**: This text is considered to be one of the foundations of classical Yoga philosophy of Hinduism. This scriptural text includes description of *ashtānga yoga* – eight limbs of Yoga, afflictions of the mind and how to practice *Kriyā Yoga* to get rid of the afflictions and colorings of the mind with *abhyāsa* (spiritual practices) and *vairāgya* (non-attachment).

A synopsis of the teachings of the **Bhagavad Gitā**: Spiritual practices, Yoga for everyday life. Role of intense attachments and aversions in one's life, practice of *Karma Yoga, Bhakti Yoga, Rāja Yoga, Jñāna (Gñāna) Yoga* and how to apply these teachings of Yoga in one's daily life.

Vedānta terms: Many Vedāntic terms such as *Māyā, Purusha* and *Prakruti*, the five *Kosha* can be difficult to grasp for a person unexposed to the systematic and long-term teaching of Vedānta. There is therefore a chapter to systematically explain these concepts to remove any confusion arising from exposure to sources not well versed in Vedānta.

Symbolism: Exploring the profound meanings of many symbols used in the world of Yoga. The purpose of this chapter is to make a practitioner understand the deeper significance of the culture and traditions of those practicing Yoga since ancient times. The significance of these symbols is explained so that the symbols and practices are treated with respect and reverence.

Pronunciations: An introduction to accurate pronunciations of various Sanskrit words. Mispronunciations of Sanskrit terminology are rampant in the world of Yoga. An effort needs to be made to learn proper pronunciations of Yoga related Sanskrit words.

One should understand and make proper use of Yoga vocabulary in order to do justice not only to the divine language, but also justice to oneself and justice to future generations by passing on a correct and an authentic version of Sanskrit language.

Why this particular book?

- Though there are innumerable books on Patañjali's Yoga Sutra or Bhagavad Gitā, most Yoga enthusiasts today find it difficult to penetrate and decipher the precise and yet difficult (and at times confusing) terminology of the scholarly works on Yoga philosophy.
- There are books with literal translation of verses from the Yoga Sutras and the Bhagavad Gitā, many times English language fails to do the justice in translating Sanskrit words and phrases. Some of the Sanskrit words are not translatable. Inappropriate translation often leads to misunderstanding and misappropriation of profound subject matters.
- Inability to read and understand books with Sanskrit language with various diacritical marks and/or transliterations, further make these books challenging to understand. Without proper teachings and guidance, it is difficult to grasp the profound symbolism of the words, mantras and symbols used in various books because these reflect a very different cultural background.
- There are many different traditions of teaching Hindu philosophy, and there are innumerable articles about the philosophy of Yoga online. Multitude of articles with varied interpretations and explanations from different traditions causes confusion and can be overwhelming.

There is a need for a proper step-by-step unfolding of Yoga philosophy teachings and systematic learning under the guidance of a competent teacher of Vedānta. There is a way to lead a beginner through *āsana* practice step by step. It takes a while for a person to relax, gain more flexibility and awareness of various muscles and bones to get comfortable with advanced *āsana*. In the same manner, there should be a step-by-step teaching and learning and of the key concepts of Yoga philosophy/Vedānta.

Yoga instructors, yoga enthusiasts and serious practitioners of Hatha yoga once exposed to the systematic teachings of Yoga philosophy, will recognize the profundity of these teachings and it will help practitioners incorporate these teaching of Yoga in their daily life. This will also help prevent further propagation of Yoga as a physical practice alone.

This book is a summary of teachings of eminent teachers from past and present, Ādi Shankarāchārya from the 8th century CE, to modern day teachers including Swāmi Sivānanda, Swāmi Chinmayānanda, Swāmi Dayānanda Saraswatī and many of Swāmi Dayānanda's eminent disciples that the author has been privileged to be a student of, for over 20 years.

This book is meant to serve as a concise introduction to the philosophy of Yoga through the teachings of Vedānta. It is meant to be a guide and companion to practitioners and teachers of Yoga, to help them root their physical practice into the deeper spiritual realm of Yoga.

It is the hope that this beginner level user friendly book will serve as segue to a deeper study of Yoga as a means of straightening and mastering the mind.

OM

ॐ भद्रं नो अपिवातय मनः ।
ॐ शान्तिः शान्तिः शान्तिः ॥

Om bhadram no apivātaya manaḥ
Om shantiḥ shantiḥ shantiḥ

"(O Lord) Please lead our minds towards auspiciousness.
Om Peace Peace Peace"

Suggestions

The spiritual knowledge presented in Yoga philosophy is vast and profound. Study of these profound teachings is study of one's own self, a lifelong spiritual journey of self-exploration. For these teachings to bring about monumental transformation at the mind level, one requires time, open mindedness to learn and an attitude of reverence and gratitude towards the teachers who have passed this knowledge to us for thousands of years.

Here are a few suggestions for this book:

- Adequate time should be given to absorb and understand the given topic thoroughly, before moving on to the next topic.

- If the subject matter seems too difficult or confusing, then it is advisable to seek the guidance of a competent teacher from an authentic lineage of teachers. Approach a teacher who has made an in-depth study of the Vedic scriptures, including Yoga Sutras and the Bhagavad Gitā and who can decipher the deeper imports of the wisdom imparted by the sages of ancient India. Some of these eminent teachers are mentioned in "Other Resources".

- Sincere efforts should be made to pronounce Sanskrit words correctly. A simplified scheme of transliterations with minimum diacritics has been used in this book. Key to pronunciations is also added before each chapter to encourage and promote correct pronunciations of Sanskrit words.

This book is an elementary level handbook introducing the basics and is in NO way meant to replace in-depth teachings presented and taught by the eminent scholars of Vedānta.

“Nearly all mankind is more or less unhappy because nearly all do not know the true Self.

Real happiness abides in Self-knowledge alone. All else is fleeting. To know one's Self is to be blissful always.”

~ Sri Ramana Maharshi

Introduction

Why Study Yoga Philosophy?

You are in your favorite yoga class, going through *sūrya namaskāra,* your body movements are synchronized with your breath, and then there are more difficult challenging postures which you handle without any stress. There is no sign of worry, no distracting thoughts. Just complete focus on your breath and on your body moving with your breath. Finally you are in *shavāsana*, corpse pose, and you let go of everything. You are rested, feel relaxed, and rejuvenated. You hear the sound "*Om shāntih shāntih shāntihi!*" You feel amazing as you roll your mat and walk out of the class towards your car. As you drive home, you are still feeling blissed out; you are an embodiment of peace and calm!

You arrive home and open the door – all of a sudden you realize that you have not completed the work assignment for an important meeting next morning. You then find out that your child is not feeling well and you see the prospect of a long night with the sick child in your arms. Then it dawns on you that as you were feeling blissed out on your drive back from yoga class, you forgot to pick up groceries on the way home and there is no food left in the refrigerator!

So many stresses! What happened to your peace, calm and *shānti* from the yoga class? The yoga class did keep you stress free and peaceful on the mat for the duration of the class and it was supposed to keep you stress free all the time.

Now that the class is over, you cannot go spread your mat and get into your favorite *āsana* to find peace and calm, or close your eyes and try to use three part yogic breathing or *nādi shodhanā prāṇayāma* to deal with the stressful situations at hand. Nor can you chant peace, peace, peace when the wailing child is in your arms. Should you just shut yourself in a dark room to find peace and calm? How do you retrieve that peaceful, calm, relaxed feeling from your mat in the yoga class? What happened to the peace you had felt earlier?

Can the yoga class practice of Hatha yoga, physical postures be the way to get lasting inner peace and silence? Could the Yoga tradition that has been passed on to us since ancient times be only about the physical postures, gaining physical beauty and fitness and maybe little peace for the time being?

Is Yoga about finding stress relief albeit for a short time, improving flexibility, relieving symptoms of osteoarthritis, diabetes, depression, a cure for insomnia, and toning our body to look good?

Or is there a deeper and profound purpose behind the physical practice of yoga?

What is Yoga about? What is the purpose of Yoga?

Yoga is essentially about straightening and mastering the mind.

As the *Upanishad* point out "peace cannot be created; peace is your natural state. You create agitation and disturb peace. Where is the agitation created? – In the mind. You keep giving momentum to the thoughts because you do not have mastery over the mind."

"You are Peace. Master the mind and stop agitations to find peace, your natural state." In order to discover the true and lasting peace, one has to take a journey inwards within one's own self. For that one needs a healthy body and a refined mind.

The philosophy of Yoga is a sophisticated psychological analysis of the human mind. The mind is the world, and the world is the mind. All problems, all conflicts – individual, domestic, social, national, international, political, religious or economic are the results of a disturbed mind. The mind is our link to the world outside as well as a link to inner peace. By itself, the mind is neither good nor bad. It all depends on how we make use of our mind. There is an immense untapped power of the mind, and therefore transformation of mind by training and conquering the mind is life's biggest adventure.

The *Upanishad* points out:

"Mana eva manushyāṇām kāraṇam bandha mokshayoḥ"

The mind is the cause of bondage (problem, unhappiness) and the mind itself is the cause of liberation (solution, happiness). The human mind is a powerful tool, controlling everything. It controls our whole life. Happiness or misery, success or failure depends upon the mind. As you think, so you become. Mastery of mind means success in all fields of life.

To achieve this mastery one must study the mind; understand its nature, habits, tricks and the effective methods of bringing it under restraint. A disciplined, focused and refined mind alone is the solution to discover lasting peace and happiness within one's own self. Thus, Yoga refers to all spiritual practices that are geared to refine, discipline and train the mind to realize the profound truth about the reality of one's own self.

The teachings from Patañjali's Yoga Sutras and the Bhagavad Gitā address the mind and its relationship to one's spiritual growth, an issue that is greatly pertinent in this day and age. Shrinking attention spans, cognitive deficits and shallow thinking increasingly rule the day. The teachings on the philosophy of Yoga offer practical advice for training the mind to manage emotions, improve focus and concentration and to practice Yoga in day to day life situations. The immediate purpose of Yoga is to help gain mastery over one's mental processes and obtain a relatively calm and contented mind. Such a mind is essential for gaining the ultimate goal, which is the lasting peace that comes with self-knowledge.

"Calming the mind is Yoga.

Not just standing on the head"

~ Swāmi Satchidānanda

What is Yoga? What is the purpose of Yoga?

Yoga (*sādhanā*, spiritual practices) is a preparatory step for gaining self-knowledge.

The following *shānti mantra* from the *Brahadāraṇyaka Upanishad* can be employed to describe the journey of a spiritual seeker who is on the path of Yoga.

"Lead us from the unreal to the real,

Lead us from darkness to light,

Lead us from death to immortality.

Om Peace, Peace, Peace!"

Life of Yoga is evolution from the unreal, ever changing world of objects, relations, ever changing body, breath and thoughts – towards the unchanging reality which supports and sustains the unreal (ever changing). "From mundane, to divine."

Life of Yoga is evolution from the darkness of ignorance about who we are, towards the light of knowledge about the truth of one's own Self.

Life of Yoga is evolution from the mortal, fleeting mind, towards immortality by dwelling in one's true nature, the source of sublime silence, source of infinite contentment and peace.

True Yoga is about evolution. It is about gaining maturity. It is about moving from functioning at the instinctive level, to being a person leading a life of values and morals, to becoming a mature person ready to discover the essence of one's own existence. A life of Yoga is training, first at the body and breath level – keeping these healthy and fit, and then understanding, restraining and disciplining the dull and distracted mind, and finally training the intellect to delve deeper within one's own self. Why should we delve deeper within? Because the permanent source of peace, security and happiness is to be discovered at the core of our being, as the true Self.

Yoga is a path to remove the root cause of all types of misery, sorrow and limitations; Yoga is about various spiritual practices which are to be practiced not just on the mat for an hour or so. Yoga is to be practiced throughout the day, off the mat, beyond *āsana, prāṇāyāma, mudrā, bandha.*

Understanding the philosophy of Yoga as taught by the ancient sages and leading a life according to this philosophy, is Yoga.

The philosophy of Yoga is something that is seldom touched upon in the Hatha yoga classes offered at most studios and health clubs. Yoga is essentially so much more than Hatha yoga, postural yoga practice and techniques, *āsana*-based classes. Without awareness of the higher goals, the physical practice of *āsana* cannot be called Yoga. In modern times, Yoga is being prescribed for its side effects (physical fitness and wellness), while it's real goal is usually being ignored.

"Yoga is the journey of the self,

to the Self, through the Self"

~ The Bhagavad Gitā

Yoga is the science of right living, and is intended to be incorporated in daily life as it works on all aspects of the person – the physical, psychological and spiritual. In traditional Yoga, the aspirant works with and trains all levels of the being, including daily activities, personal and worldly relations, body, breath, senses and mind. However, none of these are by themselves the goal of Yoga.

The sole purpose of Yoga is spiritual. The word Yoga literarily means "to join – in order to discover the divine". The word "Yoga" encompasses all spiritual practices *(sādhanā)*. The purpose of Yoga as defined in the *Veda*-s is preparation for self-knowledge. Spiritual practices that lead us closer to the higher truth, towards Self- realization, are "Yoga".

Different "types" of Yoga vs. different "styles" of Hatha yoga

Philosophy of Yoga according to Vedānta comprises of the teaching of the following "**types**" of Yoga:

- *Kriyā Yoga* and *ashtānga* (eight limbs) *yoga* as described in Patañjali's Yoga Sutras
- *Karma Yoga:* The Yoga of action while fulfilling one's duties in the external world
- *Bhakti Yoga:* The Yoga of devotion, of surrender to the divine force or Supreme principle
- *Jñāna (Gñāna) Yoga:* The Yoga of knowledge or self-enquiry, knowing oneself at all levels through a process of contemplation and introspection
- *Rāja Yoga:* The Yoga of meditative practices. (The practice of postures called *"āsana"* in *ashtānga yoga* - the eight limbs prescribed by Rishi Patañjali are part of *Rāja Yoga*).

The sages had realized that a sick, weak and impure body was an obstacle to any endeavor to sit still, become silent and focus the mind on one point for the practice of meditation. In order to advance on the path of *Rāja Yoga*, to prepare the body and mind for the practice of meditation, the yogis developed a preparatory practice, a system which is called Hatha yoga.

Thus, it should be very clear that the practice of Hatha yoga is a very small part of the entire scheme of Yoga.

There are different **"styles"** of Hatha yoga e.g. Vinyāsa style, Iyengar style, Ashtānga style, Yin or Restorative style, Kundalini style.

These various styles focus on various aspects of the physical practice of Hatha yoga. Most of the modern "styles" of Yoga did not exist a few decades ago, while Yoga itself is thousands of years old. The purpose for working with the physical body and breath is so that the body is not an obstacle in practices such as Yoga meditation, contemplation, prayer and self-discovery.

Without any awareness of the higher goals of Yoga, the physical practice of Hatha yoga on its own cannot be called Yoga, and is incomplete. The physical practice of *āsana* has to lead one towards the spiritual dimensions of Yoga, followed by the yogic wisdom which allows further exploration of the spiritual beauty within oneself.

Mr. Iyengar in his books "Light on Yoga" and "Tree of Yoga" says this about the real purpose of Yoga practice:

"To practice yoga is to unite the body with the mind. For the cultured person it is also to unite the mind with the intelligence and for the still more highly cultured person it is to unite the body, mind and intelligence with *ātman (ātmā).*"

Upon analysis, it becomes clear that Hatha yoga is a preparatory step to prepare a healthy body. With a healthy body, one is ready for work towards a healthy mind. Hatha yoga opens the door to the real purpose of Yoga, spiritual practices, to realize profound truths about the essence of everything. The peace and happiness sought by the yoga practitioner does not come from physical achievements from Hatha yoga, but from a deep and well- assimilated understanding of one's true nature.

In *Katha Upanishad*, sages describe Yoga thus:

"When the senses are stilled, when the mind is at rest, when the intellect wavers not- then, say the wise, one has reached the highest stage.

This steady control of the senses and the mind is defined as Yoga."

Seers and sages worked for Self-realization through various spiritual practices. As Swami Sivānanda says: discrimination, dispassion, determination (at the mind level) and discipline (at the body and mind level) are indispensable for the one who is on the spiritual path and these can be developed with various practices of Yoga, namely *Karma Yoga, Bhakti Yoga, Rāja Yoga* (including Hatha yoga, *ashtānga yoga*) and *Jñāna (Gñāna) Yoga.*

"Yoga is an internal practice. Rest is just a circus"

~ K. Pattabhi Jois

It is perfectly all right for one to be practicing any style of Hatha yoga and be content with one's physical practice of *āsana* and *prāṇāyāma.* It is one's choice to stop at this initial stage of Yoga and work on keeping the body healthy, fit, toned and perfect with Hatha yoga.

This would be like deciding to climb a tall mountain. Upon reaching the foothills of the mountain, one decides to stay at the foothills and not climb up the mountain. One has to be aware of the fact that the foothills are a part of the mountain no doubt, but foothills are not the mountain in its entirety. One cannot claim that one has climbed up the mountain just by staying at the foothills of the mountain!

Āsana, physical practice (of any style) with the goal of fitness, wellness and physical beauty alone, is NOT Yoga!

The history of Yoga philosophy teachings

Tradition says that yogic science was a divine gift revealed by Lord *Shiva*, the Lord of Yoga, to ancient sages for the humankind to realize their inherent divine nature.

This wisdom has been passed on for centuries through authentic teachings, through *guru-shishya* (student) *paramparā* (lineage).

Some of the first teachers who brought Yoga to the Western world were Swāmi Rama Tirtha in 1902, Paramhansa Yogānanda in 1920 and other disciples of Swāmi Sivānanda of Rishikesh. These teachers stressed upon the spiritual aspects of Yoga. They taught Vedānta as the philosophy of self-realization and presented Yoga as the methodology to achieve it.

Unfortunately, over the last few decades, physical postures, *āsana* practice has gained importance, and the philosophy of Yoga and spiritual aspects have been forgotten. Yoga masters like B.K.S. Iyengar, K. Pattabhi Jois, T. Krishnamāchārya and Swāmi Satchidānanda made it imperative that their students in the West understood Yoga philosophy through the teachings of Vedānta. Earlier Yoga teachers trained by these masters had to go through rigorous training, not just to learn various *āsana, prāṇāyāma, kriyā* or *bandha,* but also to understand the complete system of Yoga and the philosophy which lives and breathes through the physical practice.

However, present day 200, 300 or 500 hours teacher training courses, online teacher trainings and other specialized teacher training programs do not have the time and may not have the means or the expertise to delve into the teachings of Yoga philosophy.

There are various other conflicting interests at play, such as, resistance in exploring eastern scriptural based teachings, incentive to make quick and fast money, name and fame. These and other reasons dissuade many teacher training programs from spending training hours for important philosophy teachings.

Many yoga teacher training programs minimize or completely avoid, ignore or dilute the authentic teachings of Yoga. There are spiritual words and phrases like "love", "divine" "find your truth" and other words interwoven in the physical practice but essentially, the spiritual aspect of the teachings of Yoga has fallen to the sidelines. The result is that today very few Yoga teachers (and consequently Hatha yoga practitioners) know about the teachings of Yoga-Vedānta or the essence of Yoga philosophy.

It is unfortunate that there is much confusion about what Yoga is, and about the terminology. For example, many do not know the difference between *ashtānga* style of Hatha yoga versus *Ashtānga Yoga* as presented by Patañjali. There is confusion about why it is helpful to study the Bhagavad Gitā (to get an idea about how Yoga is applied in daily life).

There is confusion, for example, about the study of *pancha* (five) *kosha*, confusion between *maya* (e.g. *anna**maya**, prāṇa**maya***) meaning "composed of/made of" which is different from *Māyā (Prakruti, Shakti).*

Mispronunciations are unfortunately rampant, *"āsana"* pronounced as "asaanaa", *"ājñā"* pronounced as "aajnaa" or even "aahnaa" by few Spanish speakers. The word *"chakra"* often gets pronounced as "shakra".

Sanskrit is a very precise language.

If pronounced incorrectly, the word has absolutely no meaning or can even have a completely different meaning than the intended one. For example, there is a tremendous difference between the meaning of *mala* (waste) versus a *mālā* (string, garland)! One has to know how to read diacritical marks in order to get correct pronunciation and the meaning.

If one is to call oneself a "yogi", or teach "yoga" one should understand the philosophy and the appropriate pronunciation of the terminology at least at a basic level.

If we go to a science teacher, (who may or may not be a scientist) to learn basics of the subject of science, we still expect that science teacher to have proper and complete understanding of the subject matter, science. If we go to a ballet teacher (who may or may not be performing ballet dancer) to learn ballet, we go with the assumption that this ballet instructor knows what the purpose of practicing *demi-plié* and *relevé,* and knows how to pronounce these words properly, even if he/she is not a native speaker of French language.

The same principle should apply to an instructor of Yoga. One who teaches Yoga should be well grounded in the understanding of what Yoga is, and in the basics of Yogic wisdom.

A Yoga instructor may or may not be interested in Yoga philosophy or plan to teach Yoga philosophy in *āsana* based class, but when one calls oneself a Yogi or a Yoga teacher, it is expected that he/she should know what Yoga is about in its entirety. Even though he/she might not have learnt Sanskrit from an early age, if one is teaching Yoga, the teacher should be able to say simple Hatha yoga related words correctly and should know the meaning of these words.

Why is there a demand from a science teacher or a ballet instructor for proper training and not from a Yoga instructor? Is it because there is no authority demanding it?

Āsana practice can just be a form of exercise, aerobics, gymnastics or *āsana* practice can be a gateway to deeper spiritual teachings with a proper background of the Yogic wisdom.

Usage of relevant Yoga terms, their pronunciations, understanding and awareness of the higher goals of Yoga should be a requirement for anyone who would like to teach Yoga, even if one decides to teach just the physical aspect of *āsana* practice in a regular yoga class setting.

What about Yoga in future?

A study of the philosophy of Yoga alone will help keep the authenticity of the teachings of Yoga – teachings which we can pass on to future generations with pride. Just as it is our responsibility to preserve this earth, the environment, art and science, music and craft, so also it is our duty and responsibility to keep the authentic teaching of the philosophy of Yoga intact and pass them to future generations without diluting or destroying the essence of Yoga.

The only way this can be done is by preserving the teachings of the philosophy of Yoga in its original state and then passing it on to our children and subsequently to future generations. If there is a proper understanding of the broader aspects of Yoga, complete Yoga, then we will pass this profound complete knowledge of Yoga to our future generations.

The study of the philosophy of Yoga will ensure that people do not misappropriate a cultural heritage and taint the ancient heritage which is revered and has been passed on for generations. The knowledge of Yoga has been given freely from a teacher to a student for ages.

A question that everyone associated with modern day yoga should ask is: now after many centuries, can and should this knowledge be misappropriated and uprooted from its rich past?

"Yoga is not an ancient myth buried in oblivion.

It is the most valuable inheritance of present.

It is the essential need of today, and
the culture of tomorrow."

~ Satyananda Saraswati

If there is a serious lack of training of the basics of philosophy and language of Yoga today, we might surely derive monetary gains, name and fame now but will pass on a garbled Yoga to future generations, which does not make any sense! The choice is ours.

It is very correctly said: "Yoga in the West has only scratched the surface of the greater Yoga tradition. The Yoga community in the West is currently at a crossroads. Its recent commercial success can be used to build the foundation for a more profound teaching, aimed at changing the consciousness of humanity. Or it can reduce Yoga to a mere business that has lost connection with its spiritual heart. The choice that Yoga teachers make today will determine this future." ~ Dr. David Frawley

Should one participate in the propagation of the new modern and popular version of yoga – commodified and marketed as a physical practice and lose the character of Yoga as a spiritual discipline? The consequences of our decisions today will impact lives of future generations.

"Am I being true to Yoga?" is the question each Yoga enthusiast, each practitioner and each Yoga instructor needs to ask themselves.

OM

"A quiet mind is all you need. All else will happen rightly, once your mind is quiet."

~ Sri Nisargadatta Mahārāj

"Happiness depends on what you can give, NOT on what you can get."

~ Swāmi Chinmayānanda

"Give the world the best you have,

and the best will come back to you."

~ Swāmi Dayānanda Saraswatī

"It is NOT wrong to be an ignorant;

it is an error to CONTINUE to be an ignorant."

~ Swāmi Dayānanda Saraswatī

Chapter 1

Introduction to Sanskrit Language

How to read Diacritical marks

Pronunciation key for Sanskrit transliteration characters

All Sanskrit words in this book have been transliterated using Roman letters.

The International Alphabet of Sanskrit transliteration (IAST) uses a large number of diacritical marks which can often confuse a non-academic reader. A simplified scheme of transliterations with minimum diacritics has been used in this book to encourage and promote correct pronunciations of Sanskrit words.

Guide to pronunciation for commonly mispronounced characters:

a (short) sounds like u in sun or up.
Sanskrit "a" is **never** "a" in - at, agent, charge

ā (long) sounds like "aa" in father, car, far

i (short) sounds like "i" in pin

ī (long) sounds like "i" in pizza

u (short) sounds like "u" in put

ū (long) sounds like "u" in rule

jñ the consonant cluster found in many words is derived from the root **jña** (to know).

It can be pronounced as "nny", or "dny", or "gy", **never** j-n.

The word for wisdom *"prajñā"* is pronounced *prannyaa, pradnyaa*, or *pragyaa*.

Never as **"***praj-nyaa*" or "*praj-naa*"

ñ is a palatal nasal, sounds like "ny" in canyon

ṇ sounds like "n" in under

ḥ is a slight aspiration after a vowel, at the end of a word or before a consonant

ś or **ṣ** may both be pronounced as English "sh" in shine

c sounds like "ch" in church; **never** like "k" as in car

g is always a hard "g" as in god, **not** soft "g" as in gym

o sounds like "o" in opal, as in *loka* (world). Sanskrit "o" is **not** short like "o" in pot

ṛ sounds like "r" in grind, as in *Kṛshṇa (Krishna)*

ṃ sounds like "n" in French bon, conforms to preceding vowel

There are two other transliteration schemes used in various books. One is Harvard-Kyoto Convention system of transliterations using capital letters instead of diacritical marks, also known as ITRANS. And the other one is using all Roman letters.

Please see below a few examples of words using diacritical marks of IAST (The International Alphabet of Sanskrit Transliteration), HK (ASCII) or ITRANS and Roman letters.

Saṃskṛta (SaMskRita, Samskrita) – sounds like "r" in drama

japa – sounds like "u" in but

āsana (Asana, aasana) – sounds like "a" in father

prāṇāyāma (prANAyAma, praanaayaama) – sounds like "ṇ" in under, "a" in father

akśarāṇi (akSharANi, aksharaani) – sounds like "s" in shine, "ṇ" in under

dhyāna (dhyAna, dhyaana) – sounds like "a" in father

shakti – sounds like "u" in but

bīja (bIja, biija) – sounds like "ee" in feel

chakra – sounds like "ch" in China

ājñā (AgnyA, aagyaa or aagnyaa) – sounds like "gn" in ignite

śānti (shAnti, shaanti) – sounds like soft "t" in pasta

mahāmṛtyunjaya (mahAmRityunjaya, mahaamrityunjaya) – MahA + mRityun + jaya

pūrṇa (pUrNa, poorna) – sounds like "u" in rule, "ṇ" in under

Introduction to Sanskrit Language

The Language for Yoga

The word Sanskrit comes from *saṃskṛta* meaning refined. The word Sanskrit can be translated as "put together, well or formed; refined, adorned, highly elaborated". The pre-classical form of Sanskrit is known as *Vedic Sanskrit,* with the language of the *Rig Veda* being the oldest and most archaic stage preserved, its oldest core dating back to as early as 1500 BCE. Sanskrit is considered to be one of the oldest languages on Earth originating thousands of years ago. Sanskrit is one of the richest legacies given by the seers and sages for the benefit of the mankind.

"Sanskrit language has been universally recognized by those competent to form a judgment, as one of the most magnificent, the most perfect, the most prominent and wonderfully sufficient literary instrument developed by the human mind"

~ Sri Aurobindo

Over thousands of years, many scholars have contributed to Sanskrit literature and scriptures. The collection of Sanskrit literature encompasses poetry and drama as well as scientific, technical, philosophical, religious and spiritual texts. There is no branch of knowledge that has not been discussed in Sanskrit language. Each branch of knowledge has been thoroughly investigated and systematically documented for the benefit of entire mankind.

There are guidelines which govern the structure and writing style of a literary composition. With elaborate and perfect grammar rules, pristine poetry, wide ranging usage of synonyms and metaphors, Sanskrit language has been a linguist's and philologist's delight for many centuries. Sanskrit continues to be widely used as a ceremonial language in Hindu religious rituals and even Buddhist practices in the forms of hymns and mantras (*Oṃ maṇi padme hūṃ* is a Sanskrit mantra). Sanskrit continues to be a highly respected and revered language for the practitioners of eastern religions.

Sanskrit is spoken regularly in some villages and traditional institutions. Today Sanskrit is listed as one of the 22 scheduled languages of India and is an official language of the state of Uttarakhand in northern India.

There are ongoing efforts at making the language more accessible to everyone by organizations such as Arsha Vidya Gurukulam, Chinmaya Mission centers, Samskrita Bharati and many other renowned institutions in the East and West.

What is the importance of Sanskrit language in the practice of Yoga?

More and more people are beginning to realize that there is a deep, rich philosophy behind Hatha yoga *(āsana/prāṇāyāma)* practice and that Sanskrit is the language by which that philosophy lives, breathes, and flows.

By understanding the basics and using Sanskrit words, Hatha yoga practitioners can comprehend and express spiritual concepts that are not readily conveyed in English.

The language of Yoga is deeply intertwined with the Sanskrit language; therefore, Sanskrit should be used properly and accurately in all Yoga classes.

It is said the Sanskrit terms are believed to provide a therapeutic benefit when pronounced and heard. When Sanskrit words are pronounced correctly, the sounds articulated in various parts of the mouth and throat, strike the palate at multiple reflex points. This not only stimulates energy in numerous meridians by awakening dormant parts of the brain, but also enhances the circulation and flow of energy throughout our body. As one of the Sanskrit scholars has rightly said, the study of Sanskrit language is a study of the science of vibrations. Therefore it is advised to appreciate and embrace the sounds of Sanskrit language.

Yoga class instructors and enthusiasts are not required to learn the language with innumerable grammar rules and Sanskrit language in its entirety. However it is crucial to learn basic meanings and **correct pronunciations** of the words, vocabulary and terminology used for Yoga practice. From the very beginning, it's crucial to **avoid** the Sanskrit **mispronunciations** that are rampant in the Yoga industry in the West. Correct pronunciation will help a practitioner of Hatha yoga tap into the essence of Sanskrit and extract full benefit of its energetic vibrations.

These pronunciations might sound difficult and the idea of using these Sanskrit words might seem daunting to begin with; however as with any foreign language, what is difficult initially will get easier with time. Any new language can be learned with proper guidance, with repetitions andpractice.

It is initially difficult to learn different *āsana* (physical postures), learn difficult words of anatomy and the dos and don'ts of yoga *āsana* practice.

Similarly, using Sanskrit words will be challenging initially and will get easier with time. It will be mastering a new skill, which will have rewards and benefits like boosting brain power. As the brain works out the meaning of various words and makes full use of this new language, it will sharpen other skills such as reading, negotiating, and problem-solving. Thus the more use of the left hemisphere of the brain, the better will be one's cognitive abilities!

Correct pronunciation is the heart of Sanskrit language

Sanskrit is called "*deva bhāshā*"; "*deva*" is God and "*bhāshā*" is language. Sanskrit language is held to be of divine origin, revealed to the ancient *Rishi* along with the *Veda,* which are the first compositions in Sanskrit. Each and every syllable of the language is believed to be sacred and has a presiding deity. Thus proper care and attention must be used when speaking these divine sounds.

Linguists and various scientific studies agree that the structure of the Sanskrit language is flawless. There are 48 sounds/letters in the Sanskrit script and these are formed in five distinct areas of the mouth. The letters are arranged very scientifically so the simple vowels come first, then the diphthongs, then the consonants in uniform groups according to their point of pronunciation. This allows for perfect phonetic accuracy.

Every Sanskrit letter has a **precise sound** in every word, **all the time** (no silent alphabet or different pronunciations at different times). The precision of Sanskrit stems from the unparalleled detail on how the actual sounds of the alphabet are structured and defined. The sounds have a particular place in the mouth, nose and throat that can be defined.

From the very beginning, these sounds have not changed and will never change. This is why in Sanskrit the letters are called the "indestructible" (*aksharāṇi*).

For example in English language, there is a difference when the words "rough" and "dough" are spoken. The "ci" in "special" is different from the "ci" in "cinema". In English we have different options to pronounce the vowel "a" in words "far", "fat", "fall", "another". However in Sanskrit language, everything follows rules, and nothing is left to chance from the humble origin of a letter to the most sophisticated philosophical idea.

Sanskrit stands out for the beauty of its sound, the precision in its pronunciation and the reliability as well as thoroughness in every aspect of its structure. This is why Sanskrit has never fundamentally changed unlike all other languages. It has had no need to change being the most perfect language of mankind.

What is *sandhi,* "joining" rules?

Sanskrit language has rules that apply when two words are combined to form a single word. These are called *sandhi,* meaning "joining" rules. The *sandhi* rules specify what must be done in the case of vowels and consonants. Essentially, when a new word is formed, the vowel in the last *"akshara"* (letter) of the first word, and the starting vowel in the second word will be combined to form another vowel which will be inserted to bridge the two words.

The important primary rule of vowel *sandhi* is that two Sanskrit vowels cannot be placed together (one following the other). This means that when 2 vowels A and U are next to each other, a + u always becomes O.

Although at times OM word is grammatically deconstructed into a-u-m (when explaining the symbolism), **OM word should not be written or pronounced as "aum".** The "a" and "u" always join (as per the rules of *sandhi,* joining) to become "o".

Unlike most other languages of the world, every word in Sanskrit is derived from a root. There are 2012 roots called *"dhātu"*. Suffixes and prefixes are added to a root to create words.

To facilitate pronunciation and understanding of the names of *āsana* in yoga, it will be helpful to gain an understanding of the root words from which the names of different yoga *āsana* are derived.

The pronunciation guide and the figure on the next page show the source of different sounds, and their placement in the mouth. What follows is the alphabet chart in *Devanāgarī* script. Since the 19th century *Devanāgarī* is the main script used to write Sanskrit.

Pronunciation guide:

1- **GUTTURAL** — the back of the tongue, of or pertaining to the throat

2- **PALATAL** — the flat of the tongue, articulated with the blade of the tongue held close to or touching the hard palate

3- CEREBRAL — retroflex, articulated with the tip of the tongue curled upward and back against or near the juncture of the hard and soft palates

4- DENTAL — articulated with the tongue tip touching the back of the upper front teeth or immediately above them

5- LABIAL — involving lip articulation

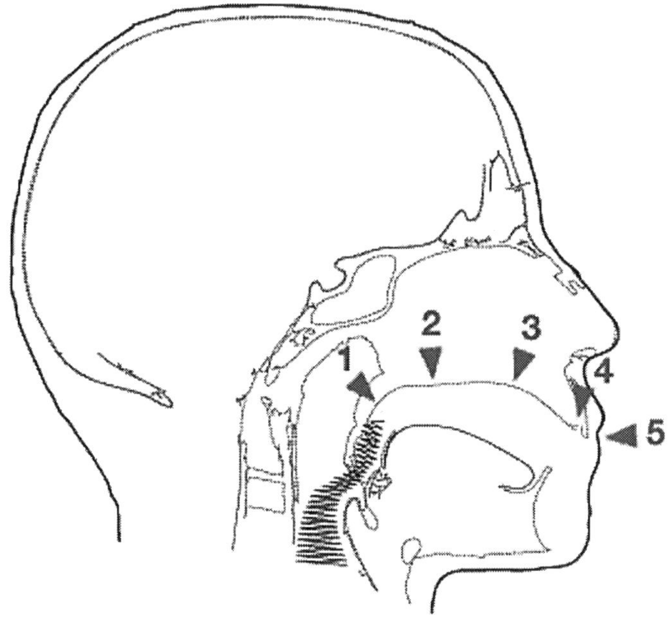

Learn to read Sanskrit characters

<u>Vowels</u>

अ	**आ**	**इ**	**ई**	**उ**	**ऊ**	**ऋ**	**ॠ**	**ऌ**	**ए**	**ऐ**	**ओ**	**औ**	**अं**	**अः**
A	**ā**	**i**	**ī**	**u**	**ū**	**ṛ**	**ṝ**	**ḷ**	**e**	**ai**	**o**	**au**	**aṁ**	**aḥ**

<u>Consonants</u>

	Hard		Soft		Nasals
	Unaspirated	Aspirated	Unaspirated	Aspirated	
Guttural	**क**	**ख**	**ग**	**घ**	**ङ**
	ka	**kha**	**ga**	**gha**	**ṅa**
Palatal	**च**	**छ**	**ज**	**झ**	**ञ**
	ca	**cha**	**ja**	**jha**	**ña**
Cerebral	**ट**	**ठ**	**ड**	**ढ**	**ण**
	ṭa	**ṭha**	**ḍa**	**ḍha**	**ṇa**
Dental	**त**	**थ**	**द**	**ध**	**न**
	ta	**tha**	**da**	**dha**	**na**
Labial	**प**	**फ**	**ब**	**भ**	**म**
	pa	**pha**	**ba**	**bha**	**ma**

Semi Vowels **य ya र ra ल la व va**

Sibilants **श śa ष ṣa स sa,** *Aspitrated* **ह ha**

Please visit:
www.yogatomasterthemind.com for a comprehensive chart

OM

असंयतात्मना योगो दुष्प्राप इति मे मतिः ।
वश्यात्मना तु यतता शक्योऽवाप्तुमुपायतः ||३६||

Asamyatātmanā yogo dushprāpa iti me matiḥ|
vashyātmanā tu yatatā shakyo vāptum upāyataḥ||

Yoga is difficult to gain for the one whose mind is not mastered.

Whereas Yoga can be gained by the one whose mind is mastered, who makes effort with proper means (with practice and objectivity).

~ The Bhagavad Gitā, chapter 6, verse 36

"The degree of freedom from unwanted thoughts and the degree of concentration on a single thought are the measures to gauge spiritual progress."

~ Sri Ramana Maharshi

"Complete peace equally reigns between two mental waves."

~ Swāmi Sivānanda

Chapter 2

Mantra

Key to correct pronunciations for Mantra chapter

Important words and their pronunciations

Mantra and *Japa* - **a** (short a) sounds like <u>u</u> in "s<u>u</u>n" or "<u>u</u>p", **not** like a in English "<u>a</u>t" or "<u>a</u>gent", also **not** ā (long a) like <u>aa</u> in "father" or "car" or "charge"

Shakti - **a** (short a) sounds like <u>u</u> in "s<u>u</u>n" or "<u>u</u>p", **not** like <u>aa</u> sound in "ch<u>a</u>rge"

kuṇdalinī - **ṇ** sounds like <u>n</u> in "u<u>n</u>der". **ī** (long i) sounds like "ee"

Om - **o** sounds like o in "<u>o</u>pal", as in *loka* (world). Sanskrit <u>o</u> is **not** similar to <u>o</u> in "p<u>o</u>t"

dhyāna, upānsanā - **ā** (long a) sounds like <u>aa</u> in "f<u>a</u>ther" or "c<u>a</u>r"

Chakra - **ch** sounds like <u>ch</u> in "<u>ch</u>ina". **Never** like <u>ch</u> in "<u>ch</u>icago"

Mūlādhāra - Moola (root) + aadhaara (support)
Svādhishthān - Sva (one's) + adhisthaana (own place)
Maṇipūra - Maṇi (precious stone) + poora (filled)
Anāhata - Anaahata (unstruck, intact)
Vishuddha - Vi + shuddha (very pure, clear)
Ajñā - aagnyaa, aagyaa (command), **never** like "j" sound in "village"
Sahasrāra - Sahasra (thousand) + aara (spoked)

Om śāntiḥ śāntiḥ śāntiḥ is pronounced as:
Om shaanti-shaanti-shaantihi

*Please see pronunciation of all mantra-s in the chapter

For more on Mantra chanting: www.yogatomasterthemind.com

Mantra

A mantra is a sound, syllable, word, or group of words that are considered capable of "creating transformation", spiritual transformation. The meaning of the Sanskrit word *mantra* is traditionally defined as that which liberates *(trāyate)* the mind *(manas)* from its troubles and limitations. It can also be derived from the verbal root *"man"* (to think) and affix *"tr"*. This derivation means "instrument of thought" or better yet, "tool or instrument for the mind". Thus a *mantra* can be considered an instrument for concentration or a tool for focusing the mind.

While some mantras may invoke certain principles (such as *shānti* or peace, wellbeing) others may invoke individual forms of the Lord, *Ishvara (Ishta devatā* such as, *Gaṇesha, Vishṇu, Shiva, Lakshmī, Durgā,* and *Sarasvatī).*

The various mantras in this section are from the four *Veda* - *Rig Veda, Yajur Veda, Sāma Veda* and *Atharva Veda* which are unparalleled teachings of *Vedic* (as per the *Veda*) knowledge and culture. These mantras were revealed through *Rishi*, sages, who discovered these prayers through their enlightened intellects. *Rishi* are held in deep reverence as seers of timeless universal truths. These teachings, universal truths in the *Veda,* are not born out of speculation, therefore should not be interpreted out of the context of the teachings of the *Veda*. These mantras, prayers are always employed with the motive of obtaining the grace of the Lord for our emotional maturity and wisdom, and not for mere material ends.

What is mantra *"japa"*?

There are various mantras, invocations, mostly in Sanskrit, which are repeated mentally for meditation. *Mantra japa* or the repetition of the mantra is perhaps the most widely used meditation technique in the Hindu tradition. The purpose of focusing one's attention on a mantra is to reach the seventh limb of the Patañjali's Yoga Sutras, *dhyāna*. In the practice of mantra *japa, dhyāna* is achieved when the attention is fixed on a stream of identical thoughts created by the repetition of the mantra. In his Yoga Sutras, Patañjali prescribes that a mantra's meaning should be contemplated upon during *mantra japa*:

YS 1.28: *"taj-japas tad-artha bhāvanam"*

"Repeat that (mantra) and contemplate on its meaning."

It is important to remember not only the words of mantra for *japa,* but the deeper meaning of the mantra has to be contemplated upon (rather than mere parrot-like repetition in the mind).

What is *mantra "shakti"*?

The traditional mantras are immensely valuable because they possess a unique capacity to draw our full attention during chanting of the mantra. This capacity is mantra *"shakti"*, its power.

These mantras are prayers. Any form of a prayer connects us to a power infinitely greater than ourselves. This infinite power is invoked when a mantra is properly recited. The prayerful dimension of a mantra is an important source of its *"shakti"*. According to the *Veda,* the vibrations and sounds of a mantra are considered extremely important.

Certain schools of thought such as *Tantra* explain how the reverberations of the mantra sound awaken the *kuṇḍalinī* and stimulate *chakras*.

How should one chant a mantra?

There are very important points to remember when chanting a mantra or practicing mantra *japa*.

One should always pay careful attention to the speed and rhythm of ones chanting, as well as the correct pronunciation, and the meaning of the mantra. It is claimed that a mantra that is **mispronounced** and used inappropriately is **"asleep"** or totally ineffective or worse, it can be detrimental. While it is certainly possible to focus attention on a meaningless mantra, they lack the prayerful meaning and inherent *"shakti"* of traditional mantras. This is especially true for mantras which are chants to purify the mind.

A mantra's whole effect is based on its sound, and to get the right effect, one has to get the sound right. Thus it is essential to have correct pronunciations, speed and rhythm while chanting a mantra.

A mantra's *shakti* stems not only from is meaning as a prayer, but also from the very sounds of its Sanskrit words. Sanskrit is called *"deva bhāshā"*, language of the gods. It is held to be of divine origin, revealed to the ancient rishis along with the *Veda*, which are the first compositions in Sanskrit. Thus **every syllable of the Sanskrit language is sacred.** Therefore proper care and attention must be taken when chanting these divine sounds.

The complete benefit of *Veda mantras* can be achieved only when the following conditions are met:

1) Correct pronunciation of syllables (words)

2) Correct duration for utterance of syllables (words)

3) Correct intonation of syllables.

The *Rishi*s insisted that any changes to these mantras (which may be as simple as altering the pitch in chanting without any change in words and duration), might not give the desired results. Furthermore, mispronunciations can even lead to diametrically opposite effects. Therefore care needs to be taken in learning these *mantras* accurately by understanding and mastering the precise nuances of Sanskrit phonetics.

OM is a mantra by itself.

For the sages of the Hindu scriptures, the *Upanishad,* the syllable OM itself constitutes a mantra. OM represents manifest and un-manifest *Brahman,* Absolute Reality because of which everything exists in the Universe and beyond the Universe.

As many *Upanishad* describe elaborately, the first manifestation of *Brahman* is the sound OM. For this reason, OM is considered to be the most fundamental and powerful mantra. Therefore it is prefixed or suffixed to all Hindu prayers.

- OM encompasses all sounds possible, starting from the sound "a" at the base of the diaphragm to "m" sound ending at the lips. Therefore OM represents *Brahman,* underlying all-encompassing Absolute Reality. Also OM sound arises from silence and merges into silence. The gap or silence between the repetitions of OM represents the Absolute Reality, from which everything arises and into which everything resolves.

- In the Sanskrit language, all words come from 2012 root words called *"dhātu"*. OM comes from the root *"av"* which means "to protect". As *Brahman,* Absolute Reality is the substratum or underlying cause of everything, *Brahman* protects existence of everything.
- OM symbolically represents the waking, dream and deep sleep states. Everyone has lifelong experiences rooted in the waking, dream and deep sleep states. According to *Mundaka Upanishad* the sound "OM" can be deconstructed for explanation purposes only, into 3 letters "a, u, m".

How is OM a symbol for *Ishvara,* the Lord as the creator, sustainer and resolver of the Universe?

The sound "a" represents the waking state – representing creation of the Universe by Lord *Brahmā* (NOT *Brahman*) who is the form of *Ishvara* as the creator. The sound "u" represents the dream state – representing sustenance of the Universe by Lord *Vishṇu,* who is the form of *Ishvara* as the sustainer. And the sound "m" represents the deep sleep state – representing resolution of the Universe by Lord *Shiva,* who is the form of *Ishvara* as the resolver, recycler of the Universe. Thus all human experiences are symbolically represented in the sound "OM".

What is *praṇava mantra?*

Praṇava is the Sanskrit name for OM, a sound symbol that represents *Brahman,* manifest and un-manifest Absolute Reality. *Brahman's* manifestation is called *Ishvara,* the Lord as the creator, sustainer and resolver of the Universe.

In sutra 1.27 of chapter 1 of Yoga Sutras, Patañjali talks about *Praṇava* as OM.

"tasya vāchakaḥ praṇavaḥ"

One needs a designation for that which cannot be experienced (perceived) like experiencing other objects and things. *"vāchaka"* is a word that stands in place of an actual thing, proxy, which has a deeper meaning. For *Ishvara* the designation *(vāchaka)* for the sake of meditation is *praṇava,* OM. OM is a sound symbol loaded with meaning.

For example, a flag is just a piece of cloth. Yet, we see that the constitution of the country and what the country stands for is deliberately superimposed and loaded on the flag of the country. Therefore, the flag symbolizes the country and respect shown to the flag is the respect shown to that country. Similarly, on the word OM, there is a deliberate superimposition of *Ishvara* and therefore OM becomes a symbol for *Ishvara.*

What are *Bīja mantra,* seed syllable mantras?

Bīja mantras are sound symbols like OM. Because they are one syllable long, they are called *bīja* - seed, *akshara* - syllables, *bījākshara. Bīja* mantras are usually associated with a particular deity as per the Tantra tradition. These *bīja* mantras are not usually chanted on their own, and often combined for a longer mantra. The chanting of *bīja* mantra by itself is called "*nāda upāsanā*", vibrations of sounds to help quieten the mind.

Below are some of the common *bīja* mantras, the deities and the energy they are associated with:

Om - praṇava - invokes *Ishvara*, Lord, also for pranic energy

Gum - *Ganapati bīja* invokes *Gaṇesha*

Hrīm - invokes goddess in all 3 forms and solar energy

Dūm - *Durgā bīja* invokes goddess *Durgā*

Aim - *Sarasvatī bīja* invokes goddess *Sarasvatī* and energy of sound

Shrīm - *Lakshmī bīja* invokes goddess *Lakshmī* and lunar energy

Krīm - *Kāli bīja* invokes goddess *Kāli* and electric energy

Klīm - invokes various deities and magnetic energy

There are *bīja mantras* for seven major *chakra*s:

Lum - Mūlādhāra chakra, *Vum* - Svādhishthāna chakra , *Rum* - Maṇipūra chakra, *Yum* - Anāhata chakra, *Hum* - Vishuddha chakra, *Om* - Ājñā (āgñā, āgnyā) chakra, *Om* - Sahasrāra chakra.

What is the meaning of *shānti mantra*, *mantra* for invoking Peace?

Shānti mantras always end with three utterances of the word *"shānti"* which can be referred to as "Peace". The reason for saying *shānti* three times is for the calming and removing obstacles in the three realms namely physical, divine and internal (within one's own self) realm.

- "Physical" realm or *Adhi-bhautika*: this realm can be source of troubles/obstacles coming from external world, such as from our surroundings – people, places and situations.
- "Divine" realm or *Adhi-daivika*: this realm can be source of troubles/obstacles coming from the laws of nature such as – storms, tornadoes, draughts and earthquakes.
- "Internal" realm or *Adhyātmika*: this realm is the source of troubles/obstacles arising out of one's own body and mind, such as – pain, diseases, laziness, absent-mindedness, stress.

According to the Hindu scriptures, sources of obstacles and troubles are in these three realms. When these disturbances are removed from the mind, what remains is *shānti,* which is the source of Peace.

ॐ शान्तिः शान्तिः शान्तिः ||

Om śāntiḥ śāntiḥ śāntiḥ (Om shānti-shānti-shāntihi) ll

Om! Let there be Peace in me!
Let there be Peace in my environment!
Let there be Peace in the forces of nature that affect me!

Commonly chanted *mantras*:

1. *Shānti mantra* from the *Yajur Veda,* dated 1400-1000 BC. This *shānti mantra* is to be recited before commencing one's education.

ॐ सह नाववतु | सह नौ भुनक्तु | सह वीर्यं करवावहै |
तेजस्विनावधीतमस्तु मा विद्विषावहै: ||
ॐ शान्तिः शान्तिः शान्तिः ||

Om saha nāvavatu, saha nau bhunaktu,
saha vīryaṃ karavāvahai
tejasvināvadhī tamastu mā vidvishāvahai
Om śāntiḥ śāntiḥ śāntiḥ
(Om shānti shānti shāntihi) ll

Om! May He protect us both (teacher and student) together;
May He nourish us both together;
May we work conjointly with great energy
May our study be vigorous and effective
May we not mutually dispute (or may we not hate any).

2. *Shānti mantra* from the *Bṛahadāraṇyaka Upanishad*

ॐ असतो मा सद्गमय । तमसो मा ज्योतिर्गमय ।
मृत्योर्माऽमृतं गमय । ॐ शान्तिः शान्तिः शान्तिः ॥

Om asato mā sadgamaya
tamaso mā jyotir gamaya
mṛtyormā amṛtaṃ gamaya
Om śāntiḥ śāntiḥ śāntiḥ (Om shānti shānti shāntihi) ll

Lead us from the unreal to the real
Lead us from darkness to light
Lead us from death to immortality
Om Peace, Peace, Peace!

3. Universal Prayers

ॐ सर्वेशां स्वस्तिर्भवतु ।
सर्वेशां शान्तिर्भवतु ।
सर्वेशां पुर्णंभवतु ।
सर्वेशां मङ्गलंभवतु ॥

Om sarveshām svastir bhavatu
sarveshām shāntir bhavatu
sarveshām poorNam havatu
sarveshām mangalam bhavatu ll

May good befall everyone
May there be peace for everyone
May all be fit for perfection
May everyone experience that which is auspicious.

सर्वे भवन्तु सुखिनः। सर्वे सन्तु निरामयाः।
सर्वे भद्राणि पश्यन्तु। मा कश्चित् दुःख भाग्भवेत्॥

sarve bhavantu sukhinaḥ
sarve santu nirāmayāḥ
sarve bhadrāṇi pashantu
mā kashchid duḥkhabhāg bhavet II

Om, May all be happy. May all be healthy.
May we all experience what is good and let no one suffer.

ॐ स्वस्तिप्रजाभ्यः परिपालयंतां । न्यायेन मार्गेण महीं महीशाः ।
गोब्राह्मणेभ्यः शुभमस्तु नित्यं ।
लोकाः समस्ताः सुखिनोभवंतु ॥

Om svasti prajābhyaḥ pari pālayantām
nyāyena mārgeṇa mahim mahishāḥ
gobrāhmaṇebhyah shubhamastu nityam
lokāḥ- samastāḥ-sukhino bhavantu
Om śāntiḥ śāntiḥ śāntiḥ (Om shānti shānti shāntihi) II

May the leaders of the earth protect us in every way by keeping to the right path. May there be goodness for those who know the earth to be sacred. And may people of the world be happy and prosperous. Om Peace Peace Peace!

लोकाः समस्ताः सुखिनोभवंतु ॥

Lokhāḥ - samastāḥ - sukhino bhavantu II

May all (*samastāh*) in the worlds (*lokhāh*) be (*bhavantu*) happy and peaceful (*sukhino*).

4. Prayer to Rishi Patañjali

योगेन चित्तस्य, पदेन वाचां । मलं शरीरस्य च वैद्यकेन ।
योऽपाकरोत् तं प्रवरं मुनीनां । पतञ्जलिं प्राञ्जलिर् आनतोऽस्मि ॥

Yogena chittasya, padena vāchāṃ
malaṃ sharīrasya cha vaidyakena I
Yo'pākarot taṃ pravaraṃ munīnāṃ
patañjaliṃ prāñjalir-ānato'smi II

To purify the mind (*chitta*), Patañjali presented the science of yoga (*yogena*) to us. To purify our use of words (*pada*) and speech (*vāchā*), he gave commentary on grammar to us (so that our use of words and way of speaking is clarified, distinct and pure). To remove the impurities (*malam*) of the body (*shariira*), he gave us the science of medicine (*vaidyakena*). Let me bow down my head with my folded hands to Rishi Patañjali.

5. Mantra on OM

From *Mahānārāyana Upanishad, Yajur Veda:*

Om tad brahma I Om tad vāyuh I Om tad ātmā I Om tat satyam I
Om tat sarvam I Om tat puror namah II

Om is *Brahman,* Absolute Reality. *Om* is *vāyu* (Air). *Om* is Self (*Ātmā*). *Om* is That. *Om* is the inherent, primal cause that existed before creation. Reverence is to that *Brahman* called by *praṇava,* OM!

Om āpo jyoti raso amṛtam brahma bhūr bhuvas svah Om II

You are water in the rivers and the ocean. You are the Sun. You are *"amṛta"*, nectar, ambrosia! You are the body of four *Veda*. You are the three-fold world, *bhūh, bhuvah* and *suvah, bhūh loka* (the physical plane), *bhuvah loka* (the astral plane) and *svah loka* (the celestial plane).

You are OM!

6. *Gāyatrī mantra*

The *gāyatrī mantra* is a highly revered mantra, based on a *Vedic* Sanskrit verse from a hymn of the *Rig Veda* 1700 – 1100 BCE, and is attributed to *rishi Vishvāmitra*. The *gāyatrī mantra* is not addressed to goddess *gāyatrī* as some might think. This mantra is addressed to *sūrya*, Lord as the Sun, who is called *"savitā"* in this mantra. The name of this mantra is derived from the poetic meter in which the mantra is composed; this meter is called *"gāyatrī chandas"*.

This mantra is more widely chanted than any other mantra. Symbolically, *Savitā* is *Ishvara*; Lord in the form of the Sun. Sun represents *Ishvara,* Lord as the source of all knowledge, especially as the source of spiritual wisdom. Thus, the *gāyatrī* mantra is a prayer for the light of spiritual wisdom, for enlightenment.

ॐ भूर्भुवस्व: | तत्सवितुर्वरेण्यम् |
भर्गो देवस्य धीमहि | धियो यो न: प्रचोदयात् ||

Om bhūr bhuvas svah, tat savitur vareṇyam
bhargo devasya dhīmahi
dhiyo yo nah prachodayāt (OM) ||

"Om Lord of earth (*bhūh*), sky (*bhuvah*) and heavens *(svah)*! We meditate (*dhiimahi*) on that (*tat*) divine (*vareṇyam*) light (*bhargas*) of the Lord (*devasya*) of *Savita* (*savituh*) in the form of the Sun. May He (*yah*) guide (*prachodayāt*) our (*nah*) minds (*dhiyah*)."

7. *Mahāmrityunjaya mantra*

The *Mahāmrityunjaya mantra*, also called the *"trayambakam" mantra*, is a verse of the *Rig Veda*. It is addressed to *Trayambaka,* "the three-eyed one", an epithet of *Rudra*, later identified with *Shiva*. The verse reoccurs in the *Yajur Veda*.

Whereas the *gāyatrī mantra* is meant for purification and spiritual guidance, the *mahāmrityunjaya mantra* is meant for healing, rejuvenation and nurturance. It is said to be beneficial for mental, emotional and physical health and is considered to be a moksha mantra which bestows longevity and immortality, freedom from the cycle of birth and death.

This mantra is addressed to Lord *Shiva* for warding off untimely death. Lord *Shiva* is the one to whom the Universe returns when the cycle of creation comes to an end. For this reason, *Shiva* is considered to be that aspect of the Absolute Reality which symbolizes time, change and transformation. This mantra is also chanted while smearing *vibhūti* (holy ashes) over various parts of the body and utilized in *japa* or *homam* (*havan*).

The energy of this mantra protects and guides the person chanting the mantra. And a regular practice of this mantra develops concentration and leads towards mental transformation.

ॐ त्र्यम्बकं यजामहे सुगन्धिंम् पुष्टिवर्धनम् ।
उर्वारुकमिव बन्धनान् मृत्योर्मुक्षीय मामृतात् ॥

Om trayambakaṃ yajāmahe sugandhiṃ pushṭi-vardhanaml
urvārukam-iva bandhanān mṛtyor mukshiiya māmṛtāt ll

Om! We worship the three-eyed *shiva (trayambaka)* who is fragrant with blessings and nurturing. Just like a fruit (called *urvāruka*) falls from the vine when ripe, free us (*muksheeya*) from the bondage of death (*mrityoh*), but not from immortality *(māmṛtāt)*.

8. *So'ham mantra*

॥ सो ऽहम् ॥ *so'ham*

So...... symbolizes inhalation, and is remembered in the mind along with that inhalation. *Hum*...... symbolizes and is the sound of exhalation, and is remembered in the mind along with that exhalation.

So'ham means - *saḥ* + *aham* - I am that. "I am that divinity, Self, *Ātmā*, unborn, uncreated, eternal consciousness, perfect, full and complete, the source of all peace and joy"

The *so'ham mantra* is a natural mantra and is called a universal mantra because the vibration of this mantra is already a part of each and every breath.

The mantra can also be inverted to *haṃ* + *sa,* from *so'ham* (*saḥ* + *aham*). Thus *so'ham mantra* is also called the *haṃsa mantra.* The word *haṃsaḥ* has also been interpreted as "I myself am the Swan", where the swan symbolizes *Ātmā.*

9. Special *shānti mantra*

From *Isha Upanishad – Yajur Veda*, this *shānti mantra* is chanted at the end of all studies.

ॐ पूर्णमदः पूर्णमिदं पूर्णात्पुर्णमुदच्यते
पूर्णस्य पूर्णमादाय पूर्णमेवावशिष्यते ॥
ॐ शान्तिः शान्तिः शान्तिः ॥

Om pūrṇamadaḥ pūrṇam-idam pūrṇāt-purṇamudachyate
pūrṇasya pūrṇamā dāya pūrṇam-eva-avashishyate

Om śāntiḥ śāntiḥ śāntiḥ (Om shānti shānti shāntihi) II

Om, That (*Brahman)* is Fullness. This (apparent creation) is fullness. From Fullness (*Brahman*) this fullness (apparent creation) comes about. Bringing (out) this (apparent creation) from Fullness, Fullness (*Brahman*) alone remains.

Om, Peace, Peace, Peace

II ओम् तत् सत् II

II *Om tat sat* II

"Om tat" literaly means "all that is", and refers to the manifest and un- manifest *Brahman,* Absolute Reality.
"Sat" means "truth or existence absolute".
Brahman, Absolute Reality is the truth of all existence.

Brahman is the material and the efficient cause of all that exists (for example, the material cause of a table is wood and the efficient cause of a table is a carpenter). *Brahman* is the truth, unchanging source and essence of all existence, and is the Absolute Reality.

Thus, *"Om tat sat"* means *Brahman,* Absolute Reality (denoted by Om) is the all-encompassing reality that gives existence to everything (including our body, our mind, our thoughts, and even our consciousness as our true self, *Ātmā*).

The sages discovered this truth and expressed it in the *Mundaka Upanishad* 1.1.6:

"That (*Brahman*) cannot be seen or grasped; it has no origin, no eyes or ears, no hands or feet. Wise ones perceive everywhere the eternal, vast, all-pervasive, utterly formless, unchanging source of existence."

OM

Arjuna says to Lord Krishna:

"In fact Krishna, the mind is unsteady, turbulent, strong and obstinate. I consider its control to be as greatly difficult as of the wind."

To this Lord Krishna replies:

"O mighty armed one, undoubtedly the mind is stubborn and restless. But Arjuna, it is brought under control through practice and detachment."

~ Bhagavad Gitā, chapter 6, verses 34 & 35

यथा दीपो निवातस्थो नेङ्गते सोपमा स्मृता |
योगिनो यतचित्तस्य युञ्जतो योगमात्मन: ||१९||

Yathā dīpo nivātastho neṅgate sopamā smṛitā
yogino yata-chittasya yuñjato yogam ātmanaḥ II19II

"Just as a lamp in a windless place does not flicker, similarly the disciplined mind of a Yogi remains steady in meditation on the Self."

~ Bhagavad Gitā, chapter 6, verse 19

Chapter 3

The Yoga-Sûtra of Patañjali

Key to correct pronunciations for Patañjali Yoga Sutras chapter

a (short a) sounds like u in "sun" or "up", **not** "at" or "agent"

ā (long ā) pronunciation is "aa", sounds like aa in "father" or "car"

Important words without diacritical marks:

Chapters: *Samaadhi Paada, Saadhanaa Paada, Siddhi Paada, Kaivalya Paada*

Eight limbs according to Rishi Patañjali - *Ashtaanga Yoga*

1) *Yama* - *a* sounds like u in "sun" or "up"
- *ahimsaa, satya, asteya, brahmacharyam, aparigraha*

2) *Niyama* - *a* sounds like u in "sun" or "up"
shaucham, santosha, tapas, svaadhyaaya, Ishvara praṇidhaanam

3) Aasana, 4) *Praṇaayaama,* 5) *Pratyaahaara,*

6) *Dhaaraṇaa,* 7) *Dhyaana,* 8) *Samaadhi*

5 states of the mind:
- *Kshiptam, Vikshiptam, Mudham, Ekaagra, Niruddham*

Mastering the mind with:
- *Abhyaasa, Vairaagya*

Impurities of the mind - *Klesha*:
- *Avidyaa* (soft d dental sound), *Asmitaa, Raaga, Dvesha, Abhinivesha*

Reduce impurities with - *Kriyaa Yoga*:
- *Tapas, Svaadhyaaya, Ishvara Praṇidhaanam*

Correct pronunciations for frequently chanted sutras

Athaḥ yogaḥ anushāsanam – soft aspirated sound *ḥ*

Yogash chitta vṛtti nirodhaḥ - subtle "sh" sound

Sthira sukham āsanam – kh as in blockhead

Tada drashtuḥ svarūpe avasthānam – u as in moon

llOM ll

A Glimpse of Patañjali's Yoga Sutras

Section 1

- What is the text "Yoga Sutras" about?

The teaching of the Yoga Sutras helps one deal with the colorings, agitations, conflicts, wrong conclusions and problems of the mind. Rishi Patañjali provides a systematic method of disciplining the mind. A disciplined and calm mind is essential for the discovery of the Self as *Purusha*, infinite *ānanda*. (See pages 70-72)

- Was Rishi Patañjali the creator of Yoga philosophy?

No, Rishi Patañjali was not the creator of Yoga philosophy. He identified all the teachings about the mind already elaborated in the *Veda* and the *Upanishad*, and presented these teachings in a precise and organized form in Yoga Sutras text.

The four *Veda*-s are the highest authoritative and ancient body of sacred Hindu texts and the *Upanishad*-s are the end part of the *Veda* (called *Vedānta*). The *Upanishad*-s are the essence of the *Veda*-s and the foundation of Hindu philosophical thought.

- What is the meaning of "Yoga" and "Sutra" in the text "Patañjali Yoga Sutras"?

Yoga is "to join – in order to discover the divine". The word "Yoga" encompasses all spiritual practices (*sādhanā*). Spiritual practices which lead us closer to the higher truth, is "Yoga".

Yoga is not about the shape or fitness of the body. Yoga is about training and disciplining the mind for self-realization. "Sutra" is a brief statement that compresses a large amount of information into a small number of words, in a very brief format. (See pages 75-77)

- What is the layout of the Patañjali's Yoga Sutras text?

There are four chapters called *"Pāda"* with over 196 verses. The topics are: *Samādhi Pāda, Sādhanā Pāda, Siddhi Pāda* and *Kaivalya* (or *Vibhūti*) *Pāda.* (See overview on pages 78-83)

- *"Chitta vritti nirodha"* disciplined and calm mind is essential for the discovery of the Self as *Purusha.* What does *"Purusha"* mean?

That which is full (*pūrṇa*) and abiding in all beings is *Purusha. Purusha* is Pure Consciousness, Being. This all-pervading Consciousness principle is *Purusha. Purusha* is the non-dual Reality due to which everything else exists. *Purusha* (known as *Ātmā* in the Bhagavad Gitā) is Awareness, Subject, Self, Divinity and is the source of all existence. Realization of the essence of oneself as *Purusha, Ātmā* is the discovery of limitless and boundless fulfillment, *ānanda*.

Section 2

- What do *"Chitta"* and *"Vritti"* mean from first two sutras of Chapter 1, *Samādhi Pāda*?

Chitta is the subconscious mind. It is the mind-stuff, mind-field. The mind includes perceptions, feelings, emotions, memory and all thinking.

It can be ideation, imagination, belief, and reasoning and also includes ego, sense of individuality, *"ahaṅkāra"*. *Vritti* is mind modifications, movement and the flow of all thoughts. (See pages 87-91)

- In the Yoga Sutras "realm of inquiry for a Yogi is MIND", what does that mean?

Yoga Sutra recognizes that mind alone is the cause for all the suffering and mind alone is the solution to end the suffering and therefore for the Yogi, the realm of inquiry has to be mind.

- What is Mind? Is the mind a powerful instrument or is it a problem?

Mind is a powerful instrument as well as a problem. For discussion on "mind", see pages 91-95.

- How do thought modifications, *"vritti"* get initiated according to Patañjali in Chapter 1 of the Yoga Sutra? What can be done with the knowledge of the fivefold mind activities? What are the five states or conditions of the mind?

Thoughts, *vritti,* get initiated from experiences, error, imagination, sleep and memory. Five conditions of the mind are distracted, dull, partially distracted, one pointed and restrained. What can be done with the knowledge of thoughts in our mind? (See pages 95-99)

- Mastering thoughts with "*abhyāsa* and *vairāgya*", what does that involve?

Abhyāsa is cultivating practices, lifestyle, actions, speech, and thoughts, all spiritual practices that lead to tranquility and equanimity of the mind. *Vairāgya* is non-attachment and objectivity. This allows the seeker to continue the journey inwards without getting sidetracked. (See pages 100-103)

- Sutra 27- 28 in Chapter 1, Rishi Patañjali describes OM, *Praṇava* as the symbol for *Ishvara*. What is the explanation of these Sutras?

OM - *Praṇava* literally means "that by which the Lord, *Ishvara* is effectively praised". OM, *Praṇava* symbol is a sacred syllable representing the Absolute Reality – omnipotent, omnipresent, and the source of all manifest existence. (Pages 104-107)

- Which distractions arise on the seat of Meditation and how to overcome them?

For the nine types of distractions on the seat of meditation and Patañjali Rishi's instructions on how to overcome them, see pages 108-109.

Section 3

- What is *Kriyā Yoga*?

Kriyā (Kriyā means actions) *Yoga* is a very effective three fold practice to be employed for weakening the mental clutter and reducing negative habits of the mind. *Kriyā Yoga's* three fold practice is the practice of *Tapas, Svādhyāya* and *Ishvara Praṇidhānam*. (Pages 111-113)

Tapas is penance or religious austerities, purifying actions which lead to training of the sense organs.

Svādhyāya is recitation or self-study in the context of the scriptures, and *Ishvara praṇidhānam* is to surrender oneself to *Ishvara* in order to reach lofty goals of *samādhi.*

- Surrender to *Ishvara*, Lord, who are we surrendering to?

The Infinite Supreme Universal principle is the Lord or *Ishvara.* The fabric of the Universe and the intelligent order of the universe is manifestation of *Ishvara.*

Ishvara manifests as space, time and the five elements. The laws sustaining and governing the universe, the intelligent order, is *Ishvara's* manifestation. Surrender to *Ishvara's* intelligent order that permeates the cosmos from a tiniest particle, to atoms, to space and beyond is *Ishvara praṇidhānam* as per the Hindu scriptures. (See pages 113-117)

- What are the five impurities (afflictions) of the mind? Impurities which bring obstruction in the mind and are the cause of all our suffering?

The five mental obstructions, (afflictions) that activate and motivate actions and thought processes in the mind are:

avidyā - ignorance of the truth, reality of oneself, *asmitā* - ego, the limited sense of "I" in relation to the body, mind and intellect, *rāga* - extreme attachments, *dvesha* - aversions and *abhinivesha* - fears and insecurities.

These five take one further and further away from *shanti,* peace and thus leads one to sorrows. (See pages 117-121)

Section 4

- What are *Yama* and *Niyama, Āsana, Praṇāyāma* and *Pratyāhāra?* Rishi Patañjali starts chapter 3 on Yoga Sutras with *Dhāraṇā, Dhyāna* and *Samādhi,* what is the meaning of these last 3 limbs of the eight limbs?

The eight limbs of Yoga are described in the *"sādhanā pāda"*. These eight limbs, *ashta anga,* deal with the total personality. Here Yoga is a spiritual practice (*sādhanā*) much more than *Āsana* and *Praṇāyāma,* physical postures and breathing techniques.

Each step or limb is a way to delve deeper into one's own self in order to get rid of impurities at the body, breath and mind level. These eight limbs are to prepare a seeker to realize the inner divinity, the essence of one's own self as *Purusha, Ātmā.* (See pages 125-148)

Section 5

- What is *Samyama?* What are *Siddhi?* Why should a practitioner stay away from various *siddhis*?

Samyama is the collective practice of *dhāraṇā* - concentration, *dhyāna* - meditation, and *samādhi* - meditative absorption. (Page 150-157)

- Concluding Chapter of the Yoga Sutra is about "*Kaivalya*", what is the meaning of *Kaivalya?*

Kaivalya is the permanent state of fullness, liberation. This is the ultimate goal for a seeker on the path of spiritual journey, as described in the text Yoga Sutras. (Pages 158-161)

- Having learnt about the mind, impurities of the mind, eight steps towards removing afflictions of the body and the mind, how should we put this in practice?

Just as fitness routines including *āsana* practice can result in a strong and healthy body, Yoga in its true sense as spiritual disciplines, can shape a secure personality and a resilient, loving mind.

The opportunities to grow stronger spiritually arise not only during Yoga *āsana* class or meditation session but throughout the day. Whether working with difficult colleagues, going out to eat, or responding to a child's needs, or juggling various responsibilities in life; mindfully incorporating Yoga teachings (from the Patañjali's Yoga Sutras and the Bhagavad Gitā) in day to day life, will help a person make better and wiser choices.

In addition to unfolding the vision of Self-realization, Yoga Sutras and the Bhagavad Gitā offer practical advice for training the mind to manage emotions, improve focus and concentration.

For a seeker who desires to understand and apply the teachings of Yoga, training and conquering the mind is life's biggest adventure. (Pages 162-165)

"Peace cannot be created; peace is your natural state. You create agitation in your mind and disturb peace"

To encounter the mind, one needs to practice Yoga, spiritual disciplines which include *ashtānga yoga, Kriyā Yoga,* and other teachings from the profound text – *The Yoga-Sûtra of Patañjali.*

OM

Prayer to Rishi Patañjali:

योगेन चित्तस्य, पदेन वाचां
मलं शरीरस्य च वैद्यकेन ।
योऽपाकरोत् तं प्रवरं मुनीनां
पतञ्जलिं प्राञ्जलिर् आनतोऽस्मि ॥

Yogena chittasya, padena vāchāṃ
malaṃ śarīrasya (sharirasya) cha vaidyakena |
Yo'pākarot taṃ pravaraṃ munīnāṃ
patañjaliṃ prāñjalir ānato'smi (praanjalihi ānatosmi) ||

"He who removes impurities (*malam*) of 3 kinds, impurities of the mind, speech and body by the teachings of Yoga, Ayurveda and Grammar, that foremost (*pravaram*) amongst the sages, Patañjali, unto him I am bowing down with folded hands (*prānjalihi*)!"

As chanted in the prayer for Rishi Patañjali, teachings in the Yoga Sutras destroy the impurities "*malam*" of the mind. Rishi Patañjali presents Yoga Sutras and defines Yoga as "*Chitta Vritti Nirodhaḥ*". "*Chitta*" is mind, "*vritti*" means flow of thoughts or thoughts proliferation or mental functions and "*nirodha*" means disciplining or regulating.

Yoga (spiritual practice) is for disciplining mental functions in order to lead an aspirant closer to the highest truth, to discover the inner divinity by realization of one's eternal and true identity as Self, *Purusha, Ātmā.*

"Yoga is the *nirodha* (regulating, mastering, integrating, coordinating, stilling or calming) **of the modifications** (gross and subtle thought patterns) **of the mind."**

Section 1:

Sutra 1.2- योगश्चित्तवृत्तिनिरोधः ॥२॥

Yogaścittavṛttinirodhaḥ //2 //

Yoga is the mastery, discipline of the thoughts of the mind. Yoga is restraining the mind stuff (*chitta*) from taking various forms (*vrtti*).

Sutra 1.12- अभ्यासवैराग्याभ्यां तन्निरोधः ॥१२॥

Abhyāsavairāgyābhyāṁ tannirodhaḥ //12 //

The discipline of these thoughts is by repetition and by non-attachment, (which together lead to contemplation and contemplative life). Restraint comes from practice and non-attachment.

Sutra 1.16- तत्परं पुरुषख्यातेर्गुणवैतृष्ण्यम् ॥१६॥

Tatparaṁ puruṣakhyāterguṇavaitṛṣṇyam //16 //

The extreme non-attachment, giving up even the qualities, shows (the real nature of) *Purusha*. When an individual has achieved complete understanding of his true self, he will no longer be disturbed by the distracting influences within and around him.

Sutra 1.51- तस्यापि निरोधे सर्वनिरोधान्निर्वीजः समाधिः ॥५१॥

Tasyāpi nirodhe sarvanirodhānnirvījaḥ samādhiḥ //51 //

The mind reaches a state when it has no impressions of any sort. It is open, clear, and simply transparent. By the restraint of even these impressions, which obstructs all other impressions (all being restrained), comes the "seedless" *samādhi, "Nirbīja samādhi".*

In this section –

- What is the text "Yoga Sutra" about?
- Who was Rishi Patañjali?
- Was Patañjali the creator of the Yoga philosophy?
- What is the meaning of *"Yoga"* and *"Sutra"*?
- What is the layout of the Patañjali's Yoga Sutras text?

What is the text Patañjali Yoga Sutras about?

The Yoga Sutras of Patañjali concisely outlines the art and science of meditation for Self-realization. Yoga Sutras is the foundation scripture for *dhyāna*, meditation based on *Saṅkhyā* Philosophy.

> Rishi Patañjali provides a systematic method of disciplining the mind.
>
> A disciplined and calm mind is essential for the inquiry "who am I?", and for the subsequent realization of the essence of oneself as the source of limitless peace and contentment, *"ānanda"*.

In our life we play different roles, we have a date of birth, a gender, our unique story of growing up, a socio-economic class, a status, a profession. We can be a wife/husband, daughter/son, teacher, manager, employee, seeker.... In order to function in life, we involuntarily identify with our roles and get caught up in creating false identities in the mind.

However, we remain ignorant of the truth, the essence of who we are beyond the imperfect body, breath and mind. Yoga Sutras guides us as we walk on the path of spiritual journey, with

Yoga, spiritual practices, that lead to the realization of our eternal and true identity as *Purusha,* (*Ātmā,* Pure Consciousness, Awareness).

That which is *Pūrṇa*, full and abiding in all beings is *Purusha. Purusha* is state of pure Being, Absolute Reality, Pure Consciousness. This all-pervading Consciousness principle is *Purusha. Purusha* is the non-dual reality due to which everything else exists. *Purusha* (known as *Ātmā* in the Bhagavad Gita) is Awareness, Subject, Self, Divinity and is the limitless source of all existence. Realization of the essence of oneself as *Purusha, Ātmā* is the discovery of infinite peace, fullness and contentment, *ānanda*. * Read more in Chapter 4, "The Bhagavad Gitā", pages 197-199 and 242-243*

We think that our identification with various transient and temporary roles we play and the story of our life is the truth of who we are. We go through life's ups and downs as we identify with the roles we play, and we identify with the wrong conclusions created through the false identifications in our mind.

The problem is the significance and importance we place on these transient and fleeting thoughts, feelings and emotions – vacillations of the mind. The colorings created by the mind keep us occupied in a continuous whirlpool of thoughts.

Patañjali's Yoga Sutras is a systematic exposition, a process of examining and encountering false identities in the mind. The Yoga Sutras help us to recognize that our final goal in life is to realize "Self", the reality and truth of who we are beyond the mask of false identifications. With this self-realization, discovery of oneself as Pure Consciousness, Awareness, *Purusha, Ātmā,* one attains liberation, absoluteness, limitless and boundless *ānanda.*

The teaching of the Yoga Sutra helps one deal with the colorings, agitations, conflicts, wrong conclusions and problems of the mind.
Yoga Sutra teachings leads one through a step by step process to finally realize the jewel of Divinity as the truth of oneself.

Scripture Yoga Sutra *(Yoga shāstra)* is about knowing oneself. The realm of inquiry in this text is the mind. The failure to recognize our true nature (due to mind-born confusion) is the source of all our problems. Without changing anything in the world, by just changing the mind alone, one can recognize Divinity as the essence of oneself.

Who was Rishi Patañjali, the author of the Yoga Sutras?

History and legend: Indian history attributes a sage (*Rishi*) named Patañjali with the authorship of Yoga Sutras. Very little is known about Rishi Patañjali because the ancient sages did not speak or write much about themselves, and the name of an author was of much less importance than what the text could teach. Consequently, most of what is known about Rishi Patañjali comes from ancient stories and legends.

There are a number of legends surrounding Patañjali. One legend describes him as the divine incarnation of the serpent named *Ananta* (meaning "the Infinite One", *Ādishesha*) who supports the whole universe. A devotee of Lord *Vishṇu*, this serpent wished to be born as a human. The legend states that once upon a time, *Gonikā,* a spiritual practitioner was praying for a worthy son. As she prayed to the Lord in the form of the sun, she scooped up a handful of water as an offering and asked for the blessing of a son.

Just as *Gonikā* was about to offer her handful of water to the sun, she glanced down at her hands and was astonished to see a tiny serpent moving about in her palms. She was even more astonished when the serpent assumed a human form. Patañjali's iconographical depiction is with a man's torso and the coiled tail of a serpent.

The name Patañjali therefore derives from the Sanskrit words *pat* (to fall) and *añjali* (prayerful gesture) because he had fallen from the abode of *Lord Vishṇu* into her hands, which had been held in the gesture of prayer.

Rishi Patañjali is also known to be the author of other works besides the Yoga Sutras. He is said to have written a commentary on *Pāṇini's* grammar sutras as well as a treatise on *Āyurvedic* medicine. There may also have been more than one individual by the name of Patañjali who could have written all the three works. Some historians have concluded that Patañjali lived sometime between 800 B.C. and 200 B.C.; however traditional descriptions place him earlier than that.

Was Patañjali the creator of the yoga philosophy?

No, Rishi Patañjali may have written the Yoga Sutras, however he did not create the philosophy of Yoga. The first sutra starts with *"atha yoga anushāsanam"*. This sutra, 1.1 is translated as "now begins the teaching of yoga." Rishi Patañjali himself points this out in this very first sutra 1.1 that he (Rishi Patañjali) did not discover (invent) the practice of Yoga. Patañjali makes it very clear that he was not presenting his own ideas or personal philosophy but he was the one who codified what was prevalent at that time in ancient India, approximately over 2500 years ago.

The word *anushāsanam* means more than just "teaching", *anushāsanam* means "in accordance with" or "following." Thus the whole word actually means "teaching in accordance with" or "to teach that which is already taught." The question then naturally arises is, "in accordance with what, or what was already taught?" The answer, of course, is that it is teaching in accordance with the *Veda.*

In accordance with the knowledge contained in the four *Veda*, Yoga Sutras does not present "new" information.

The Sutras classify and organize the information that is already presented in the *Veda* and the *Upanishad.*

Rishi Patañjali identified all the teachings about the mind in the 4 *Veda* and the *Upanishad* (the ending section of each *Veda*) and presented those teachings in the precise and organized form.

Rishi Patañjali has compiled the information about the mind, information about *Ishvara, Klesha, Karma, Guṇa, Purusha, Samādhi, Siddhi* and *Kaivalya* provided by the four *Veda* into a more clearly defined structure.

The *Veda* reveal the teachings of the immortal Self, divinity, *Ātmā*, the Supreme Reality (referred to as *Purusha* in Yoga Sutras), and that our goal in life is to realize "Self" and become liberated from the endless cycle of birth and death. That is exactly the goal of the Yoga Sutras as well.

In other words the goal prescribed in the *"Veda"* and "Patañjali's Yoga Sutras" is the same.

How does Rishi Patañjali describe "Yoga" in the Yoga Sutras?

"Yogash chitta vṛtti nirodhaḥ

Tada drashtuḥ svarūpe avasthānam"

"Yoga is the mastery of the activities of the mind.
Then the Seer rests in its true nature."

Yoga is from the Sanskrit root word *"yuj"*, which means to join or to integrate, to which English word Yoke is related. Based on this root, Yoga has two key meanings – to unite and to regulate. There are many different ways the word Yoga is described, "to come together, to unite, to tie the strands of the mind together."

A yoke is used to harness an animal to pull a plow or cart. The strong yoke serves both to regulate the animal's movement and also to join or unite it to the cart. Yoga means to bring together all the aspects of ourselves. It means to realize Reality, the all-pervading Divine, who we truly are at the deepest level, and that is to be realized through Yoga.

Once the obstacles and false identities have been temporarily set aside, the essence of one's true nature as Self, Pure Consciousness, *Purusha, Ātmā,* naturally comes shining through. The rest of the time, we are so entangled with our false identities that we literally do not even recognize that this misidentification with the limited body, mind and intellect has happened.

It is the reason that sometimes it is said that "we are asleep, and that we need to awaken". That awakening to the essence, Divinity, *Ātmā,* is the meaning of Yoga.

Yoga as a spiritual practice serves the purpose of harnessing and regulating the mind.

One of the classical descriptions of word Yoga is:
“To join - in order to discover the divine”

Although authentic Yoga is beneficial to many aspects of life, the real goal for Yoga is:

“The practice of Yoga has to culminate with the sight of *Purusha, Ātmā*.
From the fluctuations of the mind to stillness, stillness to silence and silence to the sight of *Purusha* is the journey of Yoga.”

“The purpose of Yoga is a journey within, exploring and moving through the various levels of our being.

The aim of Yoga is **NOT** physical fitness, stress management, medical treatment, **nor** a means of manifesting money.

Physical fitness, stress management or medical treatment, these are the by-products of the practice of Yoga!”
~B.K.S Iyengar

The word Yoga is used for various spiritual practices, ***Sādhanā***.

The word Yoga as *sādhanā,* spiritual practices, is used in the Bhagavad Gitā. In the Bhagavad Gitā various spiritual practices are described at length – *Karma Yoga, Bhakti Yoga, Rāja Yoga/ Upāsanā Yoga, Jñāna (Gñāna) Yoga,* all spiritual practices culminating in the discovery of divinity as one’s own true Self, *Ātmā*.

Hatha Yoga is described at length in ancient scriptures like *Hatha Yoga Pradipikā* and *Shiva Saṁhita. Laya Yoga* (absorption in the ultimate) and *Mantra Yoga* (perfection achieved through the recitation of the sacred Mantra) is talked about in texts like *Yogatattva* and *Varaha Upanishad.*

There are other *Upanishad*-s (from 4 *Veda*), for example: *Yogatattva Upanishad, Yoga Shikha, Amritabindu Upanishad* and many other *Upanishad*-s discuss at length teachings on the practice of Yoga, rules of Yoga and rewards of Yoga as a spiritual practice to realize that "the essence of all is divine". That one appears as many, just as the moon appears as many when reflected in many droplets!

What is a "Sutra"?

Sutra means thread, and this thread, or multiple threads weave a tapestry of insight. A sutra is a brief statement that compresses a large amount of information into a small number of words, in a very brief format. A sutra has very few words, yet is free from ambiguity and full of essence. This makes it easier for the student to understand and remember all the knowledge on a given topic.

Like other Hindu scriptural teachings, short and pithy words of the Sutra enabled oral transmission of the Yoga philosophy from teacher to student through the centuries. Sutras are used to teach the knowledge conveyed by the four *Veda*. Only prepared students, capable of understanding the high import of the scriptures were allowed to have instructions.

Yoga Sutras belong to the tradition of oral teachings where the knowledge was imparted from a master to a disciple first hand, which had the benefit of maintaining high standards of teaching and keeping the teachings authentic.

Layout of the Patañjali's Yoga Sutras text:

There are four *Pāda* (chapters) in the Yoga Sutra text.

***1.** Samādhi Pāda*

The first chapter of the Yoga Sutras deals with *samādhi,* which is meditative and spiritual absorption. Meditation is what comes after a great deal of preparation. It requires discipline to follow a systematic method of learning.

The introductory sutra in this chapter suggests that after our many actions in life, and whatever preparatory practices we might have performed till now finally we are ready to pursue the depths of self-exploration:

"The journey is inwards to realize *Ātmā*, Self, our eternal and true identity as *Purusha*."

Why does Rishi Patañjali begin the text with a chapter on meditative absorption?

Why does Rishi Patañjali not begin the text with discussion explaining basic concepts such as: what is mind, what is body, how do we train our body and mind to prepare for meditative absorption?

The reason is: most scriptures of ancient India address the most difficult part at the beginning of the text. This is a section for an advanced and mature student who is prepared, and understands basics from the study of various other scriptural texts. This student has a refined intellect, ready to delve into the deeper and profound truth about the mind and the Self, *Purusha*.

Mind

"The reason for suffering in life is due to the notion of bondage created by the mind. Mind alone is the cause for all the suffering and mind alone is the solution to end the suffering."

Mind comprises of mental functions, mind modifications which include perceptions, feelings, emotions, memory, all thinking - can be ideation, imagination, belief, reasoning and also includes ego, sense of individuality *"ahaṅkāra"*.

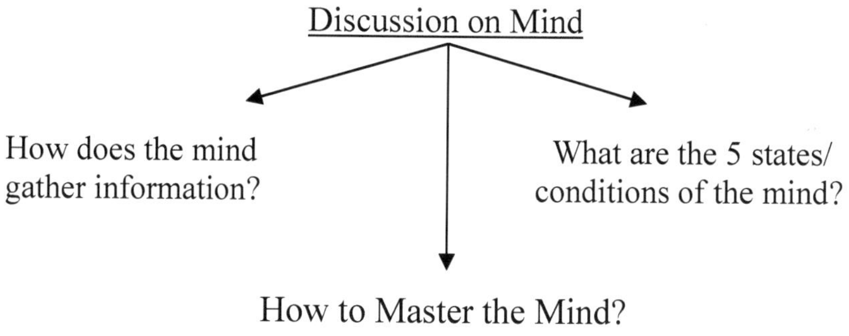

Discussion on Mind
How does the mind gather information?
What are the 5 states/ conditions of the mind?
How to Master the Mind?

This chapter describes 9 types of obstacles or distractions that arise while meditating. This chapter also explores feelings and emotions one needs to cultivate in order to counteract these obstacles.

Suggestion If one finds the first chapter to be confusing and overwhelming, a suggestion is to begin the study from the second chapter, sutra 29 of Patañjali's Yoga Sutras. With practice and perseverance, understand 8 limbs of yoga, *ashta anga,* and then study the first chapter of Patañjali's Yoga Sutras text.

2. Sādhanā Pāda

The second chapter is about the means of practice. This chapter initially discusses very important topic of *klesha,* impurities of the mind, why and how the mind collects impurities and the solution to remove the impurities of the mind.

When a novice follows the instructions given in the second chapter, the outermost sheath (body), to the innermost sheath (intellect), get purified and prepared to receive the knowledge conveyed in the other three chapters of the text.

Sutra 29 onwards talks about the first five of the eight limbs or aspects of *ashtānga* yoga. These limbs are interlinked; each has numerous facets that are revealed through study of the text and through practice.

Study and practice of these 8 limbs, *anga,* takes one to the higher stages of awareness of the body, breath and mind and finally leads one towards a life of spirituality.

1st and 2nd *anga* (limbs): *Yama* and *Niyama* prepare the ethical and moral personality of a practitioner. Integrating ethical and moral values in one's life means living a life of *dharma,* appropriate duties and responsibilities, which come with whatever role one has to lead in life.

The role of a parent, of a child, of a teacher or a student, of an employee or an employer, role as an adult, a human being, and a citizen of the society, country and of the Universe – all these roles will be played without selfish motives, without hidden agendas. Adhering to ethical and moral values will encourage a practitioner to live with a sense of responsibility and duty towards others.

3rd and 4th *anga*: *Āsana* and *Praṇāyāma* prepare the physical personality of a practitioner. A person with a healthy, fit body and a calm, quiet breath will be able to achieve much more in life than a person who is suffering from various diseases and illnesses. Freedom from the ailments of the body and breath will give a person the freedom to pursue and accomplish all the worldly goals such as pursuing health, wealth and status in society. Having pursued and accomplished goals (health and wealth) in life, one will be ready and fit to pursue the realms of the inner world, ready to take the journey inwards.

5th *anga*: *Pratyāhāra* is withdrawal of the senses from the world outside and getting ready to take a plunge within the mind by observing the functioning of the mind. Just like a turtle withdraws its head into its shell, this practitioner withdraws his/her senses, attention drawn inward to take a look within the realm or field of the mind.

6th and 7th *anga*: *Dhāraṇā* and *dhyāna* come from studying the functioning of the mind. How does the mind function, what can be done to slow down the incessant flow of thoughts? Addressing these questions will lead to concentration, and one pointed focused mind.

8th *anga*: *Samādhi* will be the culmination of all efforts and will lead to meditative absorptions with a calm, quiet and resolved mind.

As the Yogi practices and gradually attains mastery, the practice of meditative absorption will bring greater depth of experience, insight, and realization.

The eight *anga* (limbs, rungs, steps), *ashtānga* yoga, is thus a spiritual journey to prepare oneself. These eight limbs are often seen beautifully depicted as the limbs of one big tree with eight branches coming out of the same level of the trunk of a tree, where all the limbs are to be practiced simultaneously as per one's capacity. Let us now see these eight as rungs, steps (*ashtānga* pictorial depiction), like climbing the steps of a ladder. It is a step by step unfolding, each step building upon the previous step.

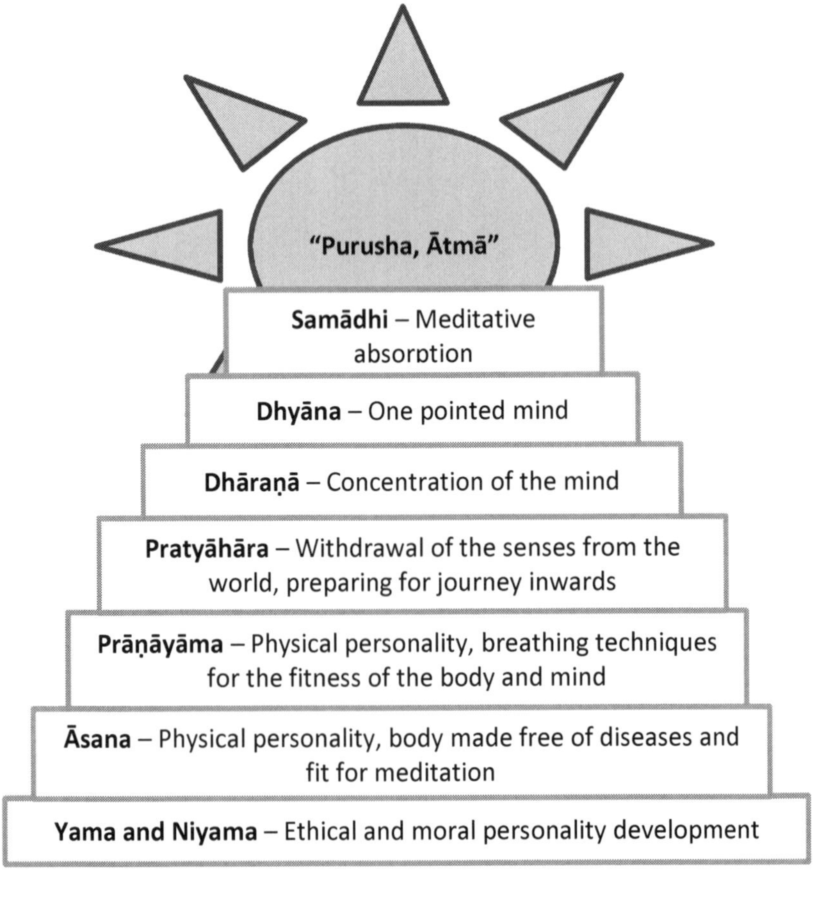

3. *Siddhi* or *Vibhūti Pāda*

The third chapter of the Yoga Sutras is about accomplishment. This chapter initially deals with the 6th, 7th and 8th limbs of *ashtānga* yoga, limbs or rungs dealing with internal *sādhanā,* the spiritual practice of *dhārṇā, dhyāna* and *samādhi*.

The later section of the third chapter discusses the wealth of effects and powers gained from the *samyama,* practice of meditation. Rishi Patañjali further goes on to explain various *siddhis*, accomplishments achieved by the training of the mind, roughly 35 effects which might be experienced by a practitioner. He also warns the practitioner that these powers can be a trap and one must not get enticed by the *siddhis* gained from the practice of meditation.

4. *Kaivalya Pāda*

The fourth and the final chapter is about liberation. It is about the subject of absoluteness. It describes discriminative knowledge that differentiates between *Purusha* and the mind. When total separation from the mind or understanding of the mind and the role of the mind takes place, *Purusha* alone remains. *Kaivalya* is reached when the Yogi realizes the ultimate spiritual reality of one's own self and that of the universe.

"When you have conquered the microcosm (the physical body, miniature universe) you have conquered the macrocosm (Universe)." ~ B.K.S. Iyengar

Kaivalya is the permanent state of liberation, of fullness. *Kaivalya* is described as total elimination of sorrow and the attainment of unsurpassable happiness. This is the ultimate goal as described by Rishi Patañjali in Yoga Sutras.

Mundaka Upanishad verse 1.16, says this about a Yogi who has realized Self:

"Wise ones perceive everywhere the eternal, vast, all-pervasive, utterly formless, unchanging source of existence."

The Bhagavad Gitā chapter 6, verse 29, Lord Krishna says to Arjuna:

"With the mind harmonized by *Yoga,* one (*Yogi*) sees the Self, abiding in all beings and all beings in the Self (*Prursha, Ātmā*); one sees the same everywhere."

Yoga Vāsishtha by *Rishi Vālmiki,* a famous Hindu text, says thus in one of the verses:

"One (*Yogi*) who has unveiled the Truth in himself, sits ever contented in enjoying nectar of his own Infinite Peace, his mind and intellect completely at rest, with no inner thought, disturbances, reveling in the Real nature of the Self."

Layout of the Yoga Sutras:

Samādhi Pāda – Meditative absorption
Discussion on Mind includes:
Source of thoughts, states/conditions of the mind
How to master thoughts, discussion on "OM"
Obstacles during meditation and ways to counteract

Sādhanā Pāda – Means of practice
Kriyā Yoga to counter *Klesha* (mental clutter)
Preparations, **external practices** (*sādhanā*)
Ethics and morals (*yama, niyama*)
Physical fitness (*āsana, prāṇāyāma*), Mental discipline (*pratyāhāra*), attention turned inwards

Siddhi (Vibhūti) Pāda – Accomplishments
Mental discipline, **internal practices** (*sādhanā*)
Spiritual practice of *dhārṇā, dhyāna* and *samādhi*
Powers gained from *samyama*, practice of meditation, warning about the trap of *Siddhi*

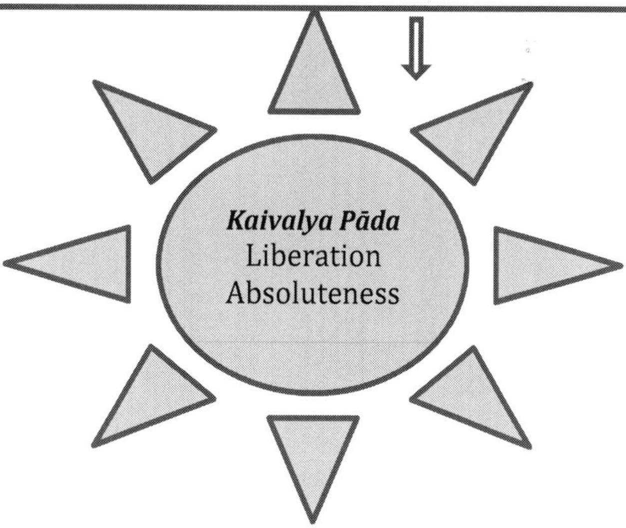

Section 2:

Sutra 1.26- पूर्वेषामपि गुरुः कालेनानवच्छेदात्॥२६॥

Pūrveṣāmapi guruḥ kālenānavacchedāt ॥26॥

That *Ishvara* is the Guru even of the former (gurus), because *Ishvara* (Lord) is not determined or limited by time. *Ishvara* is not limited by time, since *Ishvara* is the knower in the seat of intellect of all beings.

Sutra 1.37- वीतरागविषयं वा चित्तम्॥३७॥

Vītarāgaviṣayaṁ vā cittam ॥37॥

The mind also attains steadiness when it has no attachment towards objects.

Sutra 2.1- तपःस्वाध्यायेश्वरप्रणिधानानि क्रियायोगः॥१॥

Tapaḥ svādhyāyeśvara praṇidhānāni kriyāyogaḥ ॥1॥

Penance, study and full devotion to *Ishvara* is *Kriyā* Yoga. The practice of Yoga must reduce both physical and mental impurities. Yoga must develop our capacity for self-examination and help us understand that in the final analysis we are not the masters of everything we do.

In this section -

- What do *"Chitta"* and *"Vritti"* mean?
- In the Yoga Sutras "realm of inquiry for a Yogi is MIND", what does that mean?
- What is a Mind? Is mind a powerful instrument or is it a problem?
- According to Patañjali in Chapter 1 of the Yoga Sutras, how do thought modifications, *"Vritti"* get initiated? What are the five states or conditions of the mind?
- Mastering thoughts with *"abhyāsa and vairāgya"*, what does that involve?
- Sutra 27- 28 in Chapter 1, Rishi Patañjali describes OM, *Praṇava,* as the symbol for *Ishvara*. What is the detailed explanation of these Sutras?

Samadhi Pāda (Meditative absorption) – Chapter 1 of Patañjali's Yoga Sutras text

The first chapter on spiritual absorption starts with the sutra introducing the subject matter:

"athaḥ yogaḥ anushāsanam"

As per the convention of the Sanskrit language, the word *"athah"*, carries the connotation of a prayer and an auspicious beginning.

The author Patañjali indicates in this sutra, that while the subject matter is of ancient origin (*Veda*) and that he is not the originator; he has studied the teachings under a competent *guru*.

A *guru* is one who is learned and practices and lives according to the teachings of the *Veda.* The author Patañjali is now a competent teacher himself, who can share his understanding of the subject matter.

This introductory sutra 1.1 suggests that after our many actions in life, and whatever preparatory practices we might have performed till now, we are finally ready to pursue the depths of self-exploration. To practice Yoga properly requires cultivating discipline and following a systematic method oflearning.

The second sutra in the Yoga Sutras starts with this statement What is Yoga? Sutra 1.2:

"yogash chitta vritti nirodhaḥ"

"Yoga is the *nirodhaḥ"*
Yoga is regulation, channeling, integration, coordination, mastery stilling, quieting of the modifications – gross and subtle thought patterns of the mind.

In this sutra, Yoga is presented as *samādhi,* meditative absorption.

What is ***Chitta***?

The word *chitta* is derived from the root "*chit*" - to be conscious, to be aware of, and to understand. *Chitta* is the subconscious mind. It is the mind-stuff, mind-field. It is the store-house of memory and the subconscious storehouse or reservoir of all impressions. *Samskāra* or impressions of past actions and the results of the actions are imbedded in *chitt*a.

What is ***Vritti***?

Vritti is mind modifications, movement of the mind. *Vritti* are mental activities, fluctuations, modifications, changes of the mind-field. Modifications in the form of various thoughts get created when the information from the outside world is received through our sense organs namely, eyes, ears, nose, skin and tongue.

Also, the memories of the past and day to day experiences, encounters and transactions leave impressions in our mind. These impressions engraved in our mind lead to formation of various thought patterns. These memories and engraved impressions in our mind are called *"samskāra"*. And the thought modifications, flow of thoughts are the *vritti*.

Nirodha is resolving, regulating, channeling, mastering, integrating, coordinating, understanding, stilling, quieting, or setting aside of the *vritti* is "YOGA".

Can anyone remove all thoughts? Yes, in one of the forms of *samādhi, Nirvikalpa samādhi,* one can remove all thoughts. However how long can one stay in this thoughtless state? One has to, and needs to come out of this temporary state in order to conduct day to day actions and transactions with the outside world.

Thus even if the sutra says Yoga is resolving/ removing all thought modifications;

Yoga is about knowing truth of one's own self – beyond thoughts.

Yoga **"as though"** removes and resolves thoughts, when the reality of thoughts and the essence of one's own self as *Purusha, Ātmā* is realized by the spiritual seeker.

Thus *"chitta vritti nirodha"*, the 2nd sutra in the Yoga Sutras, states that the final end of Yoga is the regulation of mental operations by understanding the reality of all thought modifications.

The realm of inquiry for a *yogi* (spiritual seeker) is,

"The Mind"

The mind is the cause of all suffering. One leads a life filled with wrong conclusions about oneself due to misidentification with the physical body, mind and the thoughts in the mind. Misidentification with the physical body and the mind lead to the feeling of separation from the truth of one's own self, *Purusha, Ātmā*.

This separation from the Reality, *Purusha* leads to the feeling of incompleteness, and therefore the mind constantly tries to find the state of fulfillment and completeness by leaning upon the external sources – people, places and situations. This dependence on the outside world is the reason for all sorrow.

The goal of Yoga is to "still", to regulate *vritti,* thought modifications. When the mind is turned inwards through the practice of various spiritual disciplines (*yoga sādhanā*), a yogi (spiritual seeker) is ready to learn the technique of *samādhi*, an advanced mental discipline for the sight of *Purusha* as the truth of one's own self.

The famous metaphor of a lake is used to illustrate this concept: *Chitta,* the mind-stuff or the mind-field is the lake, and *vritti* are the impurities, waves and ripples rising in it (when external causes impinge on it). One cannot see the bottom of the lake, because its surface is covered with waves, ripples, bubbles and froth.

> "If the water is muddy, the bottom will not be seen;
> if the water is agitated all the time,
> the bottom will not be seen.
>
> It is possible for us to catch a glimpse of the bottom
> only when the turbulence has subsided, and
> the water is clean and calm.
>
> The lake is the *chitta,* and the waves, ripples, bubbles and
> froth are the *vritti,* and the bottom of the lake is
> our own true Self;"

Rishi Patañjali's discussion on the mind, source of thoughts, different states/conditions of the mind, and what should be done with the mind is given in Chapter 1 *Samādhi Pāda.*

As Yoga Sutras text is about disciplining the mind, let us begin by understanding what mind is:

What is a Mind?

Where is this mind located? Is there an organ called "mind"? Are we aware of the functioning of our mind? Is mind a powerful instrument or a problem?

There is no organ in the body called the "mind". We have an organ called the "brain" and we have various thoughts arising and subsiding and then arising again. This process goes on all the time, except in deep sound sleep. Mind is *"chitta"*. The continuous flow of thoughts is the mind field, mind stuff. Mind field or mind stuff comprises mental function and mind modifications, which include perceptions, feelings, emotions, memory, all thinking, ideation, imagination, belief, reasoning and also includes ego, a sense of individuality called *"ahaṅkāra"*.

In computer terminology mind can be thought of as software in contrast to the hardware, namely the brain. Just as a flow of water is called a "river", a flow of thoughts is the "mind".

Thoughts arise due to various impressions *(samskāra),* residue from our past actions, experiences and memories. Thoughts arise due to ego *(ahaṅkāra),* for example, I am male/female, my age is 40, the color of my eyes is brown/green, I have various qualifications, I am nice and calm, I am........ These identifications give rise to innumerable thoughts.

Samskāra, ego and intellect give rise to infinite thoughts, and the mind jumps around like a monkey! These various thought patterns lead to innumerable other thought patterns.

We fail to draw a line between the mind and our true nature.

We forget that "we HAVE a mind, we are NOT our mind".

The problem is our identification with the incessant flow of thoughts.

We will know the importance of mental discipline if we know these two important aspects:

1. First let us explore mind as a powerful tool.

We must know the greatness and powerfulness of the mind that we are born with. Mind is the most powerful instrument with which we can accomplish all goals of life. We have different sense organs for different activities; for example, to see form we have "eyes" and to hear we use another sense organ the "ears". Each sense organ is used for a particular purpose; however the mind has to be employed behind all these sensory processes. Mind is an instrument we have to use in all our activities like walking, talking, listening, eating, smelling, touching.......

> Mind is primary and powerful because mind has a unique capacity to convert a perfect state of harmony into a state of great suffering and vice versa..

A person with every luxury, ease and comfort can feel miserable and a person weighed by innumerous problems can feel wonderful. The quality of our life is dependent on the mind which is the most powerful instrument we use all the time.

2. This powerful mind also has another dimension; it has a serious problem in its nature.

We must know that though it is powerful, the mind itself faces problems. The mind has the nature of producing/generating continuous thoughts without taking permission from us. Without our will, without our permission, without our involvement, the mind (which is supposed to be an instrument for our use) generates involuntary thoughts on its own.

We are the owner of the mind but the mind acts on its own. This generation of "continuous involuntary thoughts" is a very serious problem. And because of this serious problem, several adverse consequences take place.

When there are involuntary thoughts,
the thoughts kidnap the mind!

The mind is not available for our use when we need it.

The most powerful gift given to mankind is the mind, but the involuntary thoughts encroach upon it and lessen its power. There is a property dispute which we are not even aware of! The dispute is – who is the owner of the mind?

Involuntary thoughts are the encroachers that kidnap the mind and the biggest problem is "I do not have the mind for my use most of the time". I do all the actions as an absent minded person, as a mindless person or as though "living in absentia." In all the activities we undertake, many mistakes are committed due to forgetfulness. I misplace something and waste hours searching for it – searching for a pen or book or glasses! I cannot enjoy a peaceful moment, beauty of a blooming bud, laughter of an innocent child, nor chirping of a happy bird, work of art, or harmony in a concert.

Such absent mindedness is due to the involuntary thoughts the mind produces without my permission. And it is important to recognize that the involuntary thoughts are the greatest enemies.

"Mind is engaged elsewhere and robs me of my efficiency".

When these involuntary thoughts are constantly moving in the mind, they end up producing disturbing emotions like worry, anxiety, fear, depression, regret, hurt, guilt – all these are generated in the mind without our invitation! The problem of emotional disturbance is a serious one. When these toxic emotions stay for a long time, they start affecting our health.

Loss of efficiency is the first problem.

Loss of health is the second adverse effect of involuntary thoughts in the mind.

In fact many of our modern diseases are caused by a stressful mind.

Stress results from involuntary thoughts that are continuously running in our mind and running very very fast. Our lives can become miserable because of this. We do not realize the problem and seriousness of "involuntary thoughts".

We have been given a wonderful instrument "the mind", but we are deprived of its full benefit. It is very obvious that we need to discipline and train our mind. In order to use this powerful instrument to its full extent, we first need to understand different sources from where the information is received for the thoughts to arise and for the mental process to begin.

Rishi Patañjali describes five sources from where the mind activities, *"vritti"* get initiated:

1. Experience (sensory) – comes from perceptions. Perceptions are gathered (information is received) through the sense of smell, touch, taste, seeing, hearing. Experience comes from interactions with people, places and objects in the past and present moments.

Experience also comes from the inferences drawn from scriptures, books, and other sources of knowledge.

2. Error – we can see, hear, taste, touch and smell something, however we come to a wrong conclusion depending upon the condition of our mind. For example, walking in the dark alley at night, we see a post on the side of the street but because we are in an anxious and fearful state of mind, certain emotions arise and we conclude that it is a ghost (not a post)!

3. Imagination – most of the time we imagine all kinds of scenarios for some future event that has not taken place yet. For example: we can hear winds blowing loudly and can imagine a tornado coming; we can see few clouds in the sky and imagine that there will be torrential rain coming along!

4. Sleep – sleep is the time when the mind will be busy churning out one dream after another! Dreams can arise due to the arousal of particular brain patterns. The sensory parts of our brain can play and replay fragmentary memories of our daily experiences and then brain centers weave bits and pieces together to create various dreams in a story-like fashion. Dreams can also arise as an expression of our unconscious wishes, issues or concerns buried deep within.

5. Memory – whatever has happened (in the moments before this present moment) is a moment from the past. We keep thinking about our past even though we function in the present moment. If we peek inside our mind at any given moment, there will be memories and interpretations of our memories from past experiences. There are thoughts from the past moments that constantly arise in the present moment.

Five states or conditions of the mind:

As we learn more about our mind it is important to know the five states or conditions of the mind. *Rishi Vyāsa* who has written a commentary on the Yoga Sutras, goes on to describe five states (conditions) of the mind.

Once a person starts observing the condition of his/her mind, that seeker may find the mind going through the first four states continuously. One of these conditions or combination of the first four conditions dictates a person's behavior. This can be a problem for a spiritual seeker. Anyone who wants to lead a meditative life should have a clear understanding of these following five states.

1. *Kshiptam* – distracted and confused, a mind that is always wandering. This condition of the mind can be compared to that of a monkey swinging from branch to a branch! Thoughts, feelings and emotions come and go in rapid succession. One is hardly aware of these fluctuations arising and subsiding in the mind. In fact the person is not even aware that there is such a thing as the mind at this stage. One is totally and completely taken over by the vacillations or fluctuations arising in the mind.

2. *Mūdham* – deluded mind, dull mind. Here the mind can be compared to a water buffalo, standing in one place for a very long period of time. The mind is taken over by lethargy and dullness. This state of the mind can result due to many reasons.

   For example, after eating a heavy meal, lack of sleep, lack of stimulation, depression and traumas such as, the death of a loved one, a serious illness, and natural or man-made disasters.

3. *Vikshiptam* – distracted occasionally while steady and focused at certain times. In this state of mind, a person has some direction in his/her thinking process however, occasionally gets distracted with other thoughts, feelings and emotions.

   One is able to overcome those distractions arising in the mind and move towards the goal. However the progress is slow due to various occasional distractions. This is the state of mind that one deals with in *dhāraṇā,* sixth limb of *ashtānga* yoga (Chapter 3, 1st sutra). This is the state of mind one has to deal with in order to arrive at the next state of mind, *ekāgra* focused mind.

4. *Ekāgram* – one pointed, focused, fixed on the objects of meditation. *Ekārgratā* (mind which is *ekāgra*) is able to hold one thought for a length of time which is the 7th *anga, dhyāna* explained in chapter 3 of the Yoga Sutras.

   One pointed and focused mind is what is arrived at after much preparation, detachment and discrimination.

   After taking initial steps for preparing oneself with moral and ethical values, *yama* and *niyama,* preparing the body thru *āsana* and *prāṇāyāma*, withdrawing sense organs (eyes, ears, nose, tongue and skin) from wandering around, having learned to steady the mind, one comes to the state of one pointed focus and attention.

   This is the state required for *dhyāna.* In this state of *ekāgratā,* a mind is linked completely and exclusively with the object of its attention.

5. *Niruddham* (mind in *nirodha* state) – stopped or restrained mind. When *ekāgratā* fully develops, it peaks into *niruddham,* stopped or restrained mind. The mind is so focused and absorbed that the mind and the object seem to merge. All other mental activities cease due to the total absorption of the mind. *Nirodha* is not eliminating the activities of the mind by using force or trying to use logic or by trying to get some kind of "experience". *Nirodha* is what happens when the one pointed focused mind leads to restraint "as though" stopping the mind.

According to Chapter 1, *Samādhi* (Meditative/spiritual absorption) *Pāda*, the term *samādhi* applies to the 4th state, one pointed (*ekāgram*) and the 5th state, restrained mind (*niruddham*).

The quality and quantity of all thoughts depend on the state of the mind. It is very useful to be aware of these conditions of the mind all the time. By knowing the state of mind we are in, we can guide our mind from a distracted or deluded state to a focused mind, a laser sharp one pointed mind, functioning at its level best every moment of the day.

What can be done with the knowledge of the fivefold mind activities?

1. Weaken the flow of undesirable thoughts. Create detachment.

2. Initiate a new flow of thoughts, sincere practice develops into habit. How? By watching, observing our thoughts!

Watch your thoughts > thoughts become words > words become actions > actions lead to habits > habits make the character > character becomes destiny!

3. Mind attains peace by association with good, empathizing with those who are suffering, appreciating virtues and avoiding vices. The thoughts that we choose to cultivate in our mind will either lead to disturbance and agitation or will lead to peace and calm.

Peace of mind is a matter of option.

Sutra 1.3 and 1.4 state that trained, one pointed and focused mind leads one to discover inner peace and freedom. Who can attain this *samādhi?* **1**- A person who is qualified, **2**- one who has understood the functioning of the mind, **3**- a person to whom concentration is very natural and **4**- a person who has a desire to abide in the true nature *Purusha, Ātmā.*

Mastering thoughts – with *abhyāsa* (practice) and *vairāgya* (objectivity):

In chapter 1 Rishi Patañjali talks about two core principles crucial for training the mind – practice or study *(abhyāsa)* and non-attachment *(vairāgya)*. It is through the cultivation of these two principles that the other practices evolve, finally leading towards mastery over the mind. They work together; practice leads you in the right direction, while non-attachment allows you to continue the inner journey without getting sidetracked along the way.

1. ***Abhyāsa*** – practice, repetitions and study of the scriptures.

Abhyāsa includes persistent efforts, practice to attain and maintain a state of stable tranquility. *Abhyāsa* involves cultivating lifestyle, actions, speech, and thoughts, all spiritual practices that lead to tranquility and equanimity of the mind.

Over time, with *abhyāsa,* practice, reorientation of the emotional mind takes place. When such practice is done for a long time, with full attention, without a break, and with sincere devotion, the practice becomes firmly rooted and stable, and a solid foundation for mastery in meditation.

Abhyāsa, practice, is also defined as consistent and dedicated contemplation. Rishi Patañjali has assumed that the person who is reading the Yoga Sutras has already been exposed to the teaching of the *Upanishad*s and the Bhagavad Gitā, since contemplation is the final step in the process of gaining knowledge about *Purusha, Ātmā* as the essence of oneself.

Without having any access or understanding of the scriptural teachings to contemplate upon, simply sitting with one's eyes closed and watching the breath or employing some meditation technique for a length of time will not accomplish much. Once the meditation session is over, thoughts will come rushing back in full force, and the person might again have to deal with their undisciplined mind and unruly thoughts!

Thus *abhyāsa,* practice, means bringing back to one's mind again and again the truth of one's own self as fullness, limitless *ānanda,* a reservoir of peace, happiness and contentment.

2. ***Vairāgya*** – The essential companion to practice, *abhyāsa,* is non-attachment, *vairāgya. Vairāgya* is learning to let go of the attachments, aversions, fears, and false identities that cloud the mind.

The simplest way of describing non-attachment is the gradual process of letting go. Non-attachment is not a process of suppression or repression; non-attachment is to see where our minds are attached, and then learn to systematically and mindfully let go of those attachments. This is to be accomplished by understanding the role of attachments in our life and then through various practices of yoga, work towards releasing the grip of these attachments from our minds.

Vairāgya is an attitude, an understanding born out of wisdom. Accepting things, people and situations just the way they are, and not having unrealistic expectations and being objective is *vairāgya.* Rishi Patañjali describes *vairāgya,* as mastery over one's attachments *(rāga)* and aversions *(dvesha)*. It is a cognitive process in which you gradually become aware of your"buttons", things that trigger an emotional response to situations and cause problems.

To be able to do the practices and to cultivate non-attachment, it is necessary to become better and better at discriminating between actions and thoughts which take you in the right direction and those which are a diversion and take you away from the path of spirituality.

In the Bhagavad Gitā, Lord Krishna says the very same about *abhyāsa* and *vairāgya* to Arjuna in chapter 6, verse 35:

Asamshayam mahābāho manah durnigraham chalam
abhyāsena tu kaunteya vairāgyena cha grhyate II

"Undoubtedly, O mighty-armed one, the mind is difficult to control and is restless; but, by practice, O Son of Kunti (Arjuna), and by dispassion it is restrained."

Lord Krishna admits that the mind is turbulent, strong, unyielding, and restless and that it is very difficult to control, and therefore, the goal of perfect and enduring tranquility cannot be EASILY achieved.

In the second line of this verse, Lord Krishna says that through "*abhyāsa* - practice" and "*vairāgya* - non-attachment" the mind can be brought under control in the beginning, and ultimately leading to stillness of the mind.

Once the thoughts are observed and understood and once a seeker gains one pointed focus by restraining the incessant chatter of the mind, then and only then is he/she prepared and qualified to sit in *samādhi* for a period of time.

Patañjali describes mastering the thoughts by different types of contemplation, *samādhi*.

What are the 2 main types of *samādhi* described by Rishi Patañjali?

The first type is *"saṃprajñāta" samādhi*. In this type of *samādhi,* the sense of being a meditator is present. And in the second type *"asaṃprajñāta samādhi,* even the thought "I am the meditator" is not present. In the first type *saṃprajñāta,* there is a distinction between the subject, the one who is contemplating and the object of the contemplation, while in the second one *asaṃprajñāta,* the subject-object division resolves.

It is important to note that whereas the first type of contemplation is based on the freewill of the meditator, one sits and exert effort to focus on an object of contemplation, in the second type *asaṃprajñāta samādhi* there is no exertion of freewill.

One cannot "practice" *asaṃprajñāta samādhi,* because there is no object of meditation and there is no meditator. It is a point of arrival. The mind is resolved, and is used for functional purpose only. The identification with ego, *ahaṅkāra* is gone and only divinity, *Purusha* remains. Utter fulfillment alone remains.

Once the obstacles from the mind are removed,
one abides in oneself, as oneself.

In order to reach the lofty goals of *asaṃprajñāta samādhi,* a prayer is required. Let us now explore the prayer "OM" as explained in Rishi Patañjali's Yoga Sutras.

Om (Praṇava)

Rishi Patañjali declares in sutra in chapter 1, sutra 27-28 that *Praṇava*, OM, is the symbol of *Ishvara,* Lord, Supreme universal reality and that one can attain *samādhi* by the repetition of "OM".

"tasya vāchakaḥ praṇavaḥ"

For the designation *(vāchaka)*, Lord *(Ishvara)* for the sake of meditation is *praṇava* = OM. *Praṇava* is the Sanskrit name for "OM". *Praṇava* literally means "that by which the Lord is effectively praised".

One needs a designation for that which cannot be experienced (perceived) as an object, as a feeling or a thing, "*vāchaka*" is a word that stands in place of an actual thing, proxy, that which has a deeper meaning. This *praṇava* symbol is a sacred syllable representing the non-dual Absolute Reality, omnipotent, omnipresent, and the source of all manifest existence. A symbol becomes mandatory to help us realize the formless, free of attributes, beyond time and space, and Infinite.

How is OM a symbol for the Lord, *Ishvara*?

A flag is just a piece of cloth. The constitution of the country; what the country stands for is deliberately superimposed on this piece of cloth called the flag. Therefore, the flag symbolizes the country and respect shown to the flag is the respect shown to that country.

Similarly, with the word OM, there is a deliberate superimposition of *Ishvara* and therefore it becomes a symbol.

"OM is a sound symbol representing *Ishvara*"

OM is a sound symbol full of meaning.

When OM is expanded to explain the symbolic meaning, it can be grammatically deconstructed in 3 Sanskrit letters a-u-m. This expansion is for symbolic reasons only. In Sanskrit, it is entirely <u>incorrect</u> for OM to be written or pronounced as "aum".

*For further explanation, see Chapter 1, "Introduction to Sanskrit Language" and Chapter 2, "Mantra". *

Let us see the explanations behind the deconstruction of OM in 3 Sanskrit letters:

1. "A" stands for *srishti* – create = *Ishvara* as the creator (*Brahmā*)
"U" stands for *sthiti* – sustain = *Ishvara* as the sustainer (*Vishṇu*)
"M" stands for *laya* – resolve = *Ishvara* into whom everything resolves (*Shiva*).

OM represents infinite number of cycles of creation before and after this Universe.

This fact is represented in the sequence of OM – OM – OM...

Ishvara is represented by the sound OM firstly as the source of flow of cycles of creation. The sound OM also represents that which remains changeless and is beyond time and space. This is represented by the silence after the sound of OM. Silence is the underlying reality, substratum of any sound. *Ishvara* is ever present as the underlying reality, substratum of everything.

2. Phonetically "A" is the basic sound that is produced by a human being when he tries to make a sound by opening the mouth. In most languages "A" is also the first letter of the alphabet. When a sound is produced by closing the mouth, what comes out is the sound "M". In between, when there is a rounding off of the mouth, the sound "U" is produced.

All objects are but names and all names are words. Words are made of letters and letters are made from sounds. Since sounds are produced by opening and closing the mouth, all sounds are phonetically between "A" and "M". The letter "U" is inserted in between to indicate all sounds in between.

With A, U, and M, OM sound includes all possible phonetic sounds on the vocal cords.
Thus word OM includes all letters and words (sounds) of all the languages and dialects.

As *Ishvara* is the source of everything – all names, forms and objects, OM becomes the sound symbol for *Ishvara*.

To recap what has been discussed about the mind so far:

Mind: mind stuff, mind field is *chitta* and *vritti* is thought modifications

Thoughts arise from:		Conditions of the mind
Experience	→	Kshiptam - distracted
Error	→	Mūdham - deluded and dull
Imagination	→	Vikshiptam - partially distracted
Sleep	→	Ekāgram - focused
Memory	→	Niruddham - restrained

Master thoughts (conditions of the mind) with:

Abhyāsa (choosing and cultivating that which leads to tranquility, equanimity of the mind) and *vairāgya* (non-attachment, seeing where the attachments are and systematically letting go)

Distraction on the seat of Meditation and how to overcome these distractions:

As anyone who has attempted to meditate knows all too well, the process of meditation or contemplation is filled with obstacles. To help a spiritual aspirant understand these distractions, Rishi Patañjali lists nine kinds of distractions and also gives specific instructions on how to overcome them. The list of distractions and obstructions arising on the seat of meditation are:

1. *Vyādhi* - illness
2. *Styāna* - tendency of the mind to not work efficiently
3. *Samshaya* - doubt or indecision
4. *Pramāda* - lack of attention to pursuing the means of samādhi
5. *Āalasya* - laziness in mind and body
6. *Avirati* - failure to regulate the desire for worldly objects
7. *Bhrānti-darshana* - incorrect assumptions or thinking
8. *Alabdhabhumikatva* - failing to attain stages of the practice
9. *Anavasthitatva* - instability in maintaining a level of practice once attained.

These distractions have both physical and mental consequences. As mentioned in sutra 1.31, these nine distractions result in sorrow and despair, and lead to an imbalance in the physiological functions (expressed as uneven breathing) and agitation.

Rishi Patañjali also gives instructions on how to deal with others in one's day to day life. To have healthy relationships with others, one requires a mind to be free from certain negative thought patterns and impurities of the mind such as indifference, jealousy, hatred, anger, ill will, lack of compassion. It is recommended by Patañjali that in order for the mind to be free of these impurities and to develop healthy relations, one must cultivate feelings of:

maitrī - friendliness towards those who are happy

karuṇā - compassion for those who are suffering

muditā - goodwill towards those who are virtuous and

upekshā - equanimity, non-discrimination and neutrality towards all.

The five principles and practices in sutra 19 and 20 give us a simple and straightforward outline of personal commitments needed to follow the path of Self-realization. They are:

1) Unconditional faith, trust, confidence in *Ishvara*

2) Energy to perform outward actions of friendliness, compassion, encouragement, and patience when dealing with others

3) Repeated memory of the process of stilling the mind

4) Conscious effort to focus on a given topic, and the mindfulness to stay there

5) Ongoing commitment to seek the higher state of concentration and to pursue higher knowledge and wisdom as described in sutra 1.20.

These methods help to calm the mind by removing the stimulus for the distractions. In the absence of any stimulus, the mind rests in its natural state of peace and fullness.

Section 3:

Sutra 2.6 - दृग्दर्शनशक्त्योरेकात्मतेवास्मिता ॥६॥

Dṛgdarśanaśaktyorekātmatevāsmitā ॥6॥

Egoism is the identification of the seer with the instrument of seeing. False identity results when we regard mental activity as the very source of perception.

Sutra 2.7 - सुखानुशयी रागः ॥७॥

Sukhānuśayī rāgaḥ ॥7॥

Attachment is that which dwells on pleasure. Excessive attachment is based on the assumption that it will contribute to everlasting happiness.

Sutra 2.8 - दुःखानुशयी द्वेषः ॥८॥

Duḥkhānuśayī dveṣaḥ ॥8॥

Aversion is that which dwells on pain. Unreasonable dislikes are usually the result of painful experiences in the past connected with particular objects and situations.

Sutra 2.9 - स्वरसवाही विदुषोऽपि तथारूढोऽभिनिवेशः ॥९॥

Svarasavāhī viduṣo'pi tathārūḍho'bhiniveśaḥ ॥9॥

Insecurity is the inborn feeling of anxiety for what is to come. It affects both the ignorant and the wise. "May I not cease to exist, may I live on".

In this section -

- What are *Tapas*, *Svādhyāya* and *Ishvara Praṇidhānam,* in short what is *Kriyā Yoga*?
- Surrender to *Ishvara,* Lord - who are we surrendering to?
- What are the five impurities (afflictions) of the mind? Impurities which bring obstruction in the mind and are the cause of all our suffering?

Sādhanā Pāda (Means of practice) – Chapter 2 of Patañjali's Yoga Sutras text

This chapter describes means of practice for those who have just begun their journey of spiritual development. Let us look at the methodical unfolding from the first *pāda* of the Yoga Sutras.

As we have seen so far, according to Rishi Patañjali, one should begin by understand ding what is "mind", and observe different states of mind. Then by focusing on the mind-stuff (thought modifications), work on freeing the mind from colorings, agitations, conflicts, wrong conclusions and other similar problems.

With the foundation established in chapter 1 of the Yoga Sutras, one can now begin the process of reducing the afflictions and colorings of thought patterns. In the first few sutras of *Sādhanā Pāda,* specific methods are being introduced on how to minimize the impurities, mental obstacles, *klesha* which veil the true Self.

The underlying idea behind practices described in chapter 2, *Sādhanā Pāda* (means of practice) is as follows:

Afflictions of the body lead to fluctuations in the mind and therefore by countering afflictions of the body, one counters fluctuations of the mind.

Kriyā Yoga:

The first part of the process of minimizing the *klesha,* colorings, afflictions, or impurities is called *Kriyā Yoga. Kriyā Yoga* is meant for an aspirant's early stage of journey towards *samādhi. Kriyā* (*Kriyā* means actions) *Yoga* is a very effective three fold practice to be employed for weakening the mental clutter. *Kriyā Yoga* purifies the mind by weakening (though not yet eliminating) the negative habits of mind.

Yoga in the form of action, that is *Kriyā Yoga*, involves three parts:

1. *Tapas* – penance or religious austerities, purifying actions which lead to training the senses. What is *Tapas*? All spiritual traditions value tapas, austerities. *Tapas,* practicing austerities in day to day life, on a regular basis reflects as discipline.

In the Bhagavad Gitā, Lord Krishna talks about *tapas* at length and the *Upanishad* declares "know your real true nature through *tapas*".

Tapas as a discipline of the body, mind and speech, give one the will power to say NO to oneself (and not get carried away with or indulging in irrational thoughts, inappropriate behavioral patterns or unhealthy habits), thereby promoting emotional intelligence. The practice of *tapas*, penance and austerities, helps one develop the willpower required to deal with varying external situations that might be pleasant or unpleasant, favorable or unfavorable. *Tapas* leads to alertness to recognize the problems of the body, mind and intellect and become sensitive to recognize emotions. Buddhist/ Zen teachings talk about being mindful while performing all activities such as talking, eating, walking……., being mindful each and every moment of the day.

2. *Svādhyāya* – recitation or study of the scriptures and remembrance of a sacred word or mantra. Performing *japa*, chanting mantra, chanting or studying *shāstra*/scriptures is *svādhyāya. Svādhyāya* includes self-study which is in the context of scriptural teachings. *Svādhyāya* is also studying of books and scriptures that are relevant to one's spiritual progress. Books have the power to inspire and empower all spiritual aspirants with knowledge. *Svādhyāya* also includes contemplation on what is heard, teachings of a living guru.

Svādhyāya leads to the last step of *Kriyā Yoga, Ishvara Praṇidhānam,* surrender to *Ishvara*, the Lord.

3. *Ishvara Praṇidhānam* – in Yoga Sutras all acts of worship are performed with an attitude of surrender, referred to as *Ishvara praṇidhānam.* This also can be an expression of an attitude of surrender while performing any action and it can be leading a life (performing all daily transactions) with an attitude of surrender. *Ishvara praṇidhānam* requires one to have a proper understanding of who *Ishvara* is!

Ishvara = Lord

Pra = with effort + *ṇi* = with care + *dhā* = to place

Ishvara Praṇidhānam is to surrender oneself to *Ishvara* in order to reach lofty goals of *samādhi.*

One needs to know, who am I surrendering to?

Ishvara, Lord, in Patañjali Yoga Sutras

As per the *Veda*s and subsequently in other scriptural texts and the Bhagavad Gitā, the Infinite Supreme Universal principle is Lord or *Ishvara*, the underlying reality of the Cosmos.

From Infinite Divine Reality manifests a world of innumerable names and forms. Therefore every form in the Universe is, in a sense, Divine. (And that is why we say "Namaste" recognizing that the life force, *Ishvara*'s sacred presence within, inner divinity, the Self or the Reality of who we are as *Purusha, Ātmā* is one and the same. Acknowledging this oneness with the meeting of the palms, we honor *Ishvara*'s sacred presence in the person we meet.) *See Chapter 6, "Symbolism" for details.*

Hindus worship the Supreme, the Lord of the cosmos, *Ishvara* in different forms and with different names depending upon the languages, cultures, customs and practices of different regions of India. The important point is to understand is that having different names and forms for *Ishvara* does not meant that there are many Gods! As said earlier, there is nothing that exists apart from the Absolute Reality. Hindus worship the non-dual, limitless *Ishvara* in many forms and call Lord, *Ishvara* by many differentnames. * See Chapter 5, "Vedānta Terms" for more.*

Rishi Patañjali recognizes that the fabric of the Universe and the intelligent order of the universe is a manifestation of*Ishvara.* "Just as waves arise, exist and merge back into the ocean, everything arises, exists and resolves back into the Supreme Reality."

As per the *Veda* and the *Upanishad*, names and forms and objects in this entire universe are all a manifestation of *Ishvara,* Lord. *Ishvara* manifests as space, time and the five elements. This is a dynamic creation and there are laws, *Ishvara*'s intelligent order that govern the functioning of the universe. Laws sustaining and governing the universe are *Ishvara*'s manifestation.

Let us take for example, a dream: we sustain and govern the dream world which is our own manifestation. Everything and everyone in our own dream world is our own manifestation. Similarly all the orders – physical, physiological, psychological, social, laws of gravity, various other orders and laws of nature, from the microcosm to the macrocosm, everything is *Ishvara*'s manifestation. *Ishvara*'s intelligence permeates each and everything – from a tiniest particle, to atoms, to space and beyond.

Now let us understand how we can practice *Ishvara praṇidhānam,* surrender to this intelligent order.

We as human beings are blessed to conduct ourselves with free will. When there is freedom of choice to conduct ourselves, there has to be some order and there have to be laws governing our actions. This law governing the choice, our freewill is called *dharma*. *Dharma* means understanding the right thing to do in regards to our duties and responsibilities.

Dharma is a proper way of conducting ourselves, a proper way of relating to the given situation.

Thus *dharma* is, "I am submitting myself to the order of human conduct. I gather will and push myself to commit myself to what is to be done. Committing myself to *dharma,* duty-based life is commitment to the Lord".

"What I am supposed to do versus what I feel like doing", this choice often leads to innumerous conflicts in our lives.

Dharma is using the free will to measure up the situation and doing what needs to be done, doing the right thing.

The life of *dharma* is leading a life of *Ishvara Praṇidhānam.* This is part of *Kriyā Yoga* as described by Rishi Patañjali.

This is the same as the explanation of *dharma* and life of *Karma Yoga* in the Bhagavad Gitā. When I commit myself to the duty with an attitude of surrender to *Ishvara's* order, when I follow *dharma* and I commit myself to *dharma* (*dharma* being *Ishvara*'s order), there is joy in performing the actions.

When I act according to the will of my emotions and wavering sentiments, there can be conflict, fear and guilt.

Awareness of *Ishvara* in performance of each and every action is the result of acting as per the *dharma*.

However in order to cultivate this awareness of *dharma,* awareness of *Ishvara*'s order, one has to initially make a deliberate effort. Once this awareness is achieved, there is joy in every moment, "when I do what is to be done, it is *Ishvara praṇidhānam."*

"Yoga is not just *āsana* and *prāṇāyāma* and not even *dhāraṇā, dhyāna* or *samādhi.*

First important step of yoga is *Ishvara praṇidhānam."*

"Yoga begins with *Kriyā Yoga.*"

The result of Yoga is freedom from the notion that "I am a limited, incomplete and insecure body, mind and intellect". Chapter 2, *Sādhanā Pāda,* deals with preparedness of the mind to be able to arrive at the realization that "I am not this limited, incomplete, insecure being. I am *sat chit ānanda Ātmā*". "I am liberated, full and complete" is the realization that comes about when the mind is purified to receive this knowledge.

So how do we achieve a mind that is purified (all impurities are removed) and ready to realize what the sages and various scriptures like Yoga Sutra, *Upanishad* and the Bhagavad Gitā have been saying all along? Various impurities (*klesha*) of the mind prevent one from realizing the highest truth, one's true essence, reality, "Self".

Let us begin by understanding five basic impurities of the mind as per Rishi Patañjali.

There are five basic impurities (*Klesha*), obstructions or afflictions in the mind.

These mental obstructions (afflictions) activate and motivate thought processes in the mind. These five afflictions not only deprive one from *shānti* at the mind level, but they also give rise to many more afflictions.

More and more actions get generated from these obstructions, impurities and afflictions at the mind level. This leads to more and more sorrow and this takes one further and further away from *shanti,* peace.

These five afflictions are:

1. *Avidyā*

This affliction is the root cause of the rest of the afflictions. The focus of Yoga scriptures is to ultimately remove *avidyā* *(avidyā* means ignorance) which is the source of all human suffering. Which ignorance are we talking about?

The ignorance being referred to here is ignorance of the highest truth, ultimate Reality, the truth of who we are, (which is the reality of everything) Divine, limitless, *Purusha, Ātmā.* We are ignorant of this profound truth.

> Due to our ignorance of the Reality;
> sensual pleasures, all fleeting experiences derived from objects, people and situations are taken as permanent source of happiness, peace and security.

In our ignorance we end up taking ephemeral, transient, ever changing and fleeting – body, relations, thoughts, emotions, objects and transactions to be permanent!

2. *Asmitā* – "i ness", ego, false identity

Because of the ignorance about the Reality, *avidyā,* I associate myself with the (body-mind complex) physical body and sense organs, sense perceptions, mind and intellect.

"I" am an individual self, bound by this particular body, mind and intellect this self-centered complex which gives rise to "I ness" or "ego" or *"ahaṅkāra"*. This is *asmitā.*

This "I ness", which is the ego, keeps on changing roles as the transaction, relations, duties change. "I am a wife/husband, 5/6 feet tall, light/dark colored skin, Asian/ European, MD/ Lawyer/teacher, young/old.....

Who I think I am changes depending upon gender, beliefs, qualifications, status, title, color, race, relations", this is *asmitā.*

Ignorance or *avidyā* and then *asmitā,* association with the limited body, mind and intellect (ego), leads one to perceive oneself to be a limited being.

3. *Rāga* – extreme attachments

Asmitā, ego, sense of "I" attached to the body mind complex is necessarily limited, and will remain limited no matter what we do. Due to the inherent desire to be happy, full and complete, one believes that "a particular name/form, situation or a person will make me happy, full and complete", this is *rāga. Rāga* always arises from the past experiences. In certain past moments one has experienced happiness, fullness, and completeness momentarily and it was in association with certain name/form, object, situation or a person.

During these past experiences, the thought that "I am this limited being" had disappeared and thus one attributes the happiness, fullness and completeness to that particular situation, object or person. Thus one develops *rāga* for the same. One develops an attitude of attachment towards certain objects, situations, and people, those which one associates with momentary happiness.

4. *Dvesha* – extreme aversions or dislikes

Exactly opposite of *rāga* is *dvesha.* When certain object, situations, people cause the feeling of unpleasantness; one feels uncomfortable with or uneasy with them. One develops dislike towards those objects, situations or person/persons.

These *rāga* and *dvesha* can be due to past experiences from this life or past lives *(samskāra)* or due to non-thinking on our part. Both *rāga* and *dvesha* give rise to desires and wanting. "If I get this, or if I avoid this, then I will be happy, full and complete". *Rāga* and *dvesha* give rise to anger, jealousy, and lust and finally lead to failure in adhering to moral principles. "I absolutely cannot live without……. I hate…… I despise….." all these extreme emotions and dependencies arise when *rāga, dvesha* rule our intellect.

According to all the Hindu scriptures including Yoga Sutras, "desire" per se is not an obstruction. Unless there was a desire on Rishi Patañjali's part, he would not have written 3 profound texts! Desires are *klesha,* impurities and obstruction, **only when** the desires lead to a life of unrighteousness or failure to adhere to moral principles.

5. *Abhinivesha* – insecurities, fears

Abhinivesha is the fear that comes naturally. For example, fear of death, fear of rejection, hurt, and loneliness. Fear of death is the source of the survival instinct. This instinct is very natural in all beings. Due to the fear alone we seek security. Security is sought through objects, money, latching on to people, experiences and situations. One becomes helpless and fearful in search of security.

When these fears rule our intellect, we lose self-confidence, become dependent. We get addicted or depressed. Thus this impurity (*klesha)* called *abhinivesha* in our mind, gives rise to many other *kleshas*, obstructions, and impurities.

Sutra 10 of the 2nd Chapter (*Pāda*) states that these *kleshas,* which are quite normal for all human beings, are to be reduced and made un-manifestable, and impotent like the seeds that are made non-sproutable when roasted. Roasted seeds are unable to sprout; similarly these *kleshas* are to be made non-sproutable by *Kriyā Yoga,* by the practice of *tapas*, *svādhyāya* and *Ishvara praṇidhānam.*

> By leading a life of alertness and mindfulness,
> one should not allow these mental impurities to manifest.
>
> One has to learn to manage the *klesha* at the mental level.
>
> *Kriyā Yoga* will help a person to become aware of the mental modifications, thoughts.

Usually our minds jump around from one thought to another thought like a monkey jumping from tree to tree! There is a lack of alertness. With practice of *Kriyā Yoga*, a person sees the *klesha* arising in his/her mind, and with alertness he/she will be able to manage these mental impurities.

Observing what is happening in the mind; helps a person to see thoughts covered in *klesha*. Some effort is needed to see *rāga/ dvesha,* extreme attachments and dislikes for what they are. They are created by *asmitā,* ego and *abhinivesha,* fears and insecurities.

Sutra 12 states that births – past, future and the present existing birth have their origin in actions and results of the action. *For more clarity see pages 223-226, Law of *Karma* and Theory of Reincarnation discussion in Chapter 4, "The Bhagavad Gitā".*

Actions occur due to *klesha. Avidyā,* the root cause of all mental impurities (wrong thinking based on ignorance about the reality of oneself as *"Purusha, Ātmā"*) is the cause of all actions. The *kleshas* lead to action, which leads to births, past, future and existing birth. Thus ignorance, *avidyā,* leads to other 4 *kleshas,* which in turn generate more *kleshas,* which lead to more and more actions and these actions result in more and more *kleshas* as births are taken again and again. This cycle of birth and death, the cycle of happiness and sorrow, *samsara,* continues forever.

Recap on the teachings on *klesha,* impurities of the mind.

Mind

Klesha - impurities of the mind:

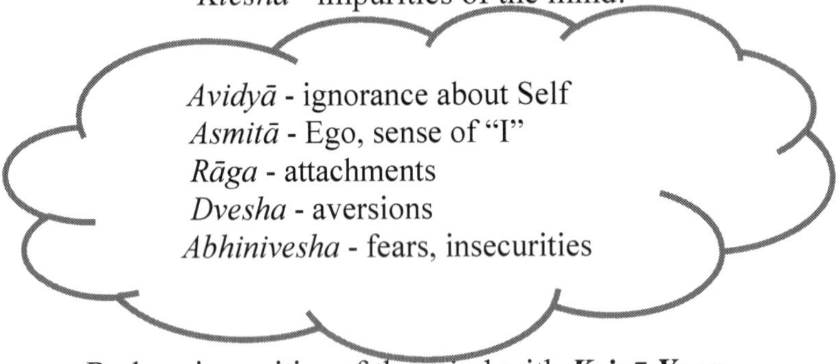

Reduce impurities of the mind with ***Kriyā Yoga.***

Three fold practice to reduce mental clutter:

- *Tapas* (purifying and training senses)
- *Svādhyāya* (self-study in the context of teachings, knowing what can or cannot be changed)
- *Ishvara praṇidhānam* (surrender what you cannot change)

Patañjali also recommends reducing mental impurities:

- With *Dhyāna* – Meditation and contemplation
- By practicing *Pratipaksha bhāvanā* – this means to contemplate and to look at the situation from another perspective, from another standpoint.

In sutra 22 of chapter 1, Rishi Patañjali says that, to be happy and liberated all the time is *Moksha*, which means enlightenment. Once *moksha*, (liberation) enlightenment is attained, one has achieved everything that is to be achieved, there is nothing more to gain or to lose.

It is for the unenlightened being that problems exist. This person suffers, gets tossed around by the ups and downs of life, life of happiness and sorrow, achievements and failures, insecurities and fears. The ultimate goal of all our pursuits in life is to be free of sorrow of any kind, and to have limitless happiness.

"I shall be happy at all times no matter what; all I want is total happiness through all my pursuits!" Whether one really understands the goals of one's life or not, what each one of us wants every moment of every day, is freedom from suffering, misery and insecurity. Each and every living being wants happiness, peace and security at all times, in all conditions and without a trace ofsorrow.

We understand now that our mind alone is the source of all sorrow. A sense of incompleteness is felt due to the ego, "I ness". We have seen the five *kleshas* particularly *avidyā,* ignorance of the true Self, as the root cause of all the obstructions and impurities at the level of the mind.

Because of the resulting ignorance and association with the limited body, mind and intellect, one perceives oneself to be a limited being.

Thus the problem is due to association. What needs to be done? Acquire "the knowledge". The knowledge about the reality of who "I" am as *sat chit ānanda Ātmā, Purusha.*

This knowledge can take place only when the mind is refined and capable of receiving this wisdom. A purified mind alone will be able to understand the profound teachings that "I am Pure Consciousness, I am fullness, and eternal happiness".

Patañjali Rishi says *"chitta vritti nirodha"*. This does **not** mean "achieve state of thoughtlessness"!

It means to see, observe, and become aware of the functioning of the mind, the thought process arising due to the 5 *kleshas,* impurities and obstructions.

Once there is an understanding of the thought process, one is able to transcend thoughts.

Once mind is regulated and *"nirodha"* is achieved, this "as though" leads to "silencing" the mind.

Section 4:

Sutra 2.26 - विवेकख्यातिरविप्लवा हानोपायः ॥२६॥

Vivekakhyātiraviplavā hānopāyaḥ ॥26॥

Clear, distinct, unimpaired discriminative knowledge is the means of liberation from this confusion.

Sutra 2.29 -
यमनियमासनप्राणायामप्रत्याहारधारणाध्यानसमाधयोऽष्टावङ्गानि॥२९॥

Yama niyamāsana prāṇāyāma pratyāhāra
dhāraṇā dhyāna samādhayo'ṣṭāvaṅgāni ॥29॥

The eight limbs of Yoga are the codes of self-regulation or restraint (*yama*), observances or practices of self-training (*niyama*), postures *(āsana)*, expansion of breath and *praṇa (praṇāyāma),* withdrawal of the senses *(pratyāhāra)*, concentration *(dhāraṇā)*, meditation *(dhyāna)*, and perfected concentration *(samādhi)*.

Sutra 2.42 - सन्तोषादनुत्तमसुखलाभः॥४२॥

Santoṣādanuttama sukhalābhaḥ ॥42॥

From *santosha* or contentment there is acquisition of unsurpassed highest happiness (*sukha*).

Sutra 2.45 - समाधिसिद्धिरीश्वरप्रणिधानात्॥४५॥

Samādhisiddhirīśvara praṇidhānāt ॥45॥

Perfection or complete attainment of *samādhi* or perfect concentration (*samādhi*) is achieved through devotion *(praṇidhānāt)* to the Lord (*īśvara*).

In this section -

- What are *Yama* and *Niyama*?
- What are *Āsana*, *Praṇāyāma* and *Pratyāhāra*?

Ashtānga* (eight limbs) *Yoga

All types of knowledge require necessary preparedness. For the knowledge about the Reality of who I am, the knowledge of *Purusha* to take place, the condition of the mind is very important. Preparedness of the person is preparedness of the mind, because the mind is the location where this knowledge takes place. The mind has to be prepared with necessary values and attitudes.

The science of Yoga is systematically described in eight (*ashta*) rungs, steps, or limbs (*anga*). Eight limbs, *ashtānga,* of Yoga are prescribed in Yoga Sutras starting from Sutra 29, 2nd *Pāda*. These 8 limbs are for preparing the mind to receive knowledge about "Self".

In order to become qualified to receive and understand the knowledge, one has to be ethically and emotionally mature. What does that mean?

> With commitment to ethics and values and mastery over whims and fancies of the mind, I have relative mastery; I am in charge of my emotions.
>
> I control what happens in my mind and not the other way around. I do not become a slave to the whims and fancies of my irrational thought process.

Yama and *Niyama* are the values and attitudes that are to be cultivated. Abiding in these values is being close to the essence of one's own Self as *Purusha*, as values are the expression of the Self. Therefore the more we abide and live a life of values; the more *ānanda*, bliss, happiness there will be in our lives because *ānanda* is an expression of the Self as *Purusha*.

Life is a struggle and full of conflicts because of innumerable *klesha*, impurities, and obstructions in the mind. When we commit to ethical and moral values, more and more *klesha*, impurities get resolved. To the extent one can give up *klesha* and wrong values, to that extent one can abide in the natural expression of the Self.

Yama

Natural tendencies of the body and mind (thoughts) are to be controlled by *Yama*. It is important to have ethical and emotional maturity in performing day to day activities, which means *yama* have to be followed. The five *yama*, abstinences, self-regulation and restraints in relation to others, external world, are *ahimsā, satya, asteya, brahmacharyam* and *aparigraha*.

1. *Ahimsā* (nonviolence)

Ahimsā is the value underlying all values. *Ahimsā* is called the value of all values because by practicing *ahimsā,* we live happily and we let others live happily. In pursuit of our desire to survive, we might deprive others and thus create *himsā,* violence. Due to free will and basic survival instincts, we might inadvertently hurt others and therefore *ahimsā* is to be practiced.

***Ahimsā* is causing least possible harm in any given situation.**

Simple examples of *himsā,* violence in our day to day life

can be – I have to take medicines, does the preparation of my medicines use trials on animals, were the animals harmed? I need to use paper; does that involve uprooting trees unnecessarily? When I speak truth, am I harming someone through my speech?

> *Ahimsā* is alertness, awareness that we keep
> our needs to bare minimum and try not to hurt others,
> as and when we pursue our own needs.

Are we creating a society of waste, taking more than we need? Wasting natural resources is violence! Minimizing need, requirements and waste is *ahimsā*. Our needs and our attitudes towards others have to be analyzed. There are many different ways we can hurt others and even cause harm to ourselves physically, with speech and with thoughts.

The more *ahimsā*, nonviolence one practices in daily life, the more one becomes sensitive in behavior and thinking. One becomes a compassionate person. Compassion is the expression of the Self, *Purusha* and violence is the expression of the ego. *Ahimsā* can be practiced by being vigilant and careful, bringing moment to moment awareness and mindfulness to thoughts, speech and actions.

2. *Satya* (speaking truth).

Speaking truth is a natural expression of the "Self, *Purusha*". Speaking untruth is an expression of the ego; it is a form of impurity of the mind. By speaking untruth, we deviate from what our common sense, understanding, wisdom and knowledge tell us to do. By speaking untruth, "I go out of my own control".

When the deviation becomes wider and wider – between what we know to be truth and what we say and how we act, we become fearful and doubts arise in our mind. When a person is split from his inner wisdom and understanding, he/she needs more and more things and objects in life to find even an iota of true happiness.

As one continues to speak untruth over and over again, one's mind gets filled with obstructions and impurities, *klesha*. It is possible that a person resorts to wrong means to pursue livelihood and in order to justify one untruth, he has to resort to many more untruths. One has to pursue a life of some comfort and leisure; however these comforts and leisure are to be achieved by truthful means and not by pursuing means which takes one away from truth.

The cycle of untruthful behavior leads one towards a life filled with manipulations, lack of trust and finally stress and fear. However, speaking truth does not mean hurting others! One has to be vigilant and practice *ahimsā,* causing least possible harm all the time.

Speaking truth, *satyam* leads one to be a person who is confident and who has an integrated personality, one who is free from conflicts.

"What I say is what I think and what I think is what I say"!

Speaking truth leads to a relaxed mind, a mind free from agitations and conflicts.

"Even if I have to die, I will not give up *ahimsā* and *satyam*" was said by Mahātmā Gāndhi. Mahātmā Gāndhi lived his life based on these two very important values.

Like Mahātmā Gāndhi, one can lead a simple life and can find happiness in simple things and simple objects; this is an indication of an integrated personality. *Ahimsā* and *satyam* are two values that give a person inner security and peace of mind.

3. *Asteya* (non-stealing)

Steya is stealing and is an expression of the ego. The meaning of *asteya* is not restricted to physically stealing; *asteya* also means not cutting corners, not being dishonest in dealing with others. One cannot argue that "I always want to be in my comfort zone and I do not care if my living in comfort is at the cost of discomfort to others". We cannot let others suffer for our comfort and pleasure. *Steyam,* stealing, is not just breaking into a house and stealing. Any unfair transaction through which we derive some benefit is *steyam.*

> One has to be a contributor in the society one lives in. If one fails to contribute to the well-being of others while pursuing one's own well-being, it is stealing from others.

From the day we were born, we receive so much from so many. We stand on innumerable shoulders to become worthy of something. After receiving from parents, family, teachers and mentors and society at large for many years, we need to become a contributor. We need to give back to the society in any and all possible ways and if we fail to give back, this is stealing.

Important example is, we have received these invaluable teachings on "Yoga" from ancient seers and sages. If we take away the credit or fail to acknowledge the roots and the origin of Yoga, the teachers or the teachings of Yoga, it is a form of stealing!

When we fail to keep the authenticity of the teachings of Yoga or we distort the teachings of Yoga to gain monetary benefits, misappropriate what has been given to us freely, that which needs to be preserved and passed along to future generations –

this is stealing from future generations!

4. *Brahmacharyam* (committed life style)

One who has committed to a lifestyle for discovery of Self as *"Brahaman"*, the Reality because of which everything exists, is a *brahmachāry. Brahmacharyam* is also explained as giving up all indecent and inappropriate attitudes towards the opposite sex. Self-denial of pleasures and complete and total focus on discovery of the essence or the presence of oneself as *"Purusha"*, by following various spiritual pursuits and not getting distracted with avoidable worldly pleasures is *brahmacharyam.*

5. *Aparigraha* (absence of possessiveness)

Absence of need to possess and capacity to part with possessions is *aparigraha. Aparigraha* is literally non-possession, and must be understood as leading a simple life.

There are two aspects to *aparigraha*: the first is, own less and the second is, having the right attitude towards whatever we own. We give up luxury, pomp, and show. We draw a line and limit our possessions to what is necessary. Simple living alone is suitable for subtle and deeper thinking. And secondly, we should also not develop possessiveness towards the possessions we have. This is even more important than owning less.

Aparigraha leads to freedom from insecurities and dependencies.

> Reminding ourselves that all that what we have belongs to the Universe at large and everything is given to us temporarily, for our personal growth.
>
> We should use our possessions by practicing gratitude towards the Universe.

Thus the practice of the five *yama* is a way of life. There is faith that I will be given what I need by the laws of nature. I need to practice alertness as I lead my daily life and interact with the world. If I wish to be a spiritual seeker, constant introspection needs to be done on the path of spirituality. I have to make sure that the above 5 *yama* are followed in my day to day life. Thus 5 *yama* are training of our actions, speech, and thoughts in relation to the external world.

One has to follow these values no matter what. Hurting and harming others in the name of religion, race and country is not following *yama.* These values/vows are to be followed at all times and in all places.

However, one has to be sensitive to others and make sure that *dharma,* righteousness, is followed causing least possible harm to the society at large.

Niyama

The five *niyama* are the observances or practices of self-training, and deal with our personal, inner world. These are ethics to be practiced with one's own self.

The five *niyama* are *shaucham*, *santosha*, *tapas*, *svādhyāya*, and *Ishvara praṇidhānam*.

1. *Shacuham* (purity) or cleanliness

We must first focus on gross or physical purity and then later concentrate on subtle or inner purity. *Shaucham* can be understood as keeping ourselves and everything around us clean. This includes our body, clothes, possessions like house, car. Physical cleanliness from self-discipline leads to mental *shaucham*, processing thoughts with *pratipaksha bhāvanā*. *Pratipaksha bhāvanā* requires us to contemplate and take another view, to look at the situation from another perspective, to get rid of negative tendencies of the mind.

Thoughts depend upon the company one keeps and therefore one needs to expose oneself to good company. Attachments and aversions can be reduced with good company and good thoughts. *Shaucham* is not only cleanliness but also orderliness in all aspects of our life, from thoughts to actions. Cleanliness is to gain control over the quality of *tamas*, dullness, to make one lead a life of alertness.

2. *Santosha* (contentment) or satisfaction

We pursue different endeavors in life, and we aspire to earn wealth and possessions. Life is a pursuit of owning and yearning and therefore *santosha* has to be developed at two levels. The first stage of contentment is at the level of owning. We need to pursue our basic needs in life.

However, complaining about what one does not have needs to be given up. Focusing on "what I do not have" takes away the joy of living. When a person is content with what he/ she possesses, such a person produces more, consumes less and creates wealth for the community, society and nation. This person is called a *karma yogi*.

The second stage of contentment focuses on yearning, stopping the cravings for more and more. Contentment at both levels of owning and yearning is called *santosha* or *trupti*. This should be practiced as a *niyama*, with a positive attitude. We should think of what we have rather than what we do not have, and thus give up beggarliness of the mind.

A contented person will readily share his wealth with others. Without *santosha*, charity (*dānam*) cannot take place. Contentment is a prerequisite for a charitable disposition.

Santosha has to be practiced at all 3 levels - body, mind and intellect. Not practicing *santosha* at an intellectual level leads to self-dissatisfaction and thus leads to problems such as low self-image and low self-esteem.

> There should be a glad acceptance of the body, mind and intellect and acceptance of limitations that come along with them. This starts with love for one's own self,
> "I accept myself with all my limitations and I own up my limitations and failures".

This does not mean one becomes insensitive and makes the same mistakes over and over again!

This means that self-condemnation, loathing, and all the complexes are to be given up by practice of *santosha* discipline.

"I accept myself and thus I am able to correct myself".

In chapter 6, verse 5 of the Bhagavad Gitā, Lord Krishna says:

"Uddharet ātmanā ātmānam, na ātmānam avasādyet
Ātmaivahyātmano bandhuḥ, ātmaiva ripuḥ ātmanaḥ"

You can lift yourself up (but) do not degrade yourself.
You only are your (true) friend and you are your own enemy."

One very important part of *santosha* is to know that *Ishvara's* grace is always present. Innumerable blessings are already available in various things, people and situations of one's life. This is the *shraddhā,* faith, with which one brings in the practice of *santosha*.

3. *Tapas* (austerity)

Tapas means austerity and like *ahimsā* and *santosha*, this word has many dimensions. Austerities practiced with understanding can lead to satisfaction and contentment, *santosha. Tapas* helps to develop will power, discipline, forbearance and tolerance. With the practice of austerities, the threshold for pain increases. *Tapas* helps one to deal with failures, adversities and unpleasant situations. *Tapas* helps to bring about much needed change.

Many problems arising in modern society result from people failing to accept and face failures and unpleasant situations. One enjoys various privileges; these privileges give a feeling of entitlement which can lead to psychological problems. One might become incapable of handling simple challenges in life, leading to unnecessary stresses and often times to depression.

Tapas helps to develop forbearance to deal with various different situations in life.

Tapas has to be practiced in all daily activities including speaking, eating and sleeping. *Tapas* is important from the religious and spiritual perspective, and also from the perspective of health and physical well-being. The grossest form of *tapas* pertains to physical activity.

4. *Svādhyāya* (spiritual study)

The study of scriptures and is a very important *niyama* to be practiced. During the time of Rishi Patañjali, *svādhyāya* in the form of a daily ritual known as *Brahma yāga* was practiced by all. *Svādhyāya* is the study in context with what the scriptures declare. Unfortunately, people today do not give much importance to spiritual study.

Study of the "Self" without having any background understanding of the scriptural teachings, will be a study of the "ego", leading to boosting of one's ego and not the study of the "Self, *Purusha"! Svādhyāya* can also be *japa*, chanting done in order to manage the mind. Yoga Sutras teaches us to use *japa* in order to restrain the mind from wandering around.

5. *Ishvara Praṇidhānam* (surrender to *Ishvara*)

Surrender to *Ishvara* is to look at every experience in our lives, favorable or unfavorable, as *Ishvara's* will. Every experience we undergo is the result of our past actions. This is called "*karma phalam*", the result or fruits of actions. Behind every *karma phalam,* result of any action, is the Law of *karma* and behind the Law of *karma* is the Lord, *Ishvara*.

Ishvara manifests as this Universe, both as the knowledge and substance of this manifestation. Laws that govern (intelligent order in the Universe) are also expression of the Lord, *Ishvara*.

> We accept the intelligent order of the Universe, *Ishvara's* order.
>
> This acceptance (total acceptance of this present moment), and surrender is called *Ishvara praṇidhānam.*

Rishi Patañjali talks about *Ishvara praṇidhānam* three times. In the first chapter there is a big section on *Ishvara* and *Ishvara praṇidhānam* following *abhyāsa* and *vairāgya*. In the second chapter, 1st sutra is *tapas, svādhyāya* and *Ishvara praṇidhānam.* Rishi Patañjali again talks about *Ishvara praṇidhānam* in the *niyama*. Thus Rishi Patañjali talks about *Ishvara* throughout Yoga Sutras.

Rishi Patañjali does not get into a discussion about the nature of *Ishvara* or the relationship of oneself to *Ishvara* in the Yoga Sutras. However, *Ishvara praṇidhānam* is stressed again and again in Yoga Sutras. This is because Rishi Patañjali assumes that one has gone through the study of other scriptural texts, *Veda* and *Upanishad,* and one has a clear idea about the basics of *Ishvara*!

What will *Ishvara praṇidhānam* do?

By living a life of surrender, *Ishvara praṇidhāna*, the whims and fancies of the mind are not followed, and there is a commitment to follow *dharma,* unconditional commitment to a duty based life. One is in harmony with the laws of nature.

> *Ishvara praṇidhānam* leads to emotional maturity and ethical maturity and thus leads to purification of the mind.
>
> A pure mind and a mind that enjoys inner freedom is a prerequisite for *samādhi,* meditative absorption!

We have learned so far:

Yoga Sutras in the very beginning of the first chapter says Yoga is *chitta vritti nirodha* – Yoga is regulation of *vritti,* thought modifications. In the second chapter Rishi Patañjali begins by saying that Yoga is *Kriyā yoga*. Then he describes *Kriyā yoga* as that which is achieved by practicing *tapas, svādhyāya* and *Ishvara praṇidhānam*. *Kriyā yoga* should thus lead to *samādhi.*

The entire Yoga Sutras text, including the second chapter is about removing *klesha,* impurities, colorings, afflictions of the mind. All eight limbs, elaborated in *sādhanā Pāda,* starting from *yama* and *niyama* to *samādhi* are to be followed in order to remove *klesha* impurities and obstructions arising in the mind.

Āsana

Out of these eight limbs prescribed by Patañjali, *āsana* is the 3rd limb. It is described in chapter 2, sutra 29 onwards. It is very clear that *āsana,* physical postures, by themselves cannot eliminate any of the *klesha*, impurities of the mind.

Āsana is a limb for yoga. Removal of *klesha* occurs only when **one learns to cut down on other unnecessary activities**. Therefore, *āsana* is given as a 3rd limb to explain the importance of cutting down, reducing unnecessary activities.

How does cutting down of the unnecessary activities help?

Cutting down or reducing unnecessary activities reduces the qualities, *guṇa* of *rajas* (extrovertedness) and *tamas* (dullness and lethargy). When one learns to sit quietly in *āsana* (posture) by using one's will power, one reduces *rajas* (extrovertedness) and *tamas* (dullness and lethargy). Only then is one able to turn the attention of the mind inwards.

Thus according to Rishi Patañjali one has to work towards turning the attention inwards (attention away from the sense pleasures, excitement derived from the outside world), with the quality of *sattva*. A subtle, focused, calm and composed mind is the aim for the practice of the 3rd limb of *āsana*.

As said by world renowned teacher, B.K.S. Iyengar:

"The practice of *āsana* purges the body of its impurities, bringing strength, firmness, calm and clarity of the mind".

Sutra 2.46 says this about *āsana*:

"sthiram sukham āsanam"

Sthira is no movement, *sukha* is comfortable and *āsana* is a particular way one keeps one's body. *Sthira* is traditionally prescribed for 48 minutes in one posture; *sukha* is comfortable which means no disturbance mental or physical. Though there were innumerable *āsana* being practiced, 16 *āsana* are mentioned in the Yoga Sutras.

How do we make these *āsana sthira* and *sukha*? Rishi Patañjali says as follows in sutra of chapter 2.47:

"prayatna-shaithilya ananta-samāpattibhyām"

"The means of perfecting the posture is that of relaxing or loosening of effort, and allowing attention to merge with endlessness, or the Infinite."

Prayatna is effort and *shaithilya* is relaxing, cutting, reducing. How do we cut unnecessary activity? By meditation on *Ishvara*, the Infinite = "*anant samāpattibhyām*". Thus by reducing unnecessary activity and meditating on *Ishvara*, Infinite alone, one can achieve *sthiram* and *sukham āsanam*.

Simply sitting in *āsana* is useful and gives therapeutic and health benefits, however it will not address the mental impurities.

Yoga is all about addressing the mind.

Sāttvika – focused, subtle, quiet and calm mind alone can work on diluting the impurities of the mind.

Sitting in *āsana* and with a mind inundated with thoughts or with a dull, lazy mind is not "*āsana siddhi*", mastery of the *āsana*. Mastery of the *āsana* is achieved only when the mind is steady calm and quiet and when the mind is able to be one with *Ishvara*.

This is what "*anant samāpattibhyām*" in sutra 2.47 means. Only by meditating on "*anant*" (Infinite) *Ishvara* will the mind become "*sāttvika*" – subtle, focused, calm and quiet.

"The movement of the body and the intelligence of the brain should synchronize and keep pace with each other"

~ B.K.S. Iyengar

***Āsana*, physical postures, held without any understanding of the functioning of the mind, or held with stormy, undisciplined mind cannot be called Yoga!**

This might help one understand the significance of *āsana* practice as the 3rd limb prescribed by Rishi Patañjali. Sutra on *āsana* says that when one has mastered *āsana* in the true sense of the word, then one is not afflicted by pairs of opposites like respect/insult, likes/dislikes, heat/cold. Sitting in any *āsana,* or holding any physical posture will not make the pairs of opposites go away on their own.

> By just holding a physical posture, *āsana,* *"chitta vritti nirodha",* regulation of the thought modifications will not take place.

If simply holding an *āsana,* physical postures makes someone a *"yogi"*, then are the peacocks, king pigeons or locusts or crows *"yogis"* as per the modern definition of Yoga?

Sthira and *sukha āsana* is held by peacocks in *pincha mayura āsana,* pigeons in *rajakapota āsana,* by locust in *shalabha āsana* or by a crane in *baka āsana*, 24 hours a day, and 7 days a week till the day they die. Does that make them a *"yogi"*?

An acrobat, a circus performer, a gymnast comfortably holds difficult physical postures for a length of time, are they practicing Yoga as per the "modern" understanding of Yoga?

If yoga is only about *sthira* and *sukha āsana,* physical

postures, by holding difficult postures, is a person practicing "yoga" as per the modern understanding and definition of yoga?

NO, the person is not practicing Yoga.

How can Yoga be only about twisting our body in different shapes? The discussion in the Yoga Sutras proves that practice of physical postures alone is,

"*āsana* practice and NOT Yoga practice"!

"*Āsana* is not a posture which you assume mechanically. It involves thought, at the end of which balance is achieved between movement and resistance" ~ B.K.S. Iyengar

How does *sthira sukha āsana* help?

- The practice of *āsana* gets rid of the impurities and ailments of the body, and thus brings about invaluable benefits to the practitioner.

- *Āsana* practice brings strength and fitness to the body and thus prepares the aspirant to sit in meditation for a length of time, with calm and clear mind.

Āsana practice can be a major "tool" for achieving higher awareness. Benefits from the physical to spiritual level will be available to a practitioner only when it becomes a holistic practice, which is positioning of the body in various postures with the total involvement of the mind.

Yogāsana practice aims at bringing different bodily functions into perfect coordination so that they work for the benefit of the entire physical body, providing stable foundation necessary for the exploration of the body, breath and finally the mind.

Praṇāyāma

Breathing in and out is a natural process, an involuntary action. When this involuntary action is converted to a voluntary action, it is called *Praṇāyāma*. Only after *āsana siddhi,* mastery of the *āsana* is achieved in the true sense, then alone *Praṇāyāma* can be practiced as the next limb.

Āyāma is not control. *Āyāma* is regulating the movement of *prāṇa*. There are 5 *prāṇa – prāṇa, apāna, udāna, vyāna* and *samāna.* If *prāṇa* does not reside in the lungs then the other 4 will not work. All five together are called *prāṇa*. *Prāṇa* requires no efforts. As long as the physiological functions of the body work, *prāṇa* will function involuntarily. *Praṇāyāma* is regulating the movement of *prāṇa* voluntarily.

Why is *Praṇāyāma* included as the 4th limb?

Of the three qualities or *"guṇa", sattva, rajas* and *tamas*, *prāṇa* comes from the *rajas guṇa,* quality. The body itself comes from the *tamas guṇa*. The Intellect comes from *sattva guṇa*. The condition of body affects *prāṇa* and mind and condition of the mind affects body and breath, *prāṇa*. It is like the stems on a plant, shake one and the other will be affected!

When the mind is disturbed, breath will get agitated and this will disturb the body, which can lead to psychosomatic problems. When the body is ill and sick, it will affect the mind. For example, a person suffering from severe flu symptoms will not be able to focus and concentrate.

All physiological activities are due to *prāṇa*. And therefore when *prāṇa* is regulated, all physical activities are regulated. Circulatory, digestive and other systems of the body can be regulated by practicing various advanced powerful techniques of *praṇāyāma* (these techniques have to be learned and performed under the guidance of a competent teacher).

Prāṇa comes from *rajas guṇa* – which means *prāṇa* is the power (*"shakti"* or energy) required for essential activities of the living body. When *prāṇa* is regulated, one obtains mastery over body and mind. Through *prāṇa* one can regulate one's mind. And by regulating *prāṇa*, activities of the mind can be resolved temporarily.

How does *praṇāyāma* help in reducing *klesha*, mental impurities?

Vritti and *klesha* (thought modifications and impurities) in the mind are not born out of breath, *prāṇa*. Therefore by regulating breath, annihilation of *klesha* will not take place.

We have seen clearly earlier that the root cause of all *klesha* is *avidyā,* ignorance, about the essence, the reality of one's own self. *Klesha* do not arise in the mind due to body or breath. *Avidyā* will not be removed with *praṇāyāma*. Unless *avidyā* is removed, permanent peace, joy and happiness will not be achieved!

So how does *praṇāyāma* help?

> By regulation of the breath, one is able to regulate the mind. Regulation of the mind leads to reducing impurities of the mind.

Mind is from *rajas guṇa* – activity oriented, and *prāṇa* (breath) is also from *rajas guṇa* – activity oriented, therefore *prāṇa* can be employed to calm the restlessness of the mind.

Prāṇa vīkashaṇa is a practice of observing breath as a tool for quietening the mind. This practice of observing the breath gives the mind something to focus on and thus the mind stops generating new thought patterns. When the mind observes one's own breath, the observing mind becomes free because the breath is free of all forms. Therefore the mind can concentrate by being quiet as the thought pattern formation is arrested for the time being.

Thinking is mechanical, thought A leads to thought B which leads to thought C and so on. A, B and C thoughts are usually unconnected to each other; the mind is always engaged in associative thinking process.

The mind per se is not a problem and deliberate thinking is an asset, a valuable tool. Only when the mind wanders around and takes us for a ride - the mind is a problem!

Prāṇa vīkashaṇa, observing breath curtails the wanderings of the mind.

Sutra 52 states that when *praṇāyāma* is done for a length of time, unnecessary activity and dullness, procrastination and laziness, namely *rajas* and *tamas* will get destroyed. As the hold of *rajas* and *tamas* reduces from the mind, the quality of *sattva* will prevail in the mind more and more.

The mind becomes relatively quiet with *praṇāyāma* and one

is able to observe unnecessary movement and dullness in the mind, and is thus able to better handle the mind.

One needs to understand that only **temporary resolution** of the mind occurs with *praṇāyāma*. The mind is arrested for the time being but the cause for incessant flow of thoughts is not gone permanently. As long as the body functions, the mind will function and thoughts will be present. One cannot get rid of thoughts. The permanent solution therefore is for the reality (basis) of the thoughts to be known. Thoughts are just flow/ modifications/ functioning of the mind which is a superimposition on Pure Consciousness.

"I am not my thoughts, I am not the mind. I am the underlying reality, Pure Consciousness, *Purusha, Ātmā* upon which the names and forms, thoughts and flow of thoughts (mind) appears and disappears".

Take for example a movie and the screen: pictures, stories, actors and actresses appear on the screen without affecting the screen. The screen here is Pure Consciousness, supporting all the functions of the movie – body, mind and intellect.

> The movie (thoughts, feelings and emotions) which appears on the screen is just a superimposition on the screen (Pure Consciousness).
>
> Movie does not affect or become a part of the screen.

What appears as thoughts (modifications of the mind), is a mere superimposition on the substratum, underlying Reality of everything, which is nothing but Pure Consciousness, *sat chit ānanda Ātmā, Purusha.*

Pratyāhāra

Prati + *āhāra* = *Pratyāhāra* = withdrawing senses from all directions. Just like a turtle with four legs and one tail withdraws within its own shell, the 5 senses – taste, touch, smell, sight and hearing are withdrawn from outward to inward. When the sense organs are withdrawn from pursuing their respective sense objects, this is *pratyāhāra.* This happens effortlessly and is not done forcibly.

Sense organs have the habit of moving (gravitating) towards sense objects. Each sense organ seeks out the sense objects of liking. For example: eyes have the liking towards particular colors and forms and therefore eyes "as though" try to seek those colors and forms. When the fancies of the mind get fulfilled through sense organs, mind becomes addicted to the respective sense objects.

Sense organs should be under the command of the mind, especially for a person who is on the path of spiritual journey. However when the sense organs get out of control and the mind loses control over the organs, the mind becomes subservient to the sense organs and subservient to likes and dislikes dictated by the eyes, ears, nose, tongue, and skin.

Sense organs if not properly controlled, will succumb to *rāga* and *dvesha,* attachments and aversions, and the sense organs will act as looters of the mind!

The solution therefore is to practice *yama, niyama, āsana* and *praṇāyāma* to gain relative purity of the mind so that the mind is able to command the sense organs. Then the sense organs effortlessly abide to the command of the mind, this is *pratyāhāra.*

A very famous example is the Chariot metaphor from the *Katha Upanishad* (*discussed in detail in Chapter 4, The Bhagavad Gitā*):

"When the mind is overruled by the sense organs (horses) and when the intellect fails to control the mind (reins controlling the horses) then, this body-mind complex (chariot) will surely be driven into the muddy ditch by the unruly sense organs (horses)!"

When sense organs are not driven by strong likes and dislikes (*rāga* and *dvesha*), the mind will be able to perform actions that are necessary on the path of spiritual journey, and this spiritual aspirant will not get distracted by attachments, aversions, anger, lust, jealousy and conceit.

When *pratyāhāra* takes place, sense organs follow the mind; sense organs do not struggle and create stress for the mind. This withdrawal will be as effortless as the tortoise drawing his head within.

Section 5:

Sutra 3.49- तद्वैराग्यादपि दोषवीजक्षये कैवल्यम्॥४९॥

Tadvairāgyādapi doṣavījakṣaye kaivalyam ॥49॥

Absoluteness, *Kaivalya,* the final goal of Yoga is attained only when the desire to acquire extraordinary knowledge is rejected and the source of obstacles is completely controlled.

Sutra 3.54- सत्त्वपुरुषयोः शुद्धिसाम्ये कैवल्यमिति॥५४॥

Sattvapuruṣayoḥ śuddhisāmye kaivalyamiti ॥55॥

When there is equality between *sāttvic buddhi* (intellect), between *sattva* and *Purusha,* then "the state of complete emancipation", *kaivalya* dawns.

Sutra 4.31- तदासवार्वरणमलापेतस्य ज्ञानस्यानन्त्याज्ज्ञेयमल्पम्॥३१॥

Tadāsarvāvaraṇamalāpetasya

jñānasyānantyājjñeyamalpam ॥31॥

When the mind is free from the clouds that prevent perception, all is known, there is nothing more to be known. Infinity comes to the knowledge which has been freed from all coverings of afflictions and actions.

Sutra 4.34- पुरुषार्थशून्यानां गुणानां प्रतिप्रसवः कैवल्यं

स्वरूपप्रतिष्ठा वा चितिशक्तिरिति॥३४॥

Puruṣārthaśūnyānāṁ guṇānāṁ pratiprasavaḥ kaivalyaṁ

svarūpapratiṣṭhā vā citiśaktiriti ॥34॥

When the highest purpose of life is achieved, the three basic qualities do not excite responses in the mind. That is freedom. In other words, the perceiver is no longer colored by the mind. *Kaivalya,* Absoluteness, is the establishment of the power of knowledge in its own nature.

In this section –

- Rishi Patañjali starts chapter 3 on Yoga Sutras with last 3 steps of the eight steps, what are they?
- What is *samyama*? What is a *siddhi*? Why should a practitioner stay away from various *siddhi*?
- Concluding Chapter of the Yoga Sutras is about "*Kaivalya*", Absoluteness – what is the meaning?
- Having learnt about the mind, impurities of the mind, eight steps towards removing afflictions of the body and the mind, how should we put this in practice?

The last three limbs of *Ashtānga Yoga* (eight limbs) are:

Dhāraṇā (concentration)

Dhyāna (meditation)

Samādhi (absorption)

Through these 3 stages, attention is progressively turned inwards (away from the outside world):

1. Attention leads to concentration (*dhāraṇā*). Concentration is the process of holding or fixing the attention of mind on one object or one place.
2. Concentration leads to meditation (*dhyāna*). Meditation is sustained concentration, whereby the attention continues to hold, stay put on the same object or place, for a length of time.
3. Meditation leads to absorption (*samādhi*). When the state of *dhyāna* is maintained for a long time without interruption, one is in *samādhi*.

Dhāraṇā

Sutra 3.1 is about *dhāraṇā,* concentration on one thing. Concentration *(dhāraṇā)* is the process of holding or fixing the attention of mind onto one object or one place, and is the sixth of the eight rungs.

Dhāraṇā takes place when the mind withdraws its backing from the senses after the 5th step of *pratyāhāra,* then the mind is able to concentrate on one single thing or at one single point, for example, on any one of the seven chakra or on the tip of the nose

Preparation for concentration: Concentration comes more easily with an effort to stabilize the mind (with *abhyāsa* and *vairāgya,* practice and non-attachment), by minimizing gross colorings of the mind through *kriyā Yoga (tapas, svādhyāya, and Ishvara praṇidhānam)*, and the first five of the eight rungs *(yama, niyama, āsana, praṇāyāma and pratyāhāra).*

Without such preparation, the efforts to concentrate the mind often will lead to an inner battle with the incessant flow of thoughts! The truth is that with proper preparation, concentration comes much more naturally, without proper preparation, very little can be achieved.

> The noisy mind leads people to say that they cannot meditate. "Meditation is very difficult. May be I should not practice meditation now when my life is full of complications"!

Actually, when one understands the tremendous value of simple concentration training, then even brief and shallower sessions of *dhāraṇā* will have a positive value. With practice and effort (*abhyāsa*) and detaching one's attention from other thoughts (*vairāgya*), by totally focusing on what one is doing (the mind remaining unmoved and unruffled); each moment of positive experience will leave its positive trace in the depth of the mind. The benefits may seem invisible at first, but those moments of concentration, *dhāraṇā,* add up over time.

Dhyāna

Sutra 3.2 is about *dhyāna,* Meditation as sustained concentration, whereby the attention is held on the same object or place without interruption. In the word *dhyāna, "dhyā"* stands for concentration. One thought, one *vritti* gets stretched out like a rubber band. The continuation of one *vritti*, thought or uninterrupted focus on one point is called absorption in meditation (*dhyāna*), and it is the 7th of the 8 limbs of *ashtāngayoga.*

We need to understand this process in detail. Usually the mind is engrossed in a thought process through associative thinking. Thought "A" leads to thought "B", and thought "B" leads to thought "C" and then to thought "D" and this process continues all the time! These are usually all unrelated thoughts, jumping around from one thought to another thought through the process of associative thinking.

> *Dhyāna* is thought "A" followed by thought "A" followed by thought "A" and so on.
>
> Finally thought "A" alone remains in the mind, flow of identical thoughts, A-A- A-A-A……

The classical example given is that of a stream of oil. When oil is poured evenly, all droplets of oil flow down in such a manner that the flow of oil droplets forms a single stream – like a silky ribbon of oil flowing down!

The repeated concentration on the object of concentration is meditation. Typically, there is a moment of concentration, followed by a distraction. In *dhyāna,* attention lets go of the distraction, then returns to the object of concentration again.

Another way of describing the process of meditation is that there is an ongoing series of individual concentrations, rather than one continuous concentration. If each of those concentrations is on the same object, that is called meditation.

For example when the *dhyāna* is on OM, there is OM … OM.... OM….. And finally it appears as there is just one OM! Whether you prefer to think of it as one continuous flow of concentration, or a series of individual concentrations on the same object, it is the unbroken or undistracted characteristic of attention that allows concentration (*dhāraṇā*) to evolve into meditation *dhyāna.*

Samādhi

Sutra 3.3 is about *samādhi,* deep absorption, wherein the essence of the object, place, or point alone shines forth in the mind. *Sam* + *ā* + *dhi* = that which is well placed.

This deserves elaboration. Fixing the mind on an object is *dhārṇā,* and flow of one identical thought is *dhyāna.* And when the object of concentration goes away, it is *samādhi.* When only the essence of that object, place, or point shines forth in the mind, as if devoid even of its own form, that state of deep absorption is called *samādhi,* which is the eighth rung. Thus *samādhi* is meditation of a higher state, a deep absorption in meditation, the state of perfected concentration.

Let us understand *samādhi* one more time. There is an "observer" of an action, who is doing the act of "observing" (of an object of meditation), which is "observed". With meditation, there is still an observer (meditator) observing the observed (object of meditation).

When the observer becomes extremely absorbed in the process of observing the object, the three collapse so that all there remains is only awareness of the object. Distance between the observer (person) and the observed (object) disappear. It is "as though" the observer is merged with the object. This is when meditation becomes *samādhi*. This is called "*nirvikalpa samādhi*" where the meditator loses his/her individual identity in the object of meditation. There are various stages and levels of *samādhi* according to sutra 1.17-1.18, 1.42.

The fact is that we have difficulty in recognizing this truth of who we are as *Purusha, Ātmā,* Pure Consciousness, Self, Being. This is because of the impurities, coloring (sutra 1.5) of the mind.

"*Samādhi* is not the end in itself, but is a tool"

A means used to discover the truth of one's own presence as *Purusha, Ātmā.*

The tool of meditation and *samādhi* is learned so that we can break away from the mind made colorings, impurities and obstructions.

How does *samādhi* work?

Transformation of the mind takes place due to *samādhi* when the chain of thoughts is stopped (associative thinking process stops) and the mind becomes steady and one-pointed.

Meditation (along with concentration and *samādhi*) is a tool for examining the inner world, a tool to work towards the realization of the core of one's own "being". Gross objects and subtle objects are systematically experienced, examined and set aside with non-attachment, gradually moving past the layers of ignorance or *avidyā*.

Samyama

Samyama is the collective practice of concentration, *dhāraṇā,* meditation, *dhyāna,* and *samādhi,* which are the sixth, seventh, and eighth *anga* of the *ashtānga yoga* in *Siddhi pāda*, chapter 3 of Patañjali's Yoga Suṭras.

The attainment of *samādhi* is not the end of practice, but is a beginning of sorts. The primary purpose of all the preparatory work and the first five limbs, rungs of Yoga are to build this tool called *samyama.*

The three processes of *dhāraṇā, dhyāna,* and *samādhi,* when taken together on the same object, place or point is *samyama.* The term *samyama* refers to a subtler practice. This tool is the means of reaching the ever subtler levels of non-attachment.

As the Yogi practices and gradually attains mastery of the process of *samyama*, his/her practice brings greater depth of experience, insight, and realization.

Samyama is like the surgeon's scalpel, the razor sharp tool of discrimination used for deep introspection.

This sharp tool of discrimination, *samyama,* eventually helps to uncover the jewel of the inner world.

This process of discrimination allows the yogi to gradually move past many forms of ignorance or *avidyā.*

This includes: 1) ignorance of taking that which is transient, body and mind, as eternal, 2) mistaking the impure for pure, 3) thinking that body mind complex, worldly objects and pleasures are the source of eternal happiness, and 4) taking that which is not-self to be Self.

Siddhi Pāda (Accomplishments) – Chapter 3 of Patañjali's Yoga Sutras text

The later part of the text is about accomplishments that result from the practices prescribed in the Yoga Sutras. This section of chapter on *siddhi* (accomplishments, attainments) speaks of the wealth of effects and powers gained from the practice of *ashtānga yoga,* about 35 effects, which might be experienced by a practitioner.

Sutra 16 onwards in chapter 3, Rishi Patañjali talks about accomplishments derived from the training of the mind. He explains various *siddhi*, accomplishments achieved by various *samyama* on different objects of meditation.

However, in sutra 37 Rishi Patañjali gives a clear warning that these powers achieved through *samyama* are obstacles on the path towards achieving the final goal of realization of "Self". *Samyama* on different objects might bring various powers which might be valuable as far as this material world is concerned but these powers obstruct progress of a spiritual seeker as far as liberation is concerned.

In sutra 50 of chapter 3, Patañjali further states that just as an ordinary person fights to get rid of afflictions, the Yogi has to fight these powers. These powers can lead to distractions, to further attachments and thus to a downward spiral of delusion. Attachment to these powers can also lead to a loss of previous achievements because this Yogi will be distracted and might lose focus and attention.

> Sutra 3.51 goes on to say that the Yogi should not be allured or wonderstruck by the courtship of various powers achieved through *samayama,* or else he will fall into the undesirable darkness of afflictions all over again!

The Yogi who has renounced everything when gets allured by the powers *(siddhi)*, he/she will then fall prey to the sense objects and desires, which are the causes of suffering. Therefore, "these powers *(siddhi)* are suitable for the foolish one" – declares Patañjali!

Only by renouncing these powers and destroying the seed of bondage will the Yogi gain liberation. When the Yogi thus discriminates, throws away the grosser forms and meditates on the finer, he attains a stage of *Kaivalya* – Absoluteness, fullness, liberation.

This stage brings knowledge of the essence, reality, Self, *Purusha.*

Kaivalya Pāda (Liberation) – Chapter 4 of Patañjali's Yoga Sutras text

Chapter 4 is about the subject of absoluteness. *Kaivalya* is the permanent state of fullness. This is the ultimate goal as described in the text Yoga Sutras.

Sutra 4.25 and 4.26 state:

"For one who has to one who has realized *Purusha* or Self - distinction between seer and the subtlest mind, the false identities and the curiosity about the nature of one's own self come to an end. Then the mind is inclined towards the highest discrimination, and gravitates towards complete liberation."

One can ask the question: why *Kaivalya*, why should the goal be absoluteness, liberation from the world around us?

The answer is: happiness and pain experienced in our life is temporary and transient. Identification with transient, imperfect body and mind will give us temporary, fleeting glimpses of happiness. However, as the body and mind can never be perfect, no matter what one does, identification with body and mind or with the roles we play in life will eventually lead to pain and suffering.

The primary reason behind all our pursuits in life is to seek permanent security, peace and happiness. *Kaivalya* is a condition of perfect peace; it is a permanent state of fullness which can never be found through worldly experiences. *Kaivalya* is when the constant seeking for security, peace and happiness ends! *Kaivalya* or liberation is fullness.

The goal according to the Yoga Sutras is to attain a permanent, everlasting source of fullness and happiness – the goal is to attain *Kaivalya. Kaivalya* is the state of utter "only-ness". The cycle of birth and death, happiness and sorrow, haves and have not's, conflicts and finally ignorance gets destroyed in the end by attainment of *Kaivalya* "Absoluteness".

When the Yogi (spiritual seeker following path of Yoga, *sādhanā*) attains final discrimination and renounces everything, nothing remains to hinder the realization of Divinity as the truth of oneself. Sutra 18 talks about *Purusha.* This sutra talks about the nature of Pure Consciousness and its relationship with the mind. Sutra 18 is about the essence of who we are as *Purusha*, the infinite, boundary-less, changeless, unborn, uncreated, observer of the mental events - that is the Subject.

"sadājñātāḥcitta-vrttayaḥtat-prabhoḥpuruṣasya-apariṇāmitvāt" ~ *Kaivalya Pād*a, sutra 18

"The true Self can always observe the thoughts (*vritti*), that which is fluctuating in human beings, because this pure Self (*Purusha,* master of the mind) is not in motion (unchanging)."

That which can be observed is an object. I can observe the objects of the world; I can observe my own body, *prāṇa,* fluctuations of the mind and the happenings in the intellect. Therefore my body, *prāṇa* or mind or my intellect are the objects. "I" possess my body, *prāṇa,* mind and intellect.

The truth of who "I" am is – not an object, "I" am the Subject. "I" am the Subject, *Purusha, Ātmā,* Pure Consciousness, thought-free observer of all objects and experiences, including my own body, *prāṇa* and the happenings of my mind.

What I possess is not the real me.

For example, I possess a pen, a dog, a house and say "my pen, my dog, my house" however I am NOT the pen, dog or the house. I possess body, *prāṇa*, mind and intellect; therefore I am NOT the body, *prāṇa*, mind or the intellect.

Then who am "I"?

The reality who "I" am is – the Subject, *Purusha, Ātmā,* Pure Consciousness, Awareness, because of which the body, *prāṇa*, mind and intellect are known.

Our mind is made up of thoughts, feelings, emotions, perceptions and experiences, modifications, waves of changing mental events which are observable. A Yogi knows the difference between *Purusha* and the mind and therefore has the knowledge that "I am not this body, mind or intellect". Ignorance about the Reality, truth of one's own self, is destroyed. Isolation from all afflictions especially from the affliction of *avidyā*, results in *Kaivalya*.

Sutras 29 to 34 talk about the mind without impurities and impediments attaining infinite knowledge about the Divinity, *Purusha, Ātmā* or the Pure Consciousness, Awareness as the essence of oneself. After having taken the journey of self-exploration, the Yogi realizes that having discovered the truth of oneself as *Prusha, Ātmā,* there is little more to know!

The essence of the existence was not so complicated after all. The recognition of this simplicity can be very inspiring for the *sādhaka* (one who treads the path of *sādhanā,* spiritual practices). It gives a comforting reassurance that, while this world of names and forms appears to be vast, there is an underlying simplicity.

When the final goal of realization of "Self" is achieved, nothing outwardly remains to be achieved. Thus a Yogi, a spiritual seeker gains enlightenment and attains liberation, *Kaivalya.*

Such an enlightened Yogi's actions are pure and spontaneous, no action is self-centered and none are initiated by selfish motives. This Yogi's actions are from the here-and-now, response to the needs of the moment in relation to the service *(sevā)* of other beings. For such a Yogi there is "no me and no other".

What remains for this enlightened Yogi is Pure Consciousness, Infinite Awareness, *Purusha,* Divinity which alone seems to play in and through various names and forms – here, there, and everywhere!

Peace cannot be created; peace is our natural state.

We create agitation and disturb peace.
Where is the agitation created? In the mind.

We keep giving momentum to the thoughts,
because we do not have mastery over the mind.

"You are Peace!"

"Master the mind and stop agitations to find peace,
your natural state." ~ The Upanishad

Summary

How can yoga enthusiasts apply the teachings of Patañjali's Yoga Sutras in day to day life?

Begin by understanding the fact that though *āsana* and *praṇāyāma* practice has invaluable benefits, this practice alone cannot be called the practice of "Yoga".

Know that being able to master different physical postures or breathing techniques alone will not make a person fit to be called a "yogi" in the true sense of the word. As per the discussion in the Yoga Sutras, Yoga has a vast and profound purpose.

1. Yoga Sutras gives detailed instructions on *ashtānga yoga,* starting with ethical principles and moral values. These *yama* and *niyama*, ethics and morals should be assimilated and followed at all times, dealing with the outside world, with others and dealing with one's own self. This is for the seeker to grow ethically and emotionally and to remove impurities at the body and mind levels.

2. Then begin the preparation of the body and mind through *āsana* and *praṇāyāma*. Unless and until the body is fit and healthy, one will not be able to go deeper into the teachings of Yoga. An unfit and unhealthy body will be a constant source of distraction. At the same time it is very important to understand that Yoga is not about the shape of the body.

   Yoga is not some kind of performance, test of flexibility of the body, nor is yoga a competition or mastering of the most difficult postures just for the sake of boosting one's ego.

3. It is very unfortunate to think that *āsana* practice, physical postures, is the final goal of Yoga. It is like learning and practicing to hold a musical instrument for years and years, never understanding what the musical instrument is for! Having learned how to hold the instrument, one needs to learn how to play music on that instrument, otherwise holding the instrument is useless.

   Work on *āsana* and *praṇāyāma* with a proper understanding of their relevance, with the understanding that Yoga is all-encompassing, and is designed for a vast and profound purpose.

4. When the afflictions and problems of the body are reduced with *āsana* and *praṇāyāma,* then identification with the body will be reduced and we will be able to discover the realm of the mind.

5. Why should we analyze the mind? Because our identification with our mind, movement of thoughts leads to suffering! All problems – personal, global, social, economic, relate to the way of thinking. We constantly seek something from outside to fix our inner problems. Better clothes, better computers and gadgets, new relations, new jobs, new situations and new places all have their shortcomings and do not solve our problems in the long run.

   New things do not make us really happy, just that the unhappy mind quietens for a few moments, and then we are off chasing other new things! Caught up on this treadmill, we find temporary satisfactions, never permanent ones. This non-stop chasing ends only by knowing one's true self. We constantly feel dissatisfied because we seek security, peace and happiness out in the world.

Real, permanent peace and contentment comes from looking within and not from outward relations, objects, or situations. Practice of *Kriyā Yoga – tapas, svādhyāya* and *Ishvara praṇidhānam* is a step in the right direction. These help us know our attachments and aversions, watching our ego at work and lead us to a proper understanding of the root cause of all impurities and colorings of the mind, *klesha*.

6. We can then analyze various conditions of the mind – distracted, dull, lazy, and sleepy or one pointed, focused. This can be done by turning our attention inwards with *pratyāhāra*, looking at our thoughts rather than getting distracted with various and enticing external distractions. And by spending time with our mind, with *dhāraṇā*.

7. As the mind stops wandering, benefits like a sharp focused mind and detachment from the happenings of the mind (in addition to our body being fit and healthy) will be derived. Once the stages of *dhyāna* and *samādhi* and *samyama* are achieved, going beyond *avidyā* (the root cause for all the impurities and colorings of the mind and the cause of all suffering), will lead to the "sight", realization of inner divinity, knowing oneself as *Purusha, Ātmā,* Pure consciousness, Awareness, boundless source of peace, fullness and happiness.

Journey of a spiritual seeker

Ethical and moral person - Established and rooted in *yama* and *niyama*

Fitness and wellbeing of the body - Practice of *āsana, praṇāyāma, mudrā, bandha* other physical practices

Towards the mind - With a fit and a healthy body, able to withdraw attention from the outwards (body, relations, objects of the world, name and fame) to delve deeper inwards, *pratyāhāra*

Understand how the mind works - Understands functioning of the mind, different states of the mind and understands colorings, afflictions, impurities *(klesha)* of the mind

Concentration - After practicing *Kriyā Yoga – tapas, svādhyāya* and *Ishvara praṇidhānam,* with the removal of the impurities of the mind, the seeker gets ready for *dhāraṇā*

Focused mind - Mastering thoughts with *abhyāsa* and *vairāgya,* the seeker gets ready for *dhyāna*

Ready for meditation - Restrained and disciplined mind leads to *samādhi*

Liberation, *Kaivalya* - Having practiced *samyama*, this seeker is finally ready for liberation, *Kaivalya.*

Quotes by the Sages of the 20th Century

"You take great care of the body. You desire that it should be clean, healthy, beautiful and strong. You take bath with sweet soaps and hot water. You regularly feed it with nourishing food. If there is the least pain or disease medicine is given. But you never give a thought to the much more important thing - MIND.

Body is only the outward appearance, a projection of the mind. If the mind is well then the body is well. If the mind is sick the body becomes ill. Mind is everything. It controls your whole life. Upon it depends your happiness or misery, success or failure."

~ Swāmi Sivānanda

"Yoga is not about twisting the body; Yoga is about straightening the mind."

~ Swāmi Chinmayānanda

"When one discovers oneself to be full and complete, all the conflicts and grief vanish; happiness becomes natural, effortless; one becomes a spontaneous person; life becomes a sport!

~ Swāmi Dayānanda Saraswatī

OM

बन्धुरात्मात्मनस्तस्य येनात्मैवात्मना जितः ।
अनात्मनस्तु शत्रुत्वे वर्तेतात्मैव शत्रुवत् ॥६-६॥

Bandurātmātmanastasya yenātmaivātmanā jitaḥ
anātmanastu shatrutve vartetātmaiva shatruvat //

"For the one who has mastered the mind, the mind is the best of friends; but for the one who has failed to do so, his very mind will be the greatest of enemies"

~ Bhagavad Gitā, chapter 6, verse 6

"Mind alone is the cause for people's bondage and liberation.

Driven by the senses, it leads to bondage. When the senses are mastered, it leads to liberation."

~ *Amrita Bindu Upanishad*

Chapter 4

The Bhagavad Gitā

Key to correct pronunciations for the Bhagavad Gitā chapter

a (short a) sounds like u in "sun" or "up"

ā (long a) sounds like aa in "father" or "car"

ñ the consonant can be pronounced as "nny "or "dny" or "gy", **not** like sound "j" in "agent"

ś or **ṣ** may both be pronounced as English sh in "shine"

c sounds like ch in "church"; **never** like k as in "car"

g is always a hard g as in "god", **not** a soft g as in "gym"

o sounds like o in "opal", as in *loka* (world). Sanskrit o is never short like o in "pot"

ṛ sounds like r in "grind", as in *Kṛshṇa (Krishna)*

Important words without diacritical marks:

Saaṅkhya - ṅ sounds like ng in "song"

Dharma / dhaarmic, Adharma/adhaarmic Ahimsaa / Himsaa

Saṃsaara - ṃ sounds like n in French "bon"

Raaga/ Dvesha

Kaama, Kṛodhah, Lobha, Moha, Mada, Maatsaryam,

Sukha/ Dukha - kh sounds like ckh in "blockhead"

Sankalap and *Samatvam* - a sound like "up" or "sun"

Karma Yoga, Raaja (Upaasanaa or *Dhyaana) Yoga, Bhakti Yoga*

Jñana (Gñāna) - jñ the consonant cluster, can be pronounced "nny" or "dny" or "gy", **not** j-n

Guṇa - ṇ sounds like the n in "under"

Sattva, Rajas, Tamas - a sounds like u in "sun" or "up", t sounds like softer t in "pasta"

II OM II

A Glimpse of the Bhagavad Gitā

Section 1

- Why is the Bhagavad Gitā often times referred to as the greatest gift to the world?

The Bhagavad Gitā has been described as a living creation rather than a book, with a new message for every age and a new meaning for every civilization. The Bhagavad Gitā teachings speak to the mind that has fought in life – fought internal battles. It is about the battles all of us face each day in our hearts and in our minds.

- What is the meaning of the word "Bhagavad Gitā"?

Bhagavad means *Bhagavān* (Lord) and *Gitā* means song. Thus Bhagavad Gitā means "song of the Lord".

- Who is the author? What are the main themes covered in this text? What is the story behind the setting of the Gitā?

For the details on the author, main themes and story behind the setting, see pages 180-186.

Section 2

- Why was the hero Arjuna, the warrior prince, distraught on the battlefield and what was the solution given to Arjuna by Lord Krishna?

Arjuna, a hero of outstanding achievements and disciplined intellect, gets overwhelmed with emotions and falls down in despair at the onset of a war. Arjuna forgets that the battle which he is supposed to fight is not between relations but the battle is between *dharma* and *adharma*, between right and wrong.

Lord Krishna's profound spiritual teachings free Arjuna from his emotional conflict and thus restore Arjuna's determination to perform his duty for *dharma* preservation. (See pages 188-190)

- What is the meaning of words *Dharma* and *Ahimsā*?

Dharma as used in Hindu scriptures is the "Law of Being". *Dharma* is righteousness, duty, a core value as a human being, core responsibilities of the role that we have to play. (Pages 191-194)

Ahimsā is the underlying value of all values. *Ahimsā* is not just "nonviolence". All-encompassing definition of *ahimsā* is "causing least possible harm in any given situation".

Section 3

- How is Arjuna's dilemma and Lord Krishna's teachings on the battlefield relevant to us at present?

Bhagavad Gitā teachings are relevant because Arjuna represents humanity of every century. The Gitā addresses the human problem of conflict and grief, a feeling of helplessness. (Page 196-197)

- Do we really know who we are? What is our problem? How does the Gitā answer the question, "who am I?"

All of us desire security, peace and happiness. Sense of inadequacy, feeling of helplessness, grief and despair arise due to the wrong conclusions "I am this physical body, limited and incomplete." This wrong conclusion about ourselves arising out of the ignorance of the reality of who we are is our problem. (See pages 197 and 200-203)

- What is the meaning of the word "*Ātmā*"?

Ātmā is the essence of who we are as unchanging, eternal Divinity, Pure Consciousness, limitless absolute Awareness. This all-pervading changeless Consciousness principle is *Ātmā.* (Pages 197-200)

For the famous Chariot allegory from *Katha Upanishad,* see pages 204-205.

Section 4

- What is the problem in pursuing happiness through appeasing strong likes *(rāga)* and dislikes *(dvesha)*? And what is Lord Krishna's advice on how to deal with fluctuations and turbulences of the mind? How do we prepare our mind to live intelligently?

We fail to see what really is, we fail to be objective, and as long as we fail to see the world objectively – we suffer.

What we need to do is to neutralize our attachments and aversions by changing strong likes and dislikes into "preferences". For *rāga* and *dvesha,* see pages (207-211 and 212-216).

Section 5

- What is *Karma Yoga*? Why practice *Karma Yoga*?

Karma Yoga is skill in action. *Karma Yoga* is dedication of performance of an action to the intelligent order of the cosmos, *Ishvara. Karma Yoga* is graceful acceptance of the results of our actions. Practice *Karma Yoga* for training and disciplining the mind. (Pages 217-222)

- What are the Law of *Karma* and the Theory of Reincarnation?

Law of *Karma* is a consequence of natural acts, a universal principle of cause and effect, action and reaction that governs all life. Law of *Karma* and the Theory of reincarnation cannot be mistaken as a system of divine reward or punishment. (Pages 223-226)

Section 6

- What do *Rāja (Upāsanā) Yoga*, *Bhakti Yoga* and *Jñana (Gñāna) Yoga* mean?

Rāja (Upāsanā) Yoga consists of different types of meditation and is recommended by Lord Krishna to quieten the mind. *Bhakti Yoga* is devotion, attitude of surrender to *Ishvara* and worship through various spiritual practices. *Jñana (Gñāna) Yoga* is all about giving up ignorance about one's own self, recognizing truth of self as limitless Awareness, *Ātmā.* (Pages227-238)

- What does the Bhagavad Gitā say about "God"?

Other words to use instead of the word "God" are – Lord, *Ishvara, Bhagavān, Parmātmā.* According to the Bhagavad Gitā, Lord, *Ishvara* is the universal principle which includes everything that exists in the Universe and beyond.

There is nothing that exists apart from *Ishvara*. Just as waves arise, exist and merge back into the ocean, everything arises, exists and merges back in *Ishvara*. (Page 231-232)

- What is achieved by practicing *Karma Yoga, Rāja (Upāsanā) Yoga, Bhakti Yoga* and *Jñana (Gñāna) Yoga*?

Purification of the mind, clear and calm mind ready to receive knowledge of the essence of oneself is achieved though *Karma Yoga, Rāja (Upāsanā) Yoga, Bhakti Yoga.* Through *Jñana (Gñāna) Yoga*, this purified mind finally realizes that "I" am full and complete – unborn, uncreated, limitless, thought-free Consciousness, Awareness, *Ātmā.* (Page 239-240)

Section 7

- What is the meaning of the word the "field" and the "Knower of the field"? What are the three *"guṇa"* attributes?

"Known", world of all known objects is the field; and the "Knower of the field" is Self, the Subject, *Ātmā.* Everyone is a mixture of three *guṇa,* attributes or qualities of *sattva, rajas* and *tamas.* The predominance of one attribute over the other two accounts for the dissimilarities among people and dissimilarities in nature. (Pages 241-245)

Section 8

- How do divine and demonic qualities shape our body and mind?

A person with divine values will become naturally calm and will have the mental poise and dispassion with an abiding mind. A person with demonic values will have pretentiousness, vanity, self-conceit, anger, harshness and ignorance of right and wrong. (Pages 246-249)

Section 9

- What was the effect of Lord Krishna's teaching on Arjuna?

Arjuna was no longer confused between right and wrong after receiving the teachings from Lord Krishna. Arjuna finally understands that his essential divine nature is *Ātmā* and decides to follow his duty as per his *dharma* as the protector of masses. (Pages 250-253)

- Concluding comments from the teachings of the Bhagavad Gitā.

The teachings of the Bhagavad Gitā are meant for anyone whose mind is unsatisfied with constant want, a mind that is alert and thinking but which has many conflicts. The teachings address the human problem of grief, a feeling of helplessness.

The teachings of the Bhagavad Gitā, when properly understood, can help us in our day to day life, giving us the strength and the wisdom to make decisions that help us to perform our duties and responsibilities and lead a virtuous life. (Page 254)

Section 10

- What are the teachings of the Bhagavad Gitā in brief?

What are the benefits derived from reading, understanding and implementing the teachings of the Bhagavad Gitā?

The teachings of the Bhagavad Gitā help a person to discover the potential power to renounce false values of life and rediscover the Divine nature as the truth of one's own self. See pages 254-261 on the teaching in brief and benefits derived by the spiritual seeker.

"The study of the Bhagavad Gitā is a positive message of hope, inspiration and joy."

- How can the Bhagavad Gitā serve as a guide to live a spiritual life?

When the teachings of the Bhagavad Gitā are followed, a calm, composed, serene and disciplined mind is achieved. Having prepared the body and the mind, one gets ready to realize the truth of one's own self as the limitless source of peace, security and happiness.

"The Gitā educated person learns to recognize a rhythm, to see beauty, and hear melody in ordinary day to day life."

OM

ॐ श्री गणेशाय नमः ॥

Section 1:

Why is the Bhagavad Gitā often times referred to as the greatest gift to the world?

"When doubts haunt me, when disappointments stare me in the face, and I see not one ray of hope on the horizon, I turn to Bhagavad Gitā and find a verse to comfort me; and I immediately begin to smile in the midst of overwhelming sorrow. Those who meditate on the Gitā will derive fresh joy and new meanings from it every day." ~ Mahātmā Gāndhi

The Bhagavad Gitā is meant for humanity. The Gitā is not meant for any one person or creed or nation. The Bhagavad Gitā teachings speak to the mind that has fought in life – fought internal battles. It is about the battles all of us face each day in our hearts and in our minds. As the famous spiritual master, philosopher, saint and poet Sri Aurobindo says~

"The Bhagavad Gitā is a true scripture of the human race, a living creation rather than a book, with a new message for every age and a new meaning for every civilization."

- The teachings are about our life situations where we have to choose between a right action and that which might not be a righteous action.
- The teachings are meant for anyone whose mind is unsatisfied with constant want, a mind that is alert and thinking but which has many conflicts.

- The teachings address the human problem of conflict and grief, a feeling of helplessness. All of us sense inadequacy and are unable to face many situations in life. A situation gets to be a problem due to the senses of inadequacy or limitation.
- The teachings of the Bhagavad Gitā, when properly understood, can help us in our day to day life, giving us the strength and the wisdom to make decisions - decisions that help us to perform our duties and responsibilities and lead a virtuous life. Leading a virtuous life will help us grow emotionally and spiritually.

The core objective of the Bhagavad Gitā is to solve the problem of sorrow in human life by means of spiritual wisdom.

In this section -

- Learn the meaning of the word “Bhagavad Gitā”
- What is in the Bhagavad Gitā, who wrote it, who gave the teaching of the Gitā?
- The main themes of the 18 chapters of the Gitā
- Story behind the setting of the Bhagavad Gitā.

What is the meaning of the word "Bhagavad Gitā"? Who is the author? What are the themes covered in this text?

Among all Hindu scriptures, the Bhagavad Gitā is by far the most widely studied. Hinduism is firmly rooted in ancient scriptures, the four *Veda*-s. The *Veda* are the oldest sacred texts, dating back to 1500 - 1000 BCE.

The central teachings of the four *Veda*, the section dedicated for spiritual wisdom is called the *Upanishad*. The *Upanishad*-s are presented in a lyrical form in the Bhagavad Gitā and therefore Bhagavad Gitā is often referred to as the "fifth *Veda*" or the essence of all the *Upanishad, "Upanishad sāra"*. The Bhagavad Gitā manages to convey the central teachings of these four *Veda* in an accessible and endearing manner.

The Bhagavad Gitā is composed by *Rishi Vyāsa.* The Bhagavad Gitā is an approximately 700 verse segment which is drawn from the middle of the Mahābhārata which is a longest known historical epic poem with 200,000 lines. The Mahābhārata is the world's longest poem composed in classical Sanskrit language! The Bhagavad Gitā shines in the middle of the epic Mahābhārata like a pendent jewel.

The Bhagavad Gitā is a dialogue taking place on the battlefield between Lord Krishna and the mighty warrior prince named Arjuna. Lord Krishna *(Kṛṣṇa)* is the 8th *avatāra* of Lord *Vishṇu* (Lord *Vishṇu* is the sustainer of all existence – one who supports, preserves, and governs the laws of the Universe). Lord Krishna is the embodiment of love and divine joy which destroys all suffering and pain. When Krishna talks in the Bhagavad Gitā, the Lord is talking. What is said in the Gitā are the words of *Bhagavān* (Lord *Vishṇu*), and *Bhagavān* is telling us what the *Veda* say!

Thus Bhagavad Gitā means "Song of the Lord", *Bhagavad* means *Bhagavān* (Lord) and *Gitā* means song.

For many people, the original *Veda* themselves are inaccessible. However, the Lord has given us a condensed version of the *Veda* in the form of the teaching of the Bhagavad Gitā imparted by Shri Krishna to the mighty warrior Arjuna. We explore the Gitā as the essence of the teachings of the four *Veda*, NOT as a work focusing on the historical personality of "Shri Krishna".

The Bhagavad Gitā is comprised of 18 chapters. In these 18 chapters, 700 verses are presented in a lyrical form, composed in classical Sanskrit language. The meter used for chanting majority of these verses is called *"anushtup cchandas"*, eight syllables in a quarter, with 4 such quarters in each verse. Chapters 2 and 18 provide an entire summary of the Gitā. These 18 chapters can be broadly divided in three groups of six chapters. The main topics are as follows:

Chapters 1 to 6 are mostly about the true nature of a person, *Ātmā* (Self): Chapter 1- Arjuna's sorrow, 2- Spiritual Wisdom, 3- *Karma Yoga*, 4- Renunciation by knowledge, 5- Renunciation, 6-Meditation

Chapters 7 to 12 are about the Lord and how the truth about the Lord can be understood: Chapter 7- Knowledge and Devotion, 8- The Supreme *Brahman*, 9- Secret Knowledge, 10- Glories of the Lord, 11- The Cosmic Form, 12- Devotion

Chapters 13 to 18 are about relationship between the individual and the Lord: Chapter 13- The field and the Knower of the field, 14- The Three Qualities, 15- The Supreme Self,

16- Divine and Demonic Traits, 17- Threefold Faith, 18- Freedom and Renunciation

The Gitā unfolds the knowledge about the nature of the Self as free of all limitations; this knowledge is known as *Brahma-vidyā* and also referred to as *Vedānta*. In order to gain this knowledge, one requires a mind that is relatively free from conflicts. The attitudes and disciplines to gain such a mind are the under the subject matter known as *Yoga-shāstra*.

Eighteen chapters of the Bhagavad Gitā

↙ ↘

Yoga –shāstra (Yoga exposition)	*Brahma- vidyā* (Self-knowledge)
rāga, dvesha (intense likes and dislikes) *Karma Yoga* (attitudes with regards to performance and results of actions) *Rāja (Upāsanā) Yoga* (practices – *ashtānga yoga, japa,* meditations) *Bhakti Yoga* (role of devotion) *3 guṇa,* divine and demonic qualities	*Jñāna (Gnyāna) Yoga* (knowledge about the reality of the Self as free of all limitations) "Known" – world of objects, the field; "Knower of the field" is Self, Subject, *Ātmā*

In this introductory condensed summary of the Bhagavad Gitā, our intention is to explain the basics about what Bhagavad Gitā is, common themes in brief and practical applications of the teachings in everyday life. This succinct study will include:

1- Explanation on the source of all human suffering, attachments (intense likes) and aversions (intense dislikes) arising from ego driven desires, how to neutralize these strong likes and dislikes by practicing *Karma Yoga.*

2- Understanding role of *Rāja (Upāsanā) Yoga,* meditation, *Jñāna (Gnyāna) Yoga* as explained by Lord Krishna to Arjuna, and understanding of *Bhakti* as the underlying attitude of devotion in practicing *Karma Yoga*, *Rāja Yoga* and *Jñāna (Gnyāna) Yoga*.

3- We will take a look into topics such as "Knower and the Known", divine and demonic attributes, 3 *guṇa*. We will also examine short discussions from the Bhagavad Gitā which will help shed light on various profound topics of philosophy.

Who is a Guru?

The study of the Bhagavad Gitā is quite extensive and this study should be undertaken with a guidance of a *"Guru"*, one who is trained by and from an authentic lineage of teachers of the *Veda.*

In modern day language the word *Guru* is very loosely used to denote all kinds of teachers. However a real *Guru* for teaching a text like the Bhagavad Gitā must be a person who has done an expansive study of the scriptures and one who is firmly rooted in the teachings of the *Veda.*

A *Guru* is a teacher who will be able to decipher profound meanings from the scriptures, one who is not driven by any ulterior motive, and is able to guide students from the darkness of ignorance towards the light of knowledge. Literal meaning of the Sanskrit word *"Guru"* is - one who dispels the darkness of ignorance by imparting spiritual wisdom.

What is the story of Mahābhārata – story behind the setting of the Bhagavad Gitā?

In a nutshell, the historical epic Mahābhārata is a story of right vs. wrong, a story of good vs. bad, a story of *dharma vs. adharma.* Two brothers Dhritarāshtra and Pāndu were the rulers in the kingdom named Hastināpur. Dhritarāshtra was blind and therefore his brother Pāndu ruled the Hastināpur kingdom. After Pāndu's death, Pāndu's five sons, called Pāndava, who were the rightful descendants to the throne were denied kingdom by Kaurava, the sons of Dhritarāshtra.

Pāndava were virtuous, intelligent, possessed all qualities fit for the righteous rulers of the land. The Kaurava were cunning, wicked and represented everything that is immoral. Kaurava wanted the kingdom for themselves and therefore called Pāndava for a game of dice.

Kaurava won the game of dice with deceit and Pāndava were humiliated and insulted and sent away to a stay in the forest, exiled for 13 years. After 13 years when Pāndava came back asking for their kingdom again, they were denied their rightful claim and asked to leave again, Kaurava denying them even a smallest piece of land to stay in the kingdom.

Pāndava, who were the embodiment of righteousness, tried to avoid the war by sending Lord Krishna to seek compromise and a solution to avoid the war. Kaurava refused to compromise and rejected all proposals for a peaceful resolution. War was declared.

As princes, the Pāndava not only had right to the kingdom, but also had a duty to see that justice was done. The Pāndava agreed to fight the war to get their kingdom back and to undo the wrong; they wished to correct the destruction and chaos created in the kingdom by the Kaurava.

Lord Krishna tried to be an intermediary between the two parties that had declared war. Kaurava shunned Lord Krishna's guidance and advice and instead asked for Lord Krishna's army to fight the war. Upon Arjuna's request, Lord Krishna offered himself as the charioteer for the mighty Arjuna's chariot.

Symbolism:

Five Pāndava symbolize five senses. Hundred Kaurava represent undesirable and destructive tendencies of the mind. Lord Krishna symbolizes the divine, our true Self. The battlefield symbolizes an internal battle resulting from the fundamental human problem of personal conflict and want, feeling of helplessness and inadequacy.

Lord Krishna (the divine) through the teaching of the Gitā guides Pāndava (five senses) on the path of *dharma*, to fight Kaurava (tendencies of the mind which distract and delude us from the path of righteousness). The teachings of the Bhagavad Gitā give the strength and the wisdom to perform duties and responsibilities with an equanimous mind, to help one lead a virtuous life.

Diagrammatic representation of the story:

Kingdom named Hastināpur

↓

Dhritarāshtra (Brothers)	Pāndu
↓	↓
Hundred Sons Kaurava	Five Sons – Pāndava (Arjuna and his 4 brothers)
↓	↓
Symbolize everything wicked and undesirable	*Dharma* protectors
↓	↓
Supported with a huge army	Supported by Lord Krishna

The war between the Kaurava and Pāndava was fought on the battlefield named "Kurukshetra".

Section 2:

Bhagavad Gitā, chapter 1 - verse 32

Arjuna's conflict –

"O Krishna! I want neither victory, nor the kingdom, nor comforts. Krishna! What is the use of kingdom or of pleasures, or of life itself to us?"

Bhagavad Gitā, chapter 2 - verse 7

"Overcome by faint-heartedness, confused about my duty, I ask you: Please tell that which is truly better for me. I am your student.

Please teach me, who has taken refuge in you."

In this section -

- Arjuna's sorrow and delusion as he stands in the midst of a battlefield
- Examine the meaning of *Dharma* and *Ahimsā*

Why was the hero Arjuna, the prince warrior, distraught on the battlefield and what was the solution given to Arjuna by Lord Krishna?

Arjuna's conflict

The excerpt forming the Bhagavad Gitā takes place in the battlefield just as the brutal war is about to begin. The Gitā recounts the dialogue between Arjuna and Lord Krishna who has volunteered to be Arjuna's charioteer.

Arjuna is the mightiest of the warriors endowed with knowledge and skills of warfare, very well known for his excellent archery skills. Arjuna is described not only as a valiant warrior and a protector of the masses, but also as a hero with an analytical mind, a clear and bright intellect.

The Gitā begins as Arjuna surveys the battlefield and sees many of his loved ones and relatives among the forces on the both sides. He falls into despair as he thinks about the destruction and impending death of many. As he stands in the midst of a battlefield, why does Arjuna refuse to fight the war? Because:

- Arjuna feels tremendous attachment towards many people on both sides of the battle. Arjuna depends upon these people for his own security, peace and happiness; and therefore he becomes weak, emotionally upset, and his intellect gets overwhelmed by emotions.
- Once Arjuna's intellect gets overwhelmed with emotions and he falls down in despair, he forgets that the battle is not between friends and relatives, but the battle is between *dharma* and *adharma*, between right and wrong.

Chapter 1, verse 30 gives a glimpse into the despair felt by Arjuna:

"My bow slips from my quaking hand, and my skin seems to burn with fire, my mind is spinning round and round, no longer can I even stand"

Attachment, sorrow, confusion is the problem of *saṃsāra* – worldly life.
This problem of *saṃsāra* is faced by Arjuna on the battlefield.

The solution in the Bhagavad Gitā

Arjuna's attachment to the world around him is very strong and hence he collapses into sorrow and despair when the battle is about to begin. Once Arjuna is in despair, he gets deluded into thinking that he will commit an immoral act by killing wrongdoers! Arjuna discovers his problem of dependence and goes through emotional turmoil. Arjuna feels the intensity of his sorrow and with tears rolling down; he drops his bow and arrow and refuses to fight. He is unable to tackle the situation and therefore surrenders to the feet of Lord Krishna.

When Arjuna refuses to fight the war, Lord Krishna advises him to fulfill his duty as a warrior.

Lord Krishna, an *avatāra*, the eighth incarnation of Lord *Vishṇu* (Lord as the sustainer of the Universe), then proceeds to impart profound spiritual teachings to Arjuna in the Bhagavad Gitā. The Bhagavad Gitā frees Arjuna from the conflict and restores his determination to fight the war for preservation of *dharma*. Arjuna in the end understands that the harm caused by not fighting the war, by not performing his duty to provide protection to the masses, will be worse than the harm caused by the war itself.

Lord Krishna's teachings guide Arjuna to fulfill his sacred duty as a warrior and fight the war for the sake of righteousness, *dharma*. One should understand that Lord Krishna is talking to a soldier; Lord Krishna is asking Arjuna to do his duty, to establish righteousness. Arjuna's aim in fighting the war is not about getting the kingdom back, but the aim is to punish the violators of social code of conduct. The mighty prince Arjuna, being a *Kshatriya* (from a warrior clan), and a ruler of the kingdom and protector of the masses, has been trained by the society and given this duty. It would be wrong on Arjuna's part to refuse to do his duty as a warrior.

The teaching in the Bhagavad Gitā is a message that all of us should do our duty and we should not shy away from what the society has trained us to do. We need to pay back society by serving the society. Our actions should not be performed with an eye on wealth or fame; actions should be performed as a duty, as per *dharma*.

Dharma and *Ahimsā*

What is *Dharma?* To begin with let us understand what "absolute truth" means. Absolute truth is that truth which is unchanging, cosmic, also considered as the laws of nature. *Dharma* is the closest approximation to the absolute Truth.

The word *dharma* in Sanskrit is derived from the Sanskrit root word, *dhṛ*, which means – to uphold, to bear, to carry or to support. That which holds together or supports is *dharma*. In a wider sense, it is *dharma* which sustains and supports the whole world. This word *dharma* has such richness of meaning and wealth of associations that, it is impossible to translate *dharma* from Sanskrit language into a single word in any other language.

Dharma encompasses all ethical, moral, social and other values or principles, code of conduct and behavior which contribute to the well-being, sustenance and harmonious functioning of individuals, societies and nations.

What is the derivation and meaning of the word *Dharma* in the Bhagavad Gitā?

Dharma is righteousness, duty, a core value as a human being, core responsibilities of the role that we play. For example, the role of a woman as a mother, the role of the king as the protector of the masses, the care giver's role in providing care.

Dharma as used in Hindu scriptures is the "Law of Being". That because of which a Thing continues to be the Thing itself, without which the Thing cannot be that Thing, is the *dharma* of the Thing.

For example, heat because of which fire maintains itself as fire, without heat fire can no more be fire. Thus in this example, heat is the *dharma*, an intrinsic property of fire. Atoms, molecules and cells all have their individual unique *dharma.* Each and every individual has his/her own unique individual *dharma* according to their roles and responsibilities in life and also *dharma* to be followed for living as human beings.

There is harmony where there is *dharma* and there is disharmony where there is violation of *dharma*. Whenever we violate *dharma,* we are violating harmony. Any stress can be traced to violation of *dharma*, which is a violation of fundamental harmony. The answer to all stress management is to live a life in keeping with *dharma*.

Lord Krishna through the teachings leads Arjuna to understand what his *dharma* as a warrior is. As Lord Krishna says in chapter 3, verse 35:

"Better is one's own imperfectly performed dharma than the well performed dharma of another. Death in one's own dharma is better. The dharma of another is fraught with fear."

What is *ahimsā* (non-violence)?

Ahimsā means avoidance of violence and injury. Does Krishna promote violence by asking Arjuna not to hesitate from fighting the war? **NO.**

Lord Krishna talks about non-violence in many verses in the Bhagavad Gitā. For example, in chapter 12, verse 13 of the Gitā, Lord Krishna describes one of the qualities as this -

"He (the ideal devotee) hates no beings. He is friendly and compassionate."

Violence is unacceptable for the sake for material gains.

However, in order to establish righteousness in the society, if all other methods have failed; people whose duty is to maintain righteousness need to do that which is necessary.

Lord Krishna talks about non-violence in chapter 17, verses 14 and 15, non-violence at all three levels - at the level of body, speech and mind respectively.

"Reverence to Deva, teachers and wise scholars,cleanliness, straightforwardness, self-discipline and not physically hurting – these constitute the penance of the body. Speaking that which is non-offensive, truthful, pleasing and beneficial, habitual study of the scriptures – these constitute the penance of the speech."

Reading these verses, one should understand that the Bhagavad Gitā does not advocate violence. The teaching of the Gitā is about non-violence and this teaching is evident from the argument which begins in chapter 2 and ends in chapter 18.

Ahimsā is the core value for all human beings.
Ahimsā is the underlying value of all values.

Understand that *ahimsā* is not just "non-violence".

An all-encompassing definition of ***ahimsā*** is:

causing least possible harm in any given situation.

If a person does not follow *dharma* and follows *adharma* (unrighteousness), if he does not change his *adhārmic* behavior with other nonviolent means, then punishment has to be employed.

In certain situations to protect larger good, it is possible that non- violence might not be followed. In this particular case, the harm caused to the masses, citizens of the kingdom would have been much more if the war on the battlefield *Kurukshetra* was not fought and those causing *adharma* were not punished.

Section 3:

Bhagavad Gitā, chapter 2 - verse 62

"The person who dwells upon objects, an attachment is born with reference to those objects. From attachment is born desire and from desire, anger is born."

Bhagavad Gitā, chapter 2 - verse 63

"From Anger comes delusion and from delusion comes the loss of memory. Because of the loss of memory, the mind becomes incapacitated and when the mind is incapacitated, the person is destroyed."

Bhagavad Gitā, chapter 2 - verse 66

"For the one who is not tranquil, there is no knowledge. For the one who is not tranquil, there is no contemplation also.

For the one who is not contemplative, there is no peace. For the one who has no peace, how can there be happiness?"

In this section -

- Relevance of the teaching of the Gitā in this day and age!
- "You are *Ātmā* – Awareness, limitless *ānanda*." What does that mean?
- Learn about the famous Chariot allegory from the *Katha Upanishad*

How is Arjuna's dilemma and Lord Krishna's teachings on the battlefield relevant to us in this day and age?

Relevance of the Bhagavad Gitā in our life at present

Why is the teaching of Lord Krishna to Arjuna, the Bhagavad Gitā read by millions of people over many centuries till this day?

The problem faced by Arjuna in the battlefield is a problem of a warrior, a hero of outstanding achievements and a disciplined intellect, who was nevertheless overwhelmed by personal conflict and a feeling of helplessness. The teachings of the Bhagavad Gitā are relevant because Arjuna represents humanity of every century. Arjuna's problem is not unique; all of us face the same problem of *saṃsāra,* worldly life, arising from attachment, sorrow and delusion.

- The Gitā addresses the human problem of conflict and grief, a feeling of helplessness. The teachings by Lord Krishna in the Bhagavad Gitā are given when Arjuna is losing his drive to perform his duty.

- This situation on the battlefield can be understood as the war we face in our day to day lives, situations where we have to choose between the right action and that which might not be a righteous action. It is about the battle we face each and every day in our hearts and our minds.

The problem of conflict, grief and feeling of helplessness is the fundamental problem. Once this problem is understood, we can now drop the story part of the Bhagavad Gitā and take the essence of the story. The story begins with the scene as follows:

Lord Krishna (as the charioteer) and Arjuna are standing in a chariot in the middle of the battlefield, about to engage in *dhārmic* war. In the midst of the battlefield, Arjuna discovers the problem of *saṃsāra* (worldly life) and the solution for this problem of *saṃsāra* (worldly life) is given by Lord Krishna in the Bhagavad Gitā.

Lord Krishna's teachings to Arjuna can help us in our daily lives, by giving us the strength and the wisdom to make right decisions and lead a virtuous life. And leading a virtuous life will help us grow emotionally and spiritually.

How do the teachings of the Gitā help us in solving our emotional problems?

We understand that all humans are constantly struggling to achieve freedom from the so-called problems in life, which are the limitations of sorrow, time, pain, suffering, ignorance. Lord Krishna says to Arjuna:

"You want to achieve freedom from the limitations of sorrow, mortality and ignorance, because you do not know that this freedom is already achieved."

This leads to the question – who is this person, the one who seeks security, peace and happiness, the person who does not want sorrow, pain, old age and suffering? What do we know about this person, what do we know about ourselves?

How does the Gitā answer the question – "who am I?"

WHO AM "I" beyond the body, breath, mind, intellect and ignorance?

WHO AM "I"?

I am not the body, nor the breath, nor my mind or intellect. I am AWARENESS. I am aware of my body and breath, aware of mind, intellect and ignorance. I am aware of the different roles I play in life; I am aware as I engage in different activities and experience different emotions and feelings. "I" am the Subject, one who is aware of this body, this breath, memories, emotions, and knowledge. All that I see hear, touch, taste, smell and see are the objects. "I" am the Subject, awareful being; as Pure Consciousness "I" am aware of all objects, including body, mind and intellect.

All objects known are limited by time, space or another object.

Absolute Awareness, "I", is limitless and non- dual, formless and all pervading.
Awareness, "I", *Ātmā,* Self is not an object and it has no dimension, no shape, no limitation.

"I" am Absolute Awareness, *ĀTMĀ*

Lord Krishna starts imparting spiritual wisdom to Arjuna who has fallen on his knees, who is in utter despair over the thought of fighting the war.

In chapter 2, verse 23 and 24 Lord Krishna says this about *Ātmā*, "I", the Subject:

"Weapons cannot cut it, fire cannot burn it, water cannot wet it, even wind cannot dry it.

It is beyond time, all pervasive, immovable, and immutable."

* The Sanskrit word *"Ātmā"* along with many other Sanskrit words, is **NOT** translatable in English language. Translating word *"Ātmā"* in English as "Spirit" or "Soul" takes away the profound meaning of the Sanskrit word, *Ātmā*. *

Let us discuss the nature of *Ātmā:*

1. *Ātmā* is the essence of who we are as limitless, boundless, unborn and uncreated unchanging Awareness, Pure Consciousness, the true SELF. *Ātmā* is a Sanskrit word used for the Divinity that shines eternally as Pure Consciousness, Absolute Awareness.

2. *Ātmā* is the unchanging reality because of which we are aware of everything around us, the reality because of which we are aware of our body, breath and happenings of our mind. This reality of who we are as *Ātmā* is the same reality of everyone and everything in the universe.

3. *Ātmā* is limitless peace, security and *ānanda* (infinite happiness). The teachings of the *Veda*, and the Bhagavad Gitā as the essence of the *Veda*, lead us to realize and recognize this truth. These spiritual teachings lead the seeker to recognize that Divinity, *Ātmā,* is not a part, product or property of the body. *Ātmā* is eternal, has always existed and will exist forever, even after the death of the body. In Absolute Awareness are space and time. And in space and time is the whole creation. Thus Lord Krishna says to Arjuna:

"You (the Reality of who you are) are full and complete – you are grieving over things that do not deserve grief".

Recognition of our true essential nature as *Ātmā,* which is beyond body, breath and mind is the true and only purpose of life. Once this profound truth is realized, all suffering ends. A person who recognizes his/her true SELF, essential nature as *Ātmā* gains freedom, liberation, enlightenment while living.

This is *Sāṅkhya,* the knowledge taught by the Bhagavad Gitā. It is not any intellectual knowledge, or a random logical theory. *Sāṅkhya* is a valid means of knowledge which makes you see what you really are.

What is our problem?

If our essential nature is full and complete *Ātmā* (infinite peace and happiness), then why do we not feel full and complete all the time? The reason is:

1. We take ourselves to be the physical body, mind and the intellect. Reasons for grief are innumerable for the body, mind and the intellect because the physical body, mind and the intellect have countless limitations.

Our intrinsic desire and basic instinct is
to be full and complete.

We want and we seek
security, peace and happiness at all times.

A sense of inadequacy, feeling of helplessness, grief and despair are due to the wrong conclusion that "I am this physical body, I am limited, I am incomplete."

The only reason we suffer and struggle in our day to day life, the reason all of us as individuals constantly have the feeling of incompleteness, inadequacy about ourselves is because:
we fail to recognize our true nature; fail to recognize the divinity, *Ātmā,* Self, unborn, changeless, thought-free consciousness – the real nature of "I".

2. Because there is a basic intrinsic need for security, peace and happiness i.e. fullness and completeness, and because we identify ourselves with the limited body, breath or thoughts in the mind, we start seeking fullness and completeness outside of ourselves. Because of ignorance about the Reality, truth of ourselves as *Ātmā*, we think that the world will provide what we are seeking. We end up thinking that some particular person, situation or object, someone or something out there will complete me, fulfill me!

All of us sense the inadequacy and are unable to face many problems in life. A situation gets to be a problem due to the feeling of inadequate self. We keep searching at the wrong places with the wrong means and come to wrong conclusions! In the futile search of ours to be full, to be complete, we end up getting attached to the outside world – attached to people, places, objects and situations.

Attachment is not a positive value. Attachment is from dependence and weakness, and attachment comes with expectations.

Understand that there is a big difference between love and attachment. Love is a positive value. Love allows oneself and others to be free. Love arises from independence.

3. Intense attachment to people, places, objects and situations is source of sorrow for all beings. Sorrow is directly proportional to attachment. The more attachment and dependence there is the more sorrow one feels. For example, death is not the cause of sorrow. If death was the source of sorrow, then we would feel sorrow when anyone dies anywhere around the world. Sorrow is immense when a loved one dies because attachment is the most with loved ones. Thus attachment leads to sorrow. Sorrow overpowers the intellect; intellect cannot function properly and this leads to confusion and delusion. Objects of attachment are different for each human being but all attachments finally lead to sorrow.

Not knowing the truth of who we are *(Ātmā);*
all of us travel from attachment to more attachments,
from birth until death.

We fail to recognize the problem of dependence, bondage (attachment) and thus fail to remove sorrow from our lives.

We constantly move from one dependence
to the next dependence and finally towards bondage.

Our problem is – we depend on others for security, peace and happiness and this leads to sorrow.

As *Amritabindu Upanishad* says:
"Mana eva manushyāṇām kāraṇam bandh mokshyoḥ"

"Mind alone is the cause of bondage and mind alone is the cause of liberation."

The problem of suffering is not out there and the solution is not out there.

It is we, our minds (thoughts) that create problems from situations and it is because of our thoughts that we suffer.

To become free and liberated, we need to refine our minds and find strength from our own refined minds.

Our problem is dependence on others for security, peace and happiness, because we do not know the truth about Self, *Ātmā.* The solution to our problem is through knowledge. Through knowledge we realize that we already possess what we are seeking!

Lasting peace and happiness is not something that can be gained from the world. Understanding one's real nature as *Ātmā,* everlasting peace and happiness, one gives up the dependence on the world outside.

As we understand from Lord Krishna's teachings (the teachings of the *Upanishad*), *Ātmā* is my real nature and it is limitless Awareness. Lord Krishna says in chapter 2, verse 55:

"When one completely renounces all the desires

entertained by the mind, satisfied in the SELF, by the SELF,

one is called a person of steady wisdom."

The famous Chariot allegory:

What is the symbolism in the Chariot metaphor?

Chapter 1.3, verse 3 to 11 of *Katha Upanishad* from the *Yajur Veda* (one of the 4 *Vedas*), has dealt with the allegoric expression of an individual as a chariot, a metaphor used to describe the relationship between the senses, mind, intellect and the Self. The chariot which Arjuna is riding can be used as a very interesting metaphor to understand the vehicle that we use - our body, sense organs, mind and intellect.

The Chariot, vehicle, is our physical body. The master of the chariot is *Ātmā,* Self, the divinity as our true self. The journey in the chariot is the journey of our life in the vehicle, in our bodies. Horses represent our sense organs – eyes, ears, tongue, skin and nose. These sense organs gather information from the world outside. Reins used to control the horses represent our mind. Once the sense organs perceive outside world of objects, they feed the information to our brain to process the information.

We however get attached to the enticing world of objects and because of this attachment to the world out there, desires arise! The horses – sense organs are then constantly dragged around in the world of objects, governed by the desires that arise in the mind. The charioteer – intellect forgets that *Ātmā,* Self is the master of the chariot and we fail to use our minds effectively to control our senses!

We have to get control of our senses using the reins of our mind wisely, using our intellect to turn our attention away from the world of objects. Having done this, we can turn our attention inwards towards *Ātmā,* Self, a permanent source of security, peace and happiness.

The famous verse from the *Katha Upanishad* chapter 1.3:

> *"He who has the understanding of the driver of the chariot and controls the rein of his mind, he reaches the end of the journey, that supreme abode of the all-pervading Ātmā."*

An enlightened person, a person who has realized the essential reality of who he/ she is as Self (*Ātmā,* Absolute Awareness, Pure Consciousness), as fullness and *ānanda*, does not depend on anything for happiness. This enlightened person lives in the world without fear or attachment, moving about as freely as air.

Enlightenment is not a state of experience in *samādhi.* Enlightenment is the realization brought about by the knowledge that one is already free from all limitations. This vision is called *Sāṅkhya*, which is presented in the 2nd chapter of the Bhagavad Gitā.

Knowledge or action – which is better?

Lord Krishna says at the end of the chapter 2 of the Bhagavad Gitā that the person from whom all desires are gone, who is free from attachment, gains happiness.

On hearing this statement of Lord Krishna, Arjuna asks: "O Lord, I want to be happy. Now I see that the objects of the world do not have the happiness that I seek. If you say that the happiness that I seek is my true nature, should I not turn away and withdraw from the world and seek happiness within?"

Arjuna feels that withdrawing from the worldly activities might be the way to gain happiness. He thinks that knowledge about the Self and engaging in worldly activities are opposed to each other.

Arjuna starts questioning the need to act and perform actions as a warrior and asks if it is a better option to leave the world of activities and retreat in the forest to sit in meditation.

Arjuna's reasoning was that the performance of any action leads to the chain of expectations, results, judgment, reactions and problems. These expectations of success and fears of failure, will lead to conflict in the mind and thus there will not be any peace when one is engaged in action. Thus Arjuna's argument against action goes this way, "why should I engage in action if the final result is conflict and problems? If I seek happiness and I know happiness is "I", my true nature, why perform actions which will not give me happiness which I seek?" Lord Krishna answers Arjuna in chapter 3, verse 8:

"Do action that is to be done because
action is superior to inaction."

In order to understand how the performance of a proper action, with a proper attitude is the answer to Arjuna's question; we need to understand the mechanics of actions, what drives us to perform actions over and over again. Lord Krishna explains how attachments (likes) and aversions (dislikes) lead to strong binding desires, and these desires in turn lead to performance of actions.

Performing proper actions with proper attitude is *Karma Yoga* and Lord Krishna discusses *Karma Yoga* in chapters 2, 3 and 4 and throughout the teachings of all 18 chapters. Let us examine *Karma Yoga* in the next chapter.

Section 4:

Bhagavad Gitā, chapter 2 - verse 47

"Your choice is in action only, never in the results thereof. Do not think you are the author of the results of action.

Let your attachment not be to inaction".

Bhagavad Gitā, chapter 3 - verse 34

"Attachment and aversion for the objects of the senses abide in the sense organs; let none come under their sway; for they are his foes."

In this section -

- Learn about the problem of attachments *(rāga)* and aversions *(dvesha)* and how the mind gets swayed by strong likes and dislikes
- Examine the difficulties in pursuing happiness through appeasing strong likes and dislikes
- Find out what Lord Krishna's advice is on how to deal with fluctuations and turbulences of the mind, arising from attachments and aversions
- Why one should practice *Karma Yoga*

What is the problem in pursuing happiness through appeasing strong likes *(rāga)* and dislikes *(dvesha)*?

Regarding the problem of attachments, strong likes *(rāga)* and aversions, strong dislikes *(dvesha)*, Lord Krishna indicates in chapter 3 of Bhagavad Gitā, verse 34 that the robber who loots away the true joys, the joy of peace of mind and the thrills of right living is within.

"Likes and dislikes can both arise, towards the objects that we perceive. Be not influenced by these two, they indeed are your enemies."

The mind gets disturbed because when stimuli reach the mind, it accepts certain types of stimuli as GOOD and certain stimuli as BAD. The mind then gets attached to the good stimuli and develops aversion for the bad stimuli. Lord Krishna advises all seekers:

"Let none come under their sway, as likes and dislikes are indeed your enemies."

Let us examine this problem of *rāga* and *dvesha.* A thinking mind is an amazing faculty available to a human being. A person with a thinking mind feels inadequate, incomplete, and unsatisfied with himself as he is, and hence needs something or someone to make him feel satisfied or pleased with himself. He seeks sense gratifications through pleasurable objects or people, or seeks ego gratification through achievement of success, power, and recognition.

All these pursuits are guided by his likes and dislikes. Likes and dislikes, or attachments and aversions, *rāga* and *dvesha* of the sense organs for their respective sense objects, are instinctive and natural in everyone.

A person feels comfortable, secure, and happy in presence of what he likes and feels the opposite in presence of what he dislikes.

> A person feels attachment towards objects, people and situations by the possession of which one feels that he/she will become happy.
> And he/she feels aversion towards objects, people and situations by the presence of which he/she will become unhappy.

A human being is thus helplessly driven to pursue what he/she likes and avoids what he dislikes. However, there are some difficulties in pursuing happiness through appeasing likes and dislikes.

1. We fail to see objects, people and situations just the way they are. We see the objects, people and situations as they appear in our mind, our mind which has peculiar likes and dislikes. In the presence of strong likes and dislikes, we fail to see what really IS, just the way it is. We color everything with the lenses of our attachments and aversions, biases of our mind. Our entire lives are driven by our desire to find what we like, and desire to get rid of what we do not like.

2. We fail to see that our strong likes and dislikes keep on changing with time, what we like today, we might dislike tomorrow and what we dislike today can become object of our liking tomorrow. Our mind remains turbulent with changing likes and dislikes as we fail to understand that these very strong likes and dislikes prevent us from living a stress free life.

3. We fail to be objective, and as long as we fail to see the world objectively – we suffer!

> The objective world, just the way it is, does not create any problem for us.
>
> Problems are caused by our minds dominated by strong likes, *rāga,* and strong dislikes, *dvesha.*

As long as we let our lives get ruled by our strong likes and dislikes, we will spend our entire lives pursuing people, objects and situations that make us feel good but in reality might not be good for us.

Only when we understand what the mind is and how the mind functions, we will be able to diffuse our strong likes and dislikes. What we need to do is to neutralize our strong likes and dislikes by changing strong likes and dislikes into "preferences". Understand that preferences are not a problem.

Let us take for example, "I love to drink coffee, a particular blend from a particular store". I go out of my way to get this blend of coffee. Just in case that particular blend is not available for some reason, I get upset, I get angry, I suffer all day long, I destroy my day and I make others around me miserable!

Suppose I change this strong liking of the coffee to a preference:

I will be pleased if and when I get that particular blend of coffee that I want, and in case I do not get it (because now it is not a strong like or dislike anymore) I will be okay getting another blend for today and be happy with the outcome, no matter what.

Until and unless strong likes and dislikes (attachments and aversions) are neutralized, one cannot own up the spiritual teachings that the reality of who I am is – limitless, full and complete, *sat chit ānanda Ātmā.* A mind ruled by likes and dislikes is unable to abide in the knowledge of *Ātmā*.

In the Bhagavad Gitā, Arjuna is afraid of performing actions, because Arjuna is afraid of his reaction to the results of his actions. Why? This is because he has intense attachment to certain people and situations, and aversion towards certain people and situations.

Lord Krishna presents to Arjuna a method of neutralizing attachments and aversions by cultivating a particular attitude towards actions and the results of actions. A contemplative mind is required for neutralizing likes and dislikes.

"Performance of right actions with proper attitude"

is

"Karma Yoga".

Karma Yoga is taught by Lord Krishna to Arjuna in the Bhagavad Gitā. This *Karma Yoga* teaching is meant to help all of us who are trying to cultivate a contemplative mind.

Section 5:

Bhagavad Gitā, chapter 2 - verse 48 & 49

"Remaining steadfast in Yoga, Dhananjaya (Arjuna), perform actions abandoning attachment and remaining the same to success and failure.

This evenness of mind is called Yoga".

"Action (based on desire) is, therefore far inferior to that performed with proper attitude of Karma Yoga. Seek refuge in this buddhi-yoga (of proper attitude) Dhanajaya (Arjuna)! Those who perform action only for the results are misers"

Bhagavad Gitā, chapter 2 - verse 22

"Just as a person gives up old clothes and takes up new ones, so does Ātmā, the one who dwells in the body, gives up old bodies and takes up new ones."

In this section -

- Learn what is *Karma Yoga*
- Examine six impurities of the mind and find out the three basic facts of life
- Learn how to prepare the mind to live intelligently
- Graceful acceptance and dedication of the performance of actions – two aspects of *Karma Yoga*
- Developing a non-reacting mind, finding the stillness of the mind and benefits from practicing *Karma Yoga*
- Law of *Karma* and the Theory of Reincarnation

What is Lord Krishna's advice on how to deal with fluctuations and turbulences of the mind?

How do we maintain equanimity of the mind when depression, guilt, pleasure and pain, various emotions, sentiments and feelings come and go? How do we maintain equanimity during turbulences of our day to day life? What prevents us from maintaining equanimity during different situations in life?

The reason we cannot maintain equanimous mind is two-fold: (a) the impurities of our minds, and (b) failure to understand three basic facts about life.

(a) Impurities of the mind here refer to variety of problems. These problems at the mind level are normally enumerated as the six fold impurities. These six impurities of our minds are an obstacle in keeping equanimity at all times and thus they are the biggest hurdle which prevents us from discovering inner joy, peace and happiness that is within. They are:

Kāma - Desire

Kṛodhah - Anger

Lobha - Greed

Moha - Delusion

Mada - Arrogance or vanity

Mātsaryam - Jealousy or competitiveness

(b) The three fundamental facts about life one should always remember:

1. Life is a mixture of *sukha* and *dukha*, filled with pleasure and pain. Life situations are never uniform and no one can avoid this pair of opposites namely pleasure and pain.

> Bhagavad Gitā does not teach how to avoid pain, but teaches how to efficiently and intelligently respond to and handle pain.

2. Our future is never predictable with regards to pleasure and pain. Every experience comes with infinite factors which are unknown. We can never predict what the future holds.

3. There are many situations beyond our control. For example, we cannot stop cyclones and tornadoes even after obtaining knowledge about weather patterns or satellite imaging technology. There are innumerous choice-less situations in life, which are painful and unavoidable.

When we understand the above three factors, we need to change our attitude towards current situations in our life and also change attitude towards situations that will arise in the future. We have to hope and plan for the best but in the case of choice-less unavoidable situations, we need to prepare our mind to accept the situations as they arise in any given moment. Strengthening of the mind needs to be done in advance.

> One cannot dig the well when the house is on fire!
>
> Put effort to strengthen the mind NOW, to face unavoidable present and to prepare for unpredictable future.
>
> This is equanimity of the mind.

How should we prepare the mind to live intelligently?

How do we get rid of the impurities of desire, anger, greed, delusion, arrogance or vanity and jealousy or competitiveness from our minds?

1. By tapping into our higher nature, infinite strength within. *Sankalpa* or auto suggestion. "As you think so you become".
2. By acknowledging that the laws of nature are *Ishvara*'s order. "Give me the strength to face whatever comes according to the laws of nature". This is a prayer to get strength to accept *Ishvara*'s order, to accept laws of nature which are very complex and beyond our understanding and control. Equanimity of the mind i.e. *samatvam* can also be maintained by invoking *bhakti,* devotion, in order to avoid anxiety and accept that which cannot be changed.

Let us now classify *Karma* (actions):

Action for material benefit

Actions for spiritual benefit or purity or spiritual fitness

❖ Actions for material benefit:

One should reduce performance of those actions which are performed to gain material benefits, because these material benefits come with 3 inherent defects:

• All material benefits come with pain. Acquiring materials requires efforts and therefore pain. "Life is spent earning for old age and when old age comes, body is not fit to enjoy any of those benefits!" Preservation of materials is painful. When we lose materials, there is again pain.

- We always remain unsatisfied with what we get. More things make us a bigger beggar. "A person with 10 dollars works for next 10, a person million dollars works for next million!" One gets into the rat race for gaining more and more.

- We get used to and then hooked on to material benefits and then become slaves of the material benefits. "They come as a guest and stay as the master!"

We need objects and materials for living, and need to work for material benefits. However, we need to know and remember the above three defects of material benefits. We need to understand that worldly possessions will not give us permanent satisfaction.

❖ Actions for spiritual benefit:

We need to perform these actions for purity of the mind, gaining spiritual benefits and spiritual progress.

These will be the actions done not for personal gains, but actions performed for the common good. These actions are performed as a way of thanking everyone and everything because of whom we are what we are today! Be thankful and grateful and then perform actions to serve *Ishvara,* the Lord, by serving elderly, serving humanity and serving environment and nature.

Thus reducing actions for material benefits and increasing actions for spiritual upliftment and mental refinement, is the process of developing equanimity of the mind.

Karma Yoga is skill in action.

In performing actions for material benefits only, there is no spiritual upliftment. And in this unskilled action, there is pain and there is addiction to action.

One is in a rat race to get more and more!

Therefore, use actions for spiritual benefits.

What is *Karma Yoga*? Why practice *Karma Yoga*?

Karma Yoga

In the 2nd, 3rd and 4th chapter of the Bhagavad Gitā, Lord Krishna describes an attitude that can diffuse strong likes and dislikes while performing actions. Here *Karma* means actions or deeds. *Karma Yoga* is:

- a healthy attitude towards performance of an action
- a healthy dependence on the world (objects, people and situations), leading to independence from the world (objects, people and situations), and leading towards a spiritual way of life
- a lifestyle because of which we learn to maintain peace, tranquility and equanimity of the mind.

1 - *Karma Yoga* as graceful acceptance

A very famous verse from the Bhagavad Gitā, 2nd chapter verse 47 says:

"You have the choice over your actions but not over the results at any time. Do not (take yourself to) be the author of the results of action; neither be attached to inaction."

The meaning of the verse is – perform action expecting results; act so that you can achieve what you desire; plan and execute your work; BUT even if the result is totally contrary to your expectations in spite of all your wishing and willing, don't react and call yourself a failure.

When you undertake to do something, you expect a result. This expectation of result, which is natural, is not a problem. The problem lies in our reaction to the results, arising out of strong likes and dislikes. It is possible to prevent such a reaction if we enjoy an attitude born of an understanding of the nature of actions and their results.

Let us examine the nature of actions and their results:

- An action produces a result that is inherent in the action itself. One cannot expect that which is not contained in the action. For example, when you drop a stone or a spoon (action on your part) – it will fall down (result of the action due to the Law of Gravity). You cannot expect it to fly upwards!

- You are not the maker of the laws of nature that govern the results of actions. You do not know all the laws that govern the results of the action, nor do you know all the laws that come into play to yield a result. For example, if you try to hit a ball on a pool table and if the table is tilted for some reason, even if you are aiming for the ball to go straight, it will not go straight because there is an additional factor involved – the table is tilted!

- One should understand that things function according to the laws of nature and that there is a harmony in the functioning of the universe. For any action, a proper result always accrues according to the laws of nature pertinent to the entire universe.

> You perform an action driven by a desire.
>
> Once you appreciate the fact that the result of action is governed by the laws of the nature, you accept the result as the "*prasāda* – blessing" from *Ishvara*, whatever may be the outcome of your action.

When a genuine effort is made in the performance of an action, there is no longer apprehension in the performance of an action as a fixed result or outcome is not expected. One keeps an open mind in receiving whatever results come, you receive and accept the result as the blessing, graceful acceptance, this is *prasāda buddhi* and this is *Karma Yoga.*

2 - *Karma Yoga* as offering actions to *Ishvara*

All activities one is engaged in arise from likes and dislikes, or from the performance of our duties and responsibilities. The focus is on the performance of action, to the best of one's capabilities. For example, if one is a great athlete, one understands that the physical capabilities that he has are due to not just from his effort, but opportunities provided to him, his genetics, and his environment – many contributions from the laws of nature.

When one performs any action, one should dedicate his actions to the laws of nature, *Ishvara* as the laws of nature.

One should focus on one's performance and performance alone and not get distracted by the worries about the results of performance. This performance comes from the understanding that *Ishvara*'s order is the reason behind ones' capabilities and therefore one is dedicating this action to the laws of nature, *Ishvara* again. This is called *Ishvara arpita buddhi* – an attitude of offering action to the *Ishvara,* towards any activity one engages in. Thus one should steady the mind against the influences of likes and dislikes.

> The focus is on performance of action to the best of one's capabilities, without getting distracted by the worries about the result of an action.

To conclude, let us examine the two defining sentences on *Karma Yoga* in the Bhagavad Gitā:

1. *"Samatvam yoga uchyate"* – equanimity (sameness) of mind is yoga. *Karma Yoga* is the graceful acceptance of the results of all actions. *Karma Yoga* is *samatvam* or equanimity towards the results (of action), whatever they are. As discussed in earlier paragraphs, results do arise from performance of action; however results depend on many other factors such as actions of others or the laws of the nature. Maintaining equanimity of mind, no matter what the result of an action is, will be possible only when the entire mechanics of action and how the results come about are understood.

Equanimity towards the results of action is *prasāda buddhi*.

2. *"Yogaḥ karmasu kaushalam"* – *Karma Yoga* is offering actions to the Lord. This second definition talks about performance of an action. In choosing to perform an action, one should be guided by what is right and wrong as determined by *dharma,* even if that choice is against personal likes and dislikes. Likes and dislikes are no longer a motivation for performance of action. Lord Krishna advises Arjuna, "change your attitude towards action and you will be a different person!"

Katha Upanishad is also notable for first introducing the term Yoga (yoking, harnessing):

> "When the five organs of perception become still, together with the mind, and the intellect ceases to be active: that is called the highest state.
>
> This firm holding back of the senses is what is known as YOGA."

Benefits of practicing *Karma Yoga*

Karma Yoga is appreciating the laws of nature, which never fail. Your likes and dislikes will not toss you between elation and despair if you accept the results of action as blessings, *prasāda.*

Your mind will be freed from agitations and impurities, your mind will become contemplative. Such a mind will be ready for the spiritual teaching. The essence of who you are is happiness and fullness - unborn, uncreated, boundary less and infinite *Ātmā.*

As Lord Krishna advises Arjuna:

- Giving up on actions is not a solution to your problems. Change your attitude towards action and the results of action and you will find happiness within. Neither action nor the results of action create bondage and suffering. No one and nothing out there in the world is the source of your problems. To be free from the bondage of feeling limited and sorrowful, one must understand that having chosen an action, one should know how to perform that action – dedicating the action to the higher power, the laws of nature, *Ishvara* the Lord and accepting the result with equanimity as the *prasāda,* blessings from *Ishvara.*

- Recognize that there are laws that produce the results of action and understand that these laws are impartial and never fail. If the result is not as per your desire, change your action and try again or accept the results as a blessing. If your actions fail, you are not a failure if you can learn from your experience.

- *Karma Yoga* will help a person to develop a non-reacting mind, a mind that is freed from the reactions of desire, anger, jealousy, greed, delusion, arrogance or vanity. *Karma Yoga* will help a person grow with every experience, even with the most painful experiences, by bringing about a calmer and more refined mind.

Real Knowledge, knowledge of the SELF takes place only when the mind is quiet, calm and clear.

As *Rishi* Patañjali's Yoga Sutras states (2nd sutra starts with this statement) - *Yogash chitta vritti nirodhaḥ* - Yoga is the regulation of all mental activities. From the fluctuations of the mind to stillness, stillness to silence and silence to the sight of *Purusha (Ātmā)* is the journey of Yoga.

What are the Law of Karma (theory) and the Theory of Reincarnation?

Having understood what *Karma* (action) is, we will explore two authentic theories, *Karma* Theory and the Theory of Reincarnation, these theories are a matter of belief. However these theories help a person to live within the moralistic framework and refrain from doing harm.

To recap from the previous chapter, *Karma* means action. And as per the laws of the nature, "for each action performed, there is always a result derived from the action called *karma-phala*, fruit of the action". These actions can be either at physical level or mental (thought) level. As the results of action arise, either we like the results or we dislike the results, which gives rise to more desires, finally resulting in performance of more actions. Thus a human being is constantly caught up in the cycle of actions and reactions to the actions.

Karma Theory

When *karma* (actions at physical or mental level) are performed but the results of the action are not derived in this current birth, one is born again to take care of the outcome of those results. Thus one is caught up in the loop of desires and actions resulting from desires, takes birth over and over again to exhaust unfulfilled results of action.

A particular action performed now is not binding to some particular, pre-determined future experience or reaction; it is not a simple, one-to-one correspondence of reward or punishment.

Law of *Karma* is **NOT** equal to the Western notion of suffering.

- *Karma* is understood as that which causes the entire cycle of cause and effect. Any conscious thought, word or action of an individual will influence the future of that individual. Human beings have the free will to choose good or bad actions and face the consequences of their actions. The effects of all actions are viewed as actively shaping past, present, and future experiences. The Law of *Karma* is the principle by which an individual's thoughts, feelings, and actions create consequences in the present and future.

Law of *Karma* is not punishment or retribution but simply an extended expression or consequence of actions.

Karma means "deed" or "act" and more broadly means the universal principle of cause and effect, action and reaction which governs all life.

- The Law of *Karma* is not fate, for humans act with free will and thus create their own destiny. According to the *Veda*s, if one sows goodness, one will reap goodness; if one sows wickedness, one will reap wickedness. This principle refers to the totality of our actions and their coincidental reactions in this and previous lives, all of which determines our future.

The conquest of *karma* lies in intelligent action and dispassionate response.

> Law of *Karma* does not imply fatalism but rather a system of consequences for one's own actions.
> *Karma* is an impartial force, like the physical laws of cause and effect.

- Law of *Karma* does not negate free will. *Karma* Theory does not say that everything is predestined. In fact doctrine of Law of *Karma* depends on free will. Free will needs to be used to understand Law of *Karma* and one can change course of action or change the goal. One can navigate *Karma* with one's free will; there is no helplessness at any time.

Theory of Reincarnation

Theory of Reincarnation is an extension of the *Karma* Theory; it is about cycle of birth and rebirth. One is born because of *Karma*, action and the result of action. *Vāsanā* or inherent desires and tendencies lead to actions, which in turn lead to the results of these action and finally this leads to taking birth over and over again – this is the Theory of Reincarnation.

The root cause of taking birth over and over again is the ignorance of the Self (reality of who you truly are as *Ātmā*). Not realizing the reality of our true nature as unborn, uncreated, changeless, infinite, *Purusha*, one will identify with the body mind complex and will perform *Karma* again and again. One will be caught up in the cycle of actions and results of action, birth and death, a cycle of pain and pleasure or *saṃsāra*!

Law of *Karma* and the Theory of Reincarnation cannot be mistaken as a system of divine reward or punishment.

These principles take no sides, and are not filtered through the divine intervention.

This birth is preceded by infinite births as there are accumulated infinite *"puṇya"* and *"pāpam"*, *karma phala*, results of the good and bad deeds. It is a continuous loop, circle of universes or manifestations. There are millions of cycles of dissolutions and manifestations of the universe and therefore there are millions of births and deaths.

Belief in the Law of *Karma* and the Theory of Reincarnation empowers one to live well.

There will be no blaming anyone as one knows that "I am living the results of my own actions".

Life is not random or arbitrary or meaningless existence.

This is a highly moralistic framework since it dissuades one from *adhārmic* (unethical, dishonest, unjust) acts. A person who understands the Law of *Karma* and Theory of Reincarnation will know that the effect of any deed will be felt in this birth or next birth or some other future birth.

Section 6:

Bhagavad Gitā, chapter 6 - verse 13

"Holding oneself firm without moving, keeping the body, head and neck in one straight line (as though) looking at the tip of one's nose (for eye position) and not looking in all directions....."

Bhagavad Gitā, chapter 6 - verse 29

"One who has his mind is resolved in SELF through Yoga, and who has the vision of sameness everywhere, sees SELF existing in everything, and everything in SELF."

Bhagavad Gitā, chapter 9 - verse 26

"Whoever offers Me with devotion – a leaf, a flower, a fruit, or water, I accept that (gift) of the pure hearted man which has been devotionally presented."

Bhagavad Gitā, chapter 9 - verse 29

"I am impartial towards all beings; to Me there is none detestable or none dear. But those who worship Me with devotion, they exist in Me, and I too exist in them."

In this section -

- What is *Rāja* (*Upāsanā*, *Dhyāna*) *Yoga* - Meditative practices
- Learn about *Bhakti Yoga* - Devotion
- Explore what is *Jñāna (Gñāna) Yoga* - Self Knowledge

What do *Rāja Yoga*, *Bhakti Yoga* and *Jñāna (Gñāna) Yoga* mean?

Rāja Yoga (*Upāsanā* or *Dhyāna Yoga*) – Meditative practices

A verse from *Katha Upanishad* that is often chanted when showing the camphor light at the altar, states:

"There (in Awareness, Self) the sun shines not, nor does the moon, nor the stars. Even lightning does not shine there; what to talk of this fire (the light of camphor)? That (Self) shining, all else shines because of it. The effulgence of that (Self) illumines the entire universe."

Through this mantra, you appreciate that the Awareness by which all the world is known, is the reality of who you are, *Ātmā*. The person who comes to realize this fact, revealed by the teaching, is wise, realized, an enlightened person.

In order to appreciate these profound teachings, you need an abiding disciplined mind, and *Karma Yoga* as discussed earlier is the means of gaining a refined, clear and abiding mind. Lord Krishna tells Arjuna that proper action with a proper attitude of *Karma Yoga* is necessary for a person who desires to pursue a contemplative mind. Lord Krishna then prescribes "Meditation" to take care of impurities at the subtler level of the mind, impurities which are caused by extrovertedness or outgoing tendency of the mind and the problem of habit!

An example can be given to explain this: suppose a beggar wins lotto jackpot. After years of being a beggar, being penniless, leaving on the streets as a homeless person, he suddenly has a car, a mansion to live in and all that money can buy.

However within a few days of winning his lotto jackpot, when he sees someone giving out free food, there is a desire in him to go run and get that which is being handed out! In the mind of this beggar-turned-rich-person, he is still poor. His beggarliness will not go away immediately. To realize his new status, he needs to meditate on the fact that he is a rich and not a beggar anymore and retain this understanding.

Similarly, we are conditioned like this beggar,
constantly seeking morsels of happiness
from someone or something out in the world!

Even after one reads Lord Krishna's message in the Gitā, which says, "the essence of who you are is fullness and happiness", one still feels inadequate and dependent. One remains a beggar in spite of being rich. This feeling of inadequacy has grown over years and many births and will take time to dissipate. This is a problem that arises due to extrovertedness and habitual thinking.

Rāja (*Upāsanā* or *Dhyāna*) *Yoga* consists of different types of meditation and is recommended by Lord Krishna in chapter 6 of the Bhagavad Gitā in order to quieten the mind. The extrovert, turbulent, restless, outgoing, wandering, fidgety mind has to find some relaxation. A stress free mind is the result of *Rāja* (*Upāsanā* or *Dhyāna*) *Yoga.* These are meditation techniques for attaining the steadiness of mind.

The subject matter of Rishi Patañjali's Yoga Sutras is also about mastering the mind. Rishi Patañjali leads through eight steps (limbs), *"ashtānga yoga",* and elaborately discusses contemplation and meditation as means for mastering the mind.

Arjuna says to Lord Krishna in verse 34:

"In fact Krishna, the mind is "agitation", a strong, well-rooted tyrant. I think of it as impossible to control as the wind."

To this Lord Krishna replies in verse 35:

"No doubt Arjuna, the mighty armed! The mind is agitated and difficult to master. But Arjuna! It is mastered by practice and objectivity."

Meditation is meant for preparing the mind to receive and assimilate the teachings; it is not prescribed for self-knowledge or for liberation. Depending on the faculty of the mind that one wants to develop, meditation can be classified into four varieties.

Preparatory meditations include:

1. Relaxation meditations for simple and deep relaxation
2. Concentration meditations to develop the faculty of focusing, directing one's mind and focusing attention on a particular object of meditation like breathing, a mantra, an image or a sound.
3. Expansion meditations with which one gains a proper perspective on problems of life. One develops a narrow, frog-in-the-well mindset by being obsessed with personal or family life all the time. To break away from this mindset one has to meditate on the totality, expand the vision and see the big picture by changing the perspective.
4. Value meditations will help in internalizing the values; universal values such as confidence, patience, compassion. This will bring about ethical and emotional maturity and transformation in performing day to day activities.

Devotional meditations, watching one's thought during meditation (*Vipassanā, Vipashyanā*) and other Vedic or Yogic meditation techniques can also be used to master the mind.

The above listed four types of meditations can be practiced by anyone. One need not be a seeker of spiritual enlightenment for practicing these. These meditations will bring about a deep transformation is one's personality which will give inner peace.

"Peace does not depend on what one has
but depends on what one is!"

As Lord Krishna in chapter 6 verse 27:

"Supreme ānanda comes to this yogi alone whose mind has become perfectly tranquil, whose rajas has been eliminated, who has become identified with Brahman and is taintless"

What does the Bhagavad Gitā say about "God"?

Hindu Scriptures give three definitions for God depending upon the spiritual maturity of a spiritual seeker.

1. God as a creator, as a personal God with a special form, called *ishta devatā*; this is for the initial stage of devotion.
2. God as the very material out of which the world is created. Since the whole universe is God, every form is God's form. God is no more a personal God but a universal God, called *Ishvara*; this is for the second stage.
3. God as the substratum, underlying reality behind innumerable names and forms. This is an impersonal God, called *Brahman.*

Other words used for "God" are – Lord, *Ishvara*, *Bhagavān*, *Parmātmā*. * See more in Chapter 6, "Symbolism". *

According to the Bhagavad Gitā, *Ishvara* is the universal principle which includes everything that exists in this universe and beyond. The physical and moral laws of the universe are the "will of *Ishvara*".

Ishvara is the essence of everything (BG Chapter 7, verses 4-7). *Ishvara* manifests as the liquidity in liquids, heat in the fire, intelligence in the intelligent, strength of the strong. (BG Chapter 7, verses 8-11). *Ishvara* is also the Pure Consciousness, Awareness that is the core of every conscious being. As Consciousness, *Ishvara* powers various living beings into activity (BG Chapter 10 verse 20, chapter 13 verse 2 and chapter 18, verse 61).

"There is nothing that exists apart from Ishvara. Just as waves arise, exist and merge back into the ocean, everything arises, exists and merges back in Ishvara."

With this understanding, *Ishvara* can be addressed by any name, and worshipped through any form and ritual (BG Chapter 7, verse 21). This depends on the context and the wish of the worshipper.

For example, when starting any endeavor, *Ishvara* is worshipped as *Gaṇesha*. When starting business endeavors, *Ishvara* is worshipped as *Devī Lakshmī*. When studying, *Ishvara* is worshipped as *Devī Sarasvatī*. When you consider yourself as the doer of action, *Ishvara* takes the role of the one who bestows the results of the action.

This leads to the discussion in chapter 9 of the Bhagavad Gitā on devotion, *bhakti*. Bhakti here is love towards the Lord. It is about developing a prayerful sense of being intimately connected with a chosen aspect of *Ishvara*, evoking feelings of reverence and adoration.

Bhakti Yoga – Devotion

All relationships in our life keep on changing; however there is one relation that does not change. "I am related to the total as an individual, to the Creator as the created". This fundamental relationship exists for every being in the world, whether you like it or not. Every creature in the world and you are related to *Ishvara*, Lord.

Bhakti is derived from the Sanskrit root *"bhaj"*, which means to "revere, honor, adore". In the Gitā too, Krishna uses the word *bhakti* in a number of contexts. Mainly, *bhakti* is used to denote two things – devotion (attitude) and worship (spiritual practice).

In the initial stages of spiritual development, 1 - *Ishvara* is introduced as a means to attain worldly prosperity; this is a lower form of *bhakti* where *Ishvara* is the means to an end. 2 - On realizing that worldly gains are ephemeral, *Ishvara* becomes the goal. The world becomes the means. This is middle form of *bhakti* where *Ishvara* is the objective. 3 - When the devotee enquires into the nature of *Ishvara*, he realizes that the Lord is the inner most core of his own existence and consciousness. He realizes that *Ishvara* is not an object, *Ishvara*, Lord is the Subject.

Thus it becomes uncultivated, natural and unconditional *bhakti*, highest level of devotion.

Lord Krishna says this in chapter 7, verse 21:

"Whoever be the devotee and in whichever form (of a deity) he wishes to worship with faith, indeed, I make that faith firm in him."

All worship aims at bringing out the devotee in oneself. There are three types of worship:

1. Worship by work (*Karma Yoga bhakti*)
2. Worship by meditation (*Rāja (Upāsanā) Yoga bhakti*)
3. Worship by enquiry (*Jñāna (Gñāna) Yoga bhakti*)

1. Dedicating all our actions as offerings to *Ishvara* is worshipping by work. As described in chapter 18 verse 46, Krishna says "worship by doing your duty". There is no distinction between secular activity and spiritual activity. Every action is a spiritual practice and the consequence of the action has to be accepted as the Lord's blessings – this is devotion through *Karma Yoga*.

2. Meditation on *Ishvara* is another form of worship. There are two options. First option is to meditate on a particular form. As seen in chapter 10 of the Gitā, the Lord can be worshipped as the natural elements like fire, natural objects like Himalayas, mantras like OM, deities like *Vishṇu,* saints and incarnations like *Rāma, Krishna,* and other *avatāra*.

The second option is to meditate on the universal form, *Ishvara* as the essence of the world. Both are options for practicing devotion through meditation.

One is NOT worshipping a form.
The worship is to *Ishvara*,
the Lord represented through a form.

3. Enquiry into the *Upanishads* (Vedic texts revealing truths about the nature of ultimate reality), to understand the true nature of the Lord. This is the highest form of worship of *Ishvara*. The knowledge of *Ishvara* is the culmination of all forms of worship – this is devotion through knowledge, *Jñāna (Gñāna)*.

Lord Krishna tells in chapter 4, verse 33:

"Better than sacrifice done with materials
is the sacrifice done as knowledge.
Without exception, all action culminates in knowledge."

Devotion is an attitude. One may sing the glory in any language; it is not the languages that matter, what matters is one's understanding and attitude. To think that path of devotion is better than the path of knowledge is immature. *Bhakti Yoga* (devotion) is the attitude which pervades the path of action and the path of knowledge.

The underlying attitude in *Karma Yoga*, *Rāja Yoga* and *Jñāna (Gñāna) Yoga* is *bhakti*, devotion. A person has to start with *Karma bhakti*, move to *Upāsanā bhakti* and culminate in *Jñāna (Gñāna) bhakti*.

Depending upon what activity is being undertaken, the action can be treated as one of the three. Thus no matter what, one can be in constant worship of *Ishvara*.

Jñāna (Gñāna) Yoga – Knowledge about the Self (Subject)

Jñāna (Gñāna) Yoga means a course of discipline meant for gaining knowledge. The question arises – knowledge of what? The word *Jñāna (Gñāna)* refers to self-knowledge i.e. knowledge regarding oneself. When we say knowledge regarding oneself, we already have some knowledge about ourselves, such as our date of birth, name of parents, height or weights. So we do have some knowledge about our superficial personality.

But what we discuss in *Jñāna (Gñāna) Yoga* is the essential nature of "I", the basic nature of "I", the real nature of "I" or the higher nature of "I". In the scriptures, the real "I" is called *Ātmā.* Hence *Jñāna (Gñāna) Yoga* means a course of discipline meant for gaining self-knowledge. As pointed out by the scriptures, the purpose of gaining the self-knowledge is, self-knowledge gives us freedom or *moksha*, liberation. *Moksha* is freedom from bondage or dependence. Self-knowledge (the real nature of "I" or the higher nature of "I"), is freedom from self-ignorance.

The next question is how can I get self-knowledge?

Jñāna (Gñāna) Yoga consists of employing a threefold exercise called *shravaṇam*, *mananam* and *nididhyāsanam* for self-knowledge.

1. The first step is comprehensive listening and learning. This is to be done by exposing oneself to the systematic teaching or handling of the scriptures by an expert *guru*, for a length of time. The study should be continuous. One has to get comprehensive teaching about the real nature of "I" from all angles, in all aspects, in its totality. And this process is called *shravaṇam.*

2. The second step is an intellectual process of inquiry called *mananam*. After comprehensively listening and being exposed to the teachings of the scriptures for a length of time, one begins to question. Hindu scriptures, especially *Vedānta* (end part of the four *Vedas*) which is the foundation of Hindu philosophical thought, encourage asking questions. Questions are to be asked until all questions subside. *Mananam* removes all obstacles in the intellect and makes the self-knowledge free from doubt and gives conviction about this knowledge.

3. The process of internalization or assimilation of the self-knowledge is called *nididhyāsanam*. This process also solves emotional problems in the light of self-knowledge. Unless emotional problems are solved, one is not able to assimilate the knowledge totally.

Internalization of the knowledge has to be done by also removing habitual behavior. Only when the habitual behavior goes away, one is able to derive the full benefit of this knowledge. One should associate with wise people – *satsanga* and stay in touch with the scriptures – *shāstra sanga*. Also, one should lead an alert life, monitoring responses and making sure that every response in every situation is governed by the teaching.

Thus the three-fold exercise of *shravaṇam*, *mananam* and *nididhyāsanam* is *Jñāna (Gñāna) Yoga* which will give self-knowledge. Self-knowledge will give *moksha* which means freedom from bondage or dependence on things, people, places and situations.

Lord Krishna says in chapter 18, verse 70, the study of the Bhagavad Gitā itself is *Jñāna (Gñāna) Yagña* (worship or offering).

If and when one wakes up from the sleep of ignorance, opens one's eyes of knowledge and sees, one shall discover the reality of this teaching – "I AM THAT".

As Consciousness, Awareness, the real essence of who I am, as the Divinity, as the Subject, *Ātmā* one realizes "I am THAT"! In chapter 8 of the Bhagavad Gitā "THAT" is defined as the Absolute Reality – imperishable, boundless, changeless, and infinite – not limited by time, space and qualities. This is the message, about the knowledge of the Self in all the *Upanishad*, the essence of the *Veda*!

I experience myself to be a limited suffering individual, why? Because,

I identify with the limited, ever changing and suffering body, mind and intellect.

This problem of limitation and suffering due to self-ignorance will not be solved by eliminating thoughts, by sitting in meditation, *samādhi*, or by various accomplishments such as raising *"kuṇdalini"* or by any other action. The darkness of ignorance about the truth of, who "I" am will be removed with this knowledge and this knowledge alone – this is *Jñāna (Gñāna) Yoga*.

Jñāna (Gñāna) Yoga is not a transformation involving any "becoming" or "change".

It is about giving up ignorance of the true Self, recognizing that, "I" am limitless Awareness, *Ātmā*.

What is achieved by practicing *Karma Yoga, Rāja (Upāsanā) Yoga, Bhakti Yoga* and *Jñāna (Gñāna) Yoga?*

As we have seen so far from the discussion, four things are achieved by Yoga.

1. Purification of the mind, freedom from strong likes (attachments) and dislikes (aversions) – achieved through *Karma Yoga.*
2. Mind that is turned inwards without seeking external objects – achieved by practicing *Rāja Yoga.*
3. Mind that is calm and free from turbulence – achieved by practicing *Bhakti Yoga.*
4. Realization that "I" the Subject is Awareness, fullness. Instead of depending on external world for happiness, realizing the truth of oneself as unborn, uncreated, changeless thought-free Consciousness – this is achieved by *Jñāna (Gñāna) Yoga.*

As Lord Krishna says in chapter 9, verse 2:

"This is the king of knowledge, the king of secrets, the most exalted of things that purifies, that which can be known directly."

This is the vision (the king of secrets) unfolded in the Bhagavad Gitā, the essence of the *Upanishads* as stated in the *Chāndogya Upanishad:*

" तत्त्वमसि "

Tattvamasi (That thou art)
"That which permeates all, which nothing transcends and which fills everything completely from within and without, that Supreme non-dual *Brahman,* that thou art."

Pictorial depiction of discussion on Yoga:

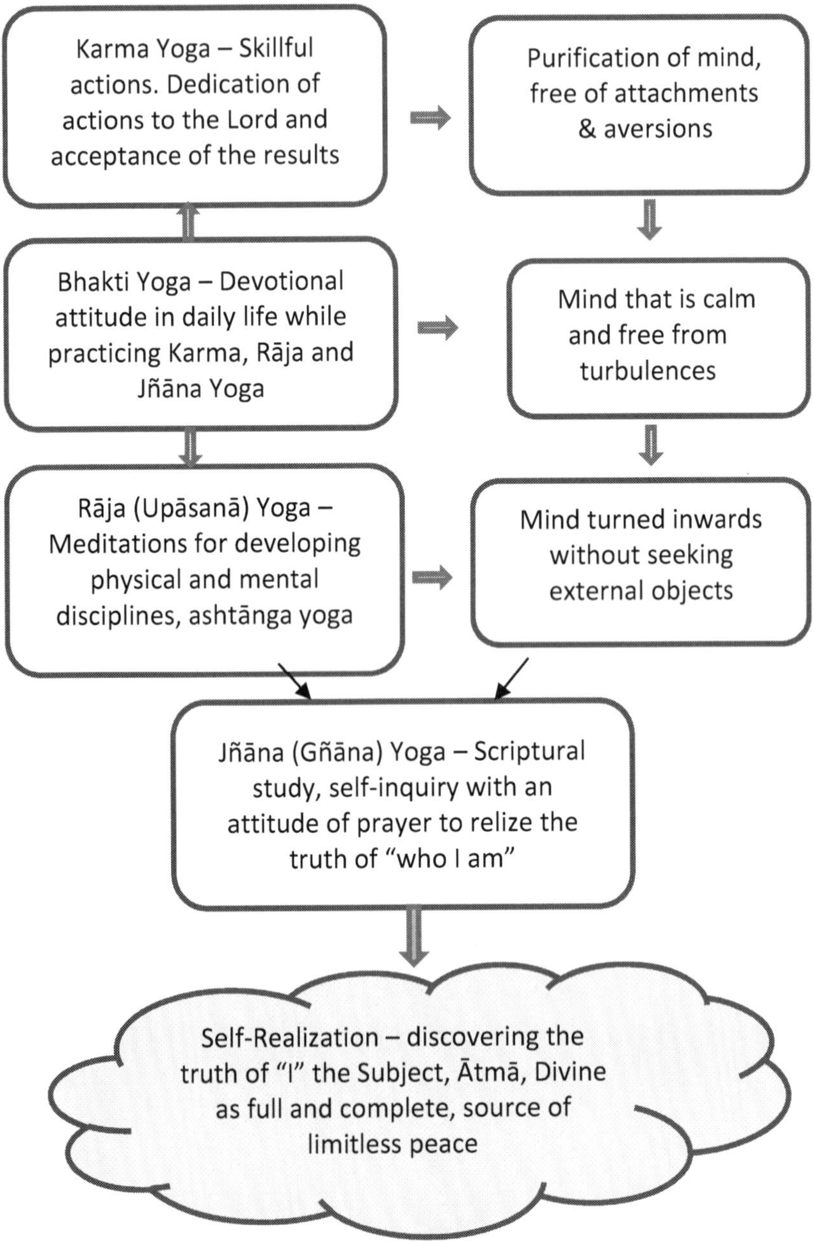
Karma Yoga – Skillful actions. Dedication of actions to the Lord and acceptance of the results
Purification of mind, free of attachments & aversions
Bhakti Yoga – Devotional attitude in daily life while practicing Karma, Rāja and Jñāna Yoga
Mind that is calm and free from turbulences
Rāja (Upāsanā) Yoga – Meditations for developing physical and mental disciplines, ashtānga yoga
Mind turned inwards without seeking external objects
Jñāna (Gñāna) Yoga – Scriptural study, self-inquiry with an attitude of prayer to relize the truth of "who I am"
Self-Realization – discovering the truth of "I" the Subject, Ātmā, Divine as full and complete, source of limitless peace

Section 7:

Bhagavad Gitā, chapter 14 - verse 6

"Arjuna, sattva, rajas and tamas, the qualities existing in Prakruti, bind as (though) the changeless indweller of the body, to the body."

Bhagavad Gitā, chapter 14 - verse 20

"Crossing these 3 guṇa (sattva, rajas, tamas) that are the cause of the body, the embodied one, released from birth, death, old age and sorrow, gains immortality."

In this section -

- What is the "field" and the "Knower of the field"
- Learn about the 3 *guṇa* (qualities or attributes) - *sattva, rajas* and *tamas*

What is the meaning of the word the "field" and the "Knower of the field"?

In chapter 13 of the Bhagavad Gitā, the discussion relates to our understanding of who we are, what this body is, and what this world is. The discussion addresses our understanding of how this body and mind are in fact our equipment, tools, that we are the users of the body and mind, that we are not the body or the mind. Let us try to understand what is the "field" of all experience, all that is known – world of objects, including our body, mind and intellect; and who is the "Knower of the field", the Self, the Subject.

Chapter 13, verse 33:

"Arjuna! Just as one Sun illumines this entire world, so too, all matter everywhere is illumined (revealed) by one Consciousness."

Even though each and every individual is unique, all individuals are an intimate mixture of two aspects **1**. Matter and energy – the changing aspect is the "field", all that is known **2**. Pure Consciousness – the changeless aspect (so far referred to as Consciousness, Awareness, *Ātmā,* Subject, Self) is the "Knower of the field".

Now let us explore the word *Purusha:*

That which is *Pūrṇa*, (which means full) and which abides in all beings is *Purusha. Purusha* is Being, Ultimate reality, Pure Consciousness. The all-pervading Consciousness principle is *Purusha. Purusha* is the omnipotent, omnipresent, non-dual reality due to which everything exists.

Purusha (Consciousness, Awareness, *Ātmā*, Subject, Self) is the limitless source of all existence.

Purusha's creative power is called *Prakruti* (*Māyā*). *Prakruti* (*Māyā*) is the basic matter and energy principle out of which the whole universe has evolved. *Prakruti* is that power (*Māyā or Shakti*) due to which *Purusha* appears as many, appears as the world of matter, the world of names and forms!

This entire world is nothing but a picture drawn with the paints of forms (physical properties of objects) and names (mental concept of objects) on the canvas of the substratum *Purusha*. If you look beyond names and forms, there is only Infinite Existence. There is no differentiation. All differentiation exists because of *Māyā* (*Prakruti*). Thus *Māyā* provides the colors and due to these colors of *Māyā*, a painting which is the world of names of forms appears.

Māyā (Prakruti) operates in three modes *(guṇa)*

Dynamic balance *(sattva),* unbalanced activity *(rajas)* and inertness (*tamas*), these three can be found everywhere innature. Lord Krishna gives a detailed explanation of how these three qualities are found in various ways in nature in chapter 14.

To recap the discussion from earlier:

Purusha or Pure Consciousness or Existence, plus the names and forms which are the result of *Prakruti (Māyā)*, gives rise to duality, names and forms that we perceive around us.

* Read more about *Purusha, Prakruti, Brahman*, *Māyā, Ishvara, Kosha* and *Guṇa* in Chapter 5 on "Vedānta Terms", page 267. *

What are the three "*Guṇa*" – attributes?

As discussed in the previous section on the *Māyā (Prakruti)*, everyone is a mixture of three "*guṇa*", attributes or qualities. The predominance of one attribute over the other two accounts for the dissimilarities among people and dissimilarities in nature.

- *Sattva* accounts for peacefulness, knowledge, inquiry and clear thinking. It is the illuminating, pure and good quality which leads to clarity and mental serenity.

- *Rajas* accounts for activity. It is the quality of mobility and movement. Any "*rajas*" tendency makes a person active and energetic, tense, hyperactive and willful.

- *Tamas* accounts for inertia, dullness. It is the dark and restraining quality which obstructs and counteracts the tendency of *"rajas* and *sattva."*

All three qualities are found in every mind. Everyone is at times contemplative, at times active, and at times dull. Human beings are blessed with the faculty of mind and intellect and thus with the use of the faculty of reasoning – all humans have the capacity and potential to develop more *sattva* quality.

A person by his constant and disciplined study of himself and his thoughts, words, actions and objects which his senses pursue, should make an effort to lead a life full of *sattva.*

One should eradicate *tamas,* move towards *rajas* and then with more effort from *rajas* one can go towards *sattva.* Pure Consciousness *Ātmā* is beyond these three *guṇa.*

One should progress from actionlessness and negativity (*tamas*) to selfish action (*rajas*) and from selfish action to selfless action, pure and good action (*sattva*).

With *sattva* predominating, all actions and thoughts are from the clarity and serenity of the mind, they are illuminating, pure and of good quality.

The mind is purified by following ethical and moral values in life, practicing *Karma Yoga*, *Hatha yoga*, *mantra japa*, singing devotional chants (*kirtan*), prayers, meditation. The purified mind is ready for further self-inquiry.

A pure mind, a subtle and a refined mind, is the prerequisite for self-inquiry and self-inquiry is a prerequisite for knowledge of the highest nature, *Ātmā (Purusha)*.

With self-inquiry and a calm, resolved, pure mind, a yogi finally moves beyond all three *guṇa*, beyond *Māyā*, towards pure existence *Ātmā* (the Divine, Pure Consciousness, Awareness).

Section 8

Bhagavad Gitā, chapter 16 - verse 5

"The divine attributes are considered the means of liberation, the demonic of bondage. Do not fear Arjuna; you are born to divine nature."

Bhagavad Gitā, chapter 16 - verse 21

"This doorway to painful experience that destroys a person is three-fold – desire, anger and greed.

Therefore, one should give up this triad."

Bhagavad Gitā, chapter 17 - verse 24

"Acts of sacrifice, charity and penance as prescribed through injunctions, of those who study the Vedas, always commence after uttering the syllable OM."

In this section -

- Learn about divine and demonic attributes
- Find out what Lord Krishna says about three-fold faith, penance and charity – *Shraddhā, Tapas, Dānam*

How do the divine and demonic qualities shape our body and mind?

In chapter 16 of the Bhagavad Gitā, there is a list of virtues to be cultivated by a person who seeks spiritual wisdom. These divine qualities are listed from verse 1 to 3 as follows:

Verse 1: fearlessness, purity of mind, commitment to knowledge, being charitable, practicing self-restraint, doing worship, study of the scriptures, performing austerities, and straightforwardness.

Verse 2: practice of non-injury, truthfulness, controlling anger, renunciation, tranquility, not speaking ill of others, compassion for all beings, lack of desire for more and more objects, gentleness, modesty, not speaking or acting needlessly.

Verse 3: continues with the list of divine qualities – not reacting internally to attack or accusation, fortitude, purity of body and mind, absence of desire to harm anyone, absence of pride.

We should assimilate these values because we see value in doing so. For example, speaking the truth, not because someone has asked us to speak the truth, but to speak the truth because, we see value in doing so. The most valuable value of all values that is to be cultivated is *ahimsā.*

What does it mean to assimilate the value of *ahimsā*? It means that we should not do unto others what we do not want others to do to us; whatever treatment we want from others is what we should give them. This is the common sense basis of all *dharma* (righteousness). If one assimilates the value of *ahimsā* completely, all other values will follow.

> Practicing the golden rule of following *ahimsā,*
> one becomes sensitive to the needs of others
> just as one is sensitive towards one's own needs.

Anyone can cultivate and assimilate these values listed above. If a person follows these values, not to oblige and please someone else, but for one's own benefit, then that person becomes divine, meaning that such a person becomes a complete human being.

Lord Krishna says in chapter 16, verse 5:

"These divine attributes, values which make a person "human" are the means of discovering freedom. If a person has these divine values, he/she will become naturally calm and will have the mental poise and dispassion with an abiding mind which will be free of likes and dislikes. The mind which is thus free of likes and dislikes alone can own up the teachings that one is fullness, is peaceful and is filled with inner joy – everything that one is fundamentally interested in achieving. Understand Arjuna that you have these divine qualities."

Those who do not follow the divine values will instead have the demonic values which are listed in chapter 16, verse 4:

"Pretentiousness, vanity, self-conceit, anger, harshness and ignorance of right and wrong – these qualities belong to one whose nature is demonic."

A person with a bloated ego (*ahaṅkāra*) is described as a demon in verse 15. All of us depend on so many others for what we are today, and what we have accomplished in this world. If one does not appreciate this fact and has a bloated ego (*ahaṅkāra*), that person has "demonic" values, as per verse 15.

Faith, penance and charity:

Having described the divine and the demonic values and earlier having described attributes with the discussion on three *guṇa* namely *sattva, rajas* and *tamas,* Lord Krishna talks to Arjuna about *shraddhā* – faith, *tapas* – austerities (physical and mental) and *dānam* – charity. Faith and austerities can be of three types each, *sattva, rajas* or *tamas,* according to the motive a person has in performing them. The same applies to the *dānam*, charities.

What is a *sattva* charity according to chapter 17, verse 20:

"That charity, which is given to someone from whom one does not expect a return, charity given in the proper place, at a proper time, and to a worthy recipient, is considered sāttvika (sattva) charity."

Lord Krishna says thus about giving *dānam,* charity:

"May you give whatever is to be given.
Don't think about it, give and then forget that you gave.
A gift is truly a gift if it blesses the one who receives it, rather than make him/her obliged to the giver."

A person, who leads his /her life by practicing divine values, and *sāttvika* values, develops a contemplative mind. A contemplative mind that is mature, calm, and simple, a mind that has nothing to long for or hate, is an abiding mind. A person with this abiding mind will discover his/her true nature as fullness, peace and limitless happiness.

Section 9:

Bhagavad Gitā, chapter 15 - verse 20

"O sinless one, this most secret scripture has thus been uttered by Me; understanding this, one becomes wise and has his duties fulfilled."

Bhagavad Gitā, chapter 18 - verse 59

"Restoring to egotism, you think, "I will not fight." This resolve of yours is false. Your disposition will impel you."

Bhagavad Gitā, chapter 18 - verse 63

"Thus the knowledge that is more secret than any secret was told by Me to you. Considering this thoroughly, you may do just as you wish."

In this section -

- Learn about how Arjuna acted after listening to Lord Krishna's teachings
- Concluding comments from the teachings of the Bhagavad Gitā

What was the effect of Lord Krishna's teaching on Arjuna?

Lord Krishna advises Arjuna in chapter 18, verse 65:

"Become one whose mind is offered to Me, one whose devotion is to Me, one whose worship is to Me; may you prostrate before Me.
You will reach Me alone. I truly promise you, because you are dear to Me."

The idea conveyed here is as follows "Appreciate Me in all your perceptions; thereby may you be My devotee. Devotion to Me is not a matter of feeling, but a matter of discovery. Let Me be the altar where you dedicate all your actions."

In the entire Bhagavad Gitā, the first person singular is used by the Lord to indicate the Supreme Self.

It is NOT Krishna as an individual, historical person who is indicated by the terms "I" and "Me".

Remember that Bhagavad Gitā is The Lord's own Song, sung to revive and guide the humankind.

This leads to the most famous and widely quoted verse from the Bhagavad Gitā, chapter 18, verse 66, where in Lord Krishna says:

"Giving up all Karmas, take refuge in Me alone. I will release you from all Karmas; do not grieve."

The meaning of this very famous verse is "understand that even while performing an action, you are action-less." How? All actions take place in the presence of the Self, "I", *Ātmā.*

The body and the organs of action perform actions such as walking, seeing, hearing, talking, but the "I" as the real Self is always action-less. The body, mind and intellect enlivened by Absolute Awareness (Pure consciousness, *Ātmā*), express dynamism and action, and create what we recognize as the manifested individuality.

Ātmā, the Divine, Pure Consciousness, Awareness in itself does not act; but in its presence matter gets vitalized and then matter seems to act.

All activities in the world are only expression of the Divine Consciousness flashing its brilliance through the body.

In all activities, be conscious of the Divine, *Ātmā,* without which no action is ever possible.

The Lord summarizes the teachings by saying: "You have been performing actions thinking that you are the doer of these actions because you have thought of yourself to be the limited body, mind and intellect with a particular name and a particular form. Now do what must be done with the attitude of *Karma Yoga*, seeing that "I" is the "Knower", "I" is the Awareness. "I" abide in all beings and all beings abide in "I" as *sat chit ānanda Ātmā.*

Then Lord Krishna concludes his teachings by saying: "once you have this knowledge, you will have no grief"! In response to the teachings at the end of the Bhagavad Gitā, Arjuna says:

"My delusion is destroyed; knowledge has been gained by me through your grace, O Krishna. I am firm, my doubts are gone. I will do as you say."

Arjuna thus agrees to take up his bow and fight for the protection of *dharma*, righteousness. Arjuna, after receiving these teachings from Lord Krishna is no longer confused between right and wrong. He now understands that his essential nature as the Subject "I", *Ātmā*, is fullness and happiness – free of longings, cravings, likes and dislikes. Arjuna is now firmly established in the abiding knowledge "I am the Awareness, Pure Consciousness". All doubts, despair, dejection, hesitations, fears are gone from Arjuna's mind and he has a clear picture of the goal of life.

At the opening of the Bhagavad Gitā, we had a warrior prince Arjuna who had declared "I shall not fight", and he had become despondent. It is the very same warrior prince Arjuna, now revived and revitalized by the spiritual wisdom gained through Lord Krishna's teachings, and he declares:

"My delusion is destroyed, I am firm, and my doubts are gone".

The narrator of the Bhagavad Gitā concludes with this final verse from chapter 18, verse 78:

"Wherever is Krishna, the Lord of all Yoga, wherever is Arjuna wielding his bow, there will be bountiful wealth, victory, prosperity and justice – which never waver.

This is my conviction".

The meaning of this verse is: where Lord Krishna and Arjuna are – where knowledge joins with proper attitude and action, there wealth, victory and glory will be ever present.

This is the teaching of the Bhagavad Gitā in brief.

Summary

Section 10:

What are the teachings of the Bhagavad Gitā covered in the previous pages? How can the Bhagavad Gitā serve as a guide to living in the most spiritually responsible manner possible?

Let us take 2 verses to summarize the teachings of the entire Gitā.

Chapter 5, verse 7:

"One whose mind is purified by being committed to a life of Karma Yoga, who has mastered the body and the sense organs, and who knows oneself to be the Self in all beings, such a person is not affected even while doing actions."

Chapter 6, verse 29:

"One whose mind is harmonized by YOGA, and one who has the vision of sameness everywhere, sees the Self existing in all beings, and all beings in the Self."

From these verses, we can derive the following lessons to summarize what has been discussed in the Bhagavad Gitā in reference to our problems and how we can apply the teaching of the Bhagavad Gitā in our day to day life.

1. What do we need in life?

If we analyze what we require in life, all our needs will boil down to three basic needs:

security (safety), peace and happiness

All humans have a basic intrinsic need to be full, complete and happy. We search for **security or safety** (the need for security, food and shelter is universal. It is present in all animals instinctively and in humans it is a sophisticated trait). And we seek **peace** and **happiness** through fulfillment.

2. What is our problem?

- We try to find security, peace and happiness from objects, people, places and situations.

Different people consider different means for attaining the above goals. For example, some consider money and objects as means of providing security, peace and happiness; whereas others consider relationships as means for providing security, peace and happiness; and yet some others seek these goals in name, fame and status.

- This misplaced search of ours leads us towards attachments, aversions, delusion and sorrow.

We look for people, places and objects to fill our inner emptiness. These things may bring brief satisfaction, but it never lasts, and it is never enough. This lust for material things, search for name and fame, and the objectification of others is the cycle of grasping and craving which continues from one life to the next life.

And so we crave more and more and finally our pursuits lead us to more attachments, to more people, places, objects and situations. This fascination with the world outside to "fulfill me, complete me, make me happy someday" results in sorrow and delusion.

- We fail to recognize our fundamental problem and therefore are unable to find a cure.

Harmony and joy cannot penetrate into our lives as long as the windows of discriminative capacity (*viveka*) in us are tightly shut. Our ego and ego-centered desires force us to pursue a life of sense gratification and ultimately bring us down to be punished by our own uncontrolled emotions. As we have no control over the mind, we become victims of circumstances. We get thrown up and down by the whim and fancy of things, people and situations around us.

3. How can the Bhagavad Gitā serve as a guide to living in the most spiritually responsible manner possible?

The most important initial step is to recognize the fact that we have a problem! Many of us fail to even see that there is a problem. Many continue to live their lives just the way they have lived for many years – they complain and cry, seek momentary refuge from the problems latching on to people, places, objects and situations, get frustrated and delusional. However they still fail to see the real problem of *saṃsāra,* worldly life.

Recognition of the fundamental problem – the problem of attachment, sorrow and delusion we face in our everyday life is a very important first step. Once we recognize that we have a problem, we can then start working towards solving this problem of *saṃsāra* worldly life.

Once the fundamental problem is recognized, the following are the solutions from the teachings of the Gitā: tackle likes and dislikes, the problem attachments (*rāga*) and aversions (*dvesha*).

What needs to be done according to the Bhagavad Gitā?

We need to stop nourishing, preserving and also promoting strong likes and dislikes and convert these strong attachments and aversions to "preferences".

-Practice *Karma Yoga* to remove the first layer of gross impurities. *Karma Yoga* is a lifestyle consisting of proper action and proper attitude. Any action which will primarily contribute to reduction of desire, anger, greed, delusion, vanity and jealousy is termed "proper action". Proper attitude is the right attitude towards an action, and result of this action. This will help one grow with every experience, even through the most painful ones.

Result of *Karma Yoga* – achieve a discriminative, dispassionate and detached mind.

-Practice *Rāja (Upāsanā) Yoga* to remove subtle impurities arising from extrovertedness of the mind. This Yoga consists of various practices to remove mental restlessness, and to quiet down a wandering, extrovert, turbulent, restless, outgoing, fidgety mind. *Rāja (Upāsanā) Yoga* includes different types of meditation practices. *Upāsanā Yoga* includes the practice of 8 limbs, *ashtānga yoga* as presented in Patañjali's Yoga Sutras.

All different forms of meditation will help in quietening the mind. A stress-free mind, a focused, steady and tranquil mind is the result of *Rāja (Upāsanā) Yoga*.

Result of *Rāja Yoga* – achieve disciplined and focused mind.

The desire for inner freedom will then arise in this disciplined mind.

-Practice *Jñāna (Gñāna) Yoga* to remove the subtlest layers of impurities. Impurities here refer to ignorance of the knowledge of Self, *Ātmā*. Thus ignorance of the true Self, *Ātmā* is the subtlest of all impurities. *Jñāna (Gñāna) Yoga* consists of an enquiry into one's real nature, Self, *Ātmā*. It is the contemplation upon the *Mahāvākya* (concise statement from *Upanishads*):

"You are eternal, uncreated, unborn, limitless, infinite, changeless, attribute-less, all-pervading divine, *Ātmā*."

Eternal source of fullness, security, peace and happiness is found as the Truth of one's own self by the realization of the divinity, *Ātmā,* Self.

Result of *Jñāna (Gñāna) Yoga* – achieve inner FREEDOM!

Inner freedom is freedom from lack, seeking and want and freedom from constant dependence on something and someone for lasting peace, security and happiness.

4. Which attributes do we need to cultivate for practicing Yoga?

We need devotion. We should have an attitude of *bhakti*. The underlying attitude of *bhakti* is vital in performing all three – *Karma Yoga*, *Rāja Yoga* and *Jñāna (Gñāna) Yoga*.

Unless and until we recognize, reconnect and restore our connection with the changeless all-pervading Reality, call it as God or Lord, *Ishvara* or *Bhagavān,* we will not be able to practice any one of the 3 Yoga mentioned above.

We should inculcate divine qualities such as: practice of non-injury, truthfulness, controlling anger, renunciation, tranquility, not speaking ill of others, compassion for all beings, lack of desire for more and more objects, gentleness, modesty, not speaking or acting needlessly and many other divine qualities listed in chapter 16, verse 1, 2 and 3. Inculcating these divine qualities will result in a non-reactive mind.

We need an understanding of the 3 *guṇa*, and need an understanding of how these 3 *guṇa* play a role in the way we think, behave and perform actions. We should aim to make progress from actionlessness and negativity (*tamas*) to selfish action (*rajas*) and then from selfish action to selfless action,pure and good action (*sattva*). With *sattva* predominating, the result will be that all actions and thoughts will come from clarity and serenity of the mind. All actions and thoughts will be illuminating, pure and of good quality.

We should understand what the ego, *ahaṅkāra,* is and then recognize when the ego comes into play in our thoughts, speech and actions. We tend to create an identification with our body, mind and intellect, and create a false sense of individuality, ego. It is this "ego" that suffers and sighs. The Bhagavad Gitā says with great insistence that we need to renounce the ego and act. The ego is the cause of all our sense of imperfections and sorrows.

5. What are the benefits derived from understanding and implementing the teachings of the Bhagavad Gitā?

The benefits are infinite for a person who gains spiritual wisdom, self-realization, and gains *moksha* (liberation or enlightenment) from understanding and implementing the teachings of the Bhagavad Gitā. This enlightened master will revel in the pure light of wisdom. This liberated person will realize inner freedom, and will be filled with peace and joy, devoid of any and all bondage and suffering. This wise person will continue to do his/her duties according to the requirements of his/her *dharma* and will perform actions with the supreme goal of working towards good and welfare of the masses.

Chapter 2, verse 71 says this about an enlightened, liberated, wise person:

"That person attains peace who, after rejecting all desires, moves about free from longing, without the idea of "I-ness and my-ness", and devoid of pride."

The teachings of the Bhagavad Gitā, when properly understood, can help a spiritual seeker *(sādhaka)* in day to day life. These teachings will give the strength and the wisdom to perform duties and responsibilities with an equanimous mind and help one lead a virtuous life.

Studying the Bhagavad Gitā will give direction and purpose to an otherwise purposeless life of "a journey form womb to tomb". The study of the Bhagavad Gitā is a positive message of hope, inspiration and joy.

"The Gitā educated person learns to recognize rhythm, to see beauty, and hear melody in ordinary day to day life."

Chapter 4, verse 18 of the Bhagavad Gitā:

"The one who finds inaction in action and action in inaction, that one is wise among human beings. That person is engaged in Yoga, one who has done everything that is to be done."

A person on the path of spiritual journey can read the teachings of the Bhagavad Gitā again and again, reflect upon and remember the teachings in order to discover the potential power to renounce false values and rediscover the Divine in each one of us.

OM

"Happiness is your nature. It is not wrong to desire it. What is wrong is seeking it outside when it is inside."

~ Sri Ramana Maharshi

"Mind is consciousness which has put on limitations.
You are originally unlimited and perfect. Later you take on limitations and become the mind."

~ Sri Ramana Maharshi

Chapter 5

Vedānta terms for Yoga

Key to correct pronunciations for Vedānta terms chapter

Important words without diacritical marks:

Veda, Aayurveda - sounds like e in "pr<u>e</u>y", <u>a</u> is like <u>u</u> in "s<u>u</u>n" or "<u>up</u>", and soft <u>d</u> dental sound

Vedaanta - sounds like <u>d</u> in "<u>d</u>art" - dental sound

Upanishad - <u>a</u> sounds like <u>u</u> in "s<u>u</u>n" or "up"

Aatmaa

Aananda - sounds like soft <u>d</u> sound dental sound of "the"

Kirtan - sounds like <u>t</u> in "pas<u>t</u>a" - cerebral sound

Sattva, Rajas, Tamas - sounds like <u>t</u> in "pas<u>t</u>a" - cerebral sound

Maayaa

In *Pancha Kosha*, "maya" in *Annamaya, Prāṇamaya....* is **NOT** the same as the word *Māyā - maayaa*. Here *"maya"* (not *māyā)* means "composed of, made of".

Anna + maya, Praaṇa + maya, Mano + maya, Vijñāna (never j-n sound) *Vignyaana + maya, Aananda + maya*

Shariira Trayam - three bodies: *Sthoola shariiram, Sukshma shariiram, Kaaraṇa shariiram*

Pancha Praaṇa:
Praaṇa, Apaana, Vyaana, Samaanaḥ, Udaanaḥ - soft "ḥ" as in hum

Four activities of the mind:
Manaḥ, Buddhi, Chittam, Ahaṅkaara

II OM II

Vedānta terms for Yoga

Explanation of *Guṇa* (three qualities), *Pancha* (five) *Kosha* and *Sharīra trayam* (three bodies) based on the teachings of *Vedānta.* Understand the basics of *Veda* and *Upanishad* (*Vedānta*), *Brahman, Ātma, Ishvara, Purusha, Prakruti, Māyā.*

The Vedic knowledge tradition: *Veda* and *Upanishad*

Shruti – "that which is heard": teachings by ancient sages which were transmitted orally.

Veda, "Knowledge". The body of knowledge containing eternal truths and thoughts about the sacred and the secular, the four *Veda* are: *Rig Veda, Yajur Veda, Sāma Veda* and *Atharva Veda*. Each *Veda* consists of two parts:

1. *Karma kānda-* "means and ends", this section consists of *mantra* and rituals.

2. *Jñāna (Gñāna) kānda-* **Upanishad** are about "Self-Knowledge", the highest philosophical knowledge. There are over 108 *Upanishad-s.*

Smriti – "that which is remembered", Literature and sciences derived from the *Veda.*

1. *Sutra* Literature – *Yoga Sutra* and many other *Sutras*

2. *Purāṇa* – Mythology and *Bhakti* towards the Lord is described, includes *Kirtan*

3. *Itihāsa* – Historical epics namely the *Mahābhārata* - *Bhagavad Gitā, Rāmāyaṇa*

4. *Upveda* – Sciences derived from the *Vedas: Āyurveda* - Medicine, *Dhanurveda* - Warfare, *Vāstuveda* - Architecture, *Gāndharvaveda* - Music.

Yoga, Vedānta, Upanishad

Yoga *sādhanā*, spiritual practices, and *Vedānta* are not separate from one another but in fact are one and the same. Yoga explains that personality (*Prakruti*) or the body-mind-sense complex, which is made of matter, is insentient by nature. What is it that brings about this sentiency, life in the body-mind-sense complex? It is the person (*Purusha, Ātmā*) or the Self, Consciousness, Awareness.

What Yoga teaches us and *Vedānta* helps us to understand is that we are not merely the personality, body-mind-senses. The personality (*Prakruti*) is, in fact, the vehicle for the manifestation of the person (*Purusha, Ātmā*). Just as the union of electricity and filament brings about a phenomenon called light, similarly, the union of the Self and the non-self or the Consciousness (*Purusha, Ātmā*) and the physical matter, personality (*Prakruti*), results in a phenomenon called 'life'.

Vedānta (Veda + anta (end) is *Vedānta*) is the final portion of the four *Veda*, comprising of what are called the *Upanishad.* The *Upanishad*-s *(Vedānta)* embody the highest philosophical knowledge of the four *Veda*-s.

The one central idea throughout all the *Upanishad, Vedānta* is that of Self-realization. Understanding "Pure Existence Consciousness" is the subject-matter of *Vedānta.*

When one inquires "who am I? Who am I at the deepest level – beyond body, mind and personality"? The central teachings of the *Upanishad* answer this question as "You are that! You are *sat chit ānanda Ātmā*".

Your true Self, *Sat* (Existence) is not a thing, an object, among other objects of the Universe. Your true Self, *Chit* (Pure Consciousness) is not an experience, yet all experiences shine in *Chit. Chit* is the consciousness illumining every thought, every experience. You are *ānanda* (the very pinnacle of happiness and contentment), and all worldly happiness is a particle of the ocean of your own *ānanda*, your true Self.

The Pure Consciousness as the individual self (*Jiva* + *ātmā*) is the same pure existence consciousness, the universal Self (*Param*+ *ātmā*). The great statements from the *Upanishad, mahā-vākya*, "You are That"- *Tattvamasi*, is the declaration of the *Guru.* And "I am That Infinite, Absolute"- *Aham Brahmāsmi,* is the realization of the student.

According to *Vedānta*, the realization of this oneness/identity of the individual Self *(ātmā)* and the universal Self *(Paramātmā)* is called liberation, *moksha.* Attaining this liberation is the ultimate end and purpose of human existence and *Vedānta* declares that this liberation is possible within this very lifetime.

The teachings of *Vedānta* and Yoga have come down for generations in the form of *Guru* (teacher) / *shishya* (student) tradition. It has been carefully preserved to the present day.

This teaching is to be handled by a competent teacher who has been exposed to the teachings of Yoga and *Vedānta* for a length of time.

Pictorial depiction of the Vedic knowledge tradition:

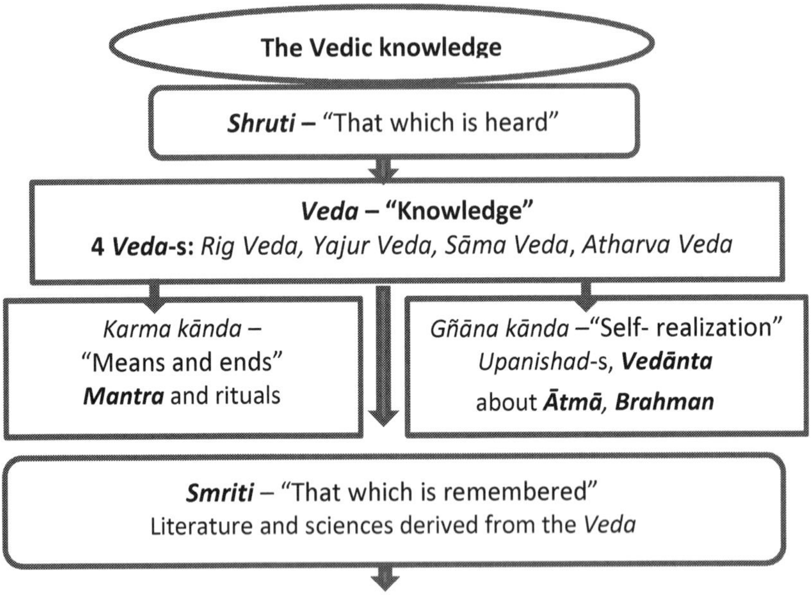

- *Sutra* Literature – ***Yoga Sutras*** and different *Sutra* scriptures
- *Purāṇa* – Mythology, stories about forms of *Ishvara*, songs, glories, ***Kirtan***.
- *Itihāsa* – Historical epics, *Mahābhārata* - ***Bhagavad Gitā, Rāmāyaṇa***
- *Upveda* – near to *Veda,* sciences derived from the *Veda,* for example: ***Āyurveda*** – Medicine, *Dhanurveda* – Warfare, *Vāstuveda* – Architecture, *Gāndharvaveda* – Music

According to the *Upanishad* (*Vedānta*), God is not a separate mysterious entity to be intimidated or afraid of, but God is the underlying reality of everything, present right here right now and above and beyond the Universe.

The divine presence that permeates all existence as Awareness, Pure Consciousness can be realized in this present birth itself. Other words to use for the word "God" are, "*Bhagavān, Parmātmā, Ishvara, Prabhu*" or Lord or other words in different regional languages according to the understanding of a devotee. The *Upanishads*' (*Vedānta*) understanding of God as the Absolute Reality is explained below.

In the Bhagavad Gitā, Lord Krishṇa talks about the two aspects of Lord's nature – Subject and Object:

1. The Subject, which is Awareness (Pure Consciousness), the higher nature, is called *Brahman* at the universal level (macrocosm), and *Ātmā, Purusha* at body/mind level (microcosm).

2. The Object, matter, which is insentient (inanimate), is called the lower nature *Māyā* or *Prakruti.* The fundamental nature of everything as the Absolute Reality is the essence of the Bhagavad Gitā and the essence of the *Veda.*

Let us understand these terms in detail:

Brahman

Bhagavad Gitā chapter 13, verse 13:

> *"Brahman, which is limitless and beginning-less,*
> *is said to be neither existent nor non-existent."*

Brahman is Absolute Reality – Infinite, Awareness, Existence. *Brahman* is beyond all duality. *Brahman* is the eternal, unchanging, all pervading macrocosmic principle which is the divine ground of all matter, energy, time, space, being, and everything beyond the Universe.

Brahman (*note: *Brahman* word is a different word than *Lord Brahmā*. *Lord Brahmā* is the Lord as the creator of the Universe) is the material and the intelligent cause of everything in the Universe and beyond. *Brahman* is infinite, undivided, and changeless principle; *Brahman* is the limitless source of all existence and consciousness. All pervading macrocosmic principle *Brahman* is omnipotent, omnipresent, non-dual reality due to which everything else exists.

Ātmā (Ātman)

Brahman is the totality of the Universe; *Ātmā* is the totality of the Universe (all-pervading principle) as it is present within all beings, at microcosm level. *Ātmā* (Subject, Self, Pure consciousness, Awareness in the context of an individual body mind complex) as described in the Bhagavad Gitā is the same *Purusha* as described in the Yoga Sutras. *See pages 199-200, Chapter 4, "The Bhagavad Gitā", for more on this topic.*

Purusha

That which is *Pūrṇa*, full and which abides in all beings is *Purusha*. *Purusha* is Pure Consciousness, truth of one's own self, that unchanging reality, "truth of who I am, and that because of which I know my thoughts".

Nature of *Ātmā, Purusha*

(Pure Consciousness, Awareness, Self, all pervading microcosmic principle in the context of an individual body-mind):

1. *Ātmā* is not a part, product, property of a body, **2.** *Ātmā* is an independent entity which pervades and enlivens the body, **3.** *Ātmā* is not limited by the boundaries of the body, extends beyond body, not bound by space and therefore all pervading,

4. *Ātmā* continues to exist even after the fall of the body; *Ātmā* is not bound by time and therefore eternal, **5.** *Ātmā* is that because of which one is conscious of thoughts, feelings, and sensations like touch, taste, hearing, smell and sight.

Māyā (Prakruti)

It is the basic matter and energy principle out of which whole universe has evolved. When we use word *Purusha* for the ultimate Reality (Awareness, Pure Consciousness), we use word *Prakruti* to show that which is not *Purusha.* With the same exact meaning in mind, when the word *Brahman* is used instead of the word *Purusha,* we use word *Māyā* instead of the word *Prakruti* to show the ignorance, disturbance and qualities (matter and energy).

Brahman's (*Purusha*) creative power is called *Māyā* (*Prakruti*). *Māyā* is that power (*Prakruti* or *Shakti*) due to which the underlying reality – *Brahman* (*Purusha*), appears as many, appears as world of matter, world of names and forms!

This entire world is nothing but a picture drawn with the paints of forms (physical properties of objects) and names (mental concept of objects) on the canvas of the underlying reality, *Brahman.* Beyond names and forms there is only Infinite Existence, there is no differentiation. All differentiation exists because of *Māyā* (*Prakruti*). Thus *Brahman* is the substratum and *Māyā* provides the colors and a painting in the form of this world (duality) appears.

Māyā (*Prakruti*) manifesting as names and forms is the basic energy and the world of matter we see around us. *Māyā* (*Prakruti*) includes our body, breath, mind, intellect and also objects and things we perceive in this universe.

> *Māyā (Prakruti)* prevents us from recognizing *Brahman (Purusha)* as the truth of who we are.

Māyā (*Prakruti*) operates in three modes (*Guṇa*-s) – dynamic balance (*Sattva*), unbalanced activity (*Rajas*) and inertness (*Tamas*). These three can be found everywhere in nature. Lord Krishna gives detailed explanation of how these three qualities are found in various ways in nature in chapter 14 of the Bhagavad Gitā.

Ishvara

Brahman as Absolute Reality with the power of *Māyā* is known as *Ishvara*. The manifestation of the impersonal *Brahman* as the Universe, i.e. creator of the cosmos is known as *Ishvara* (and thus known as the universal God). The fabric of the Universe and the intelligent order of the Universe is manifestation of *Ishvara*. *Ishvara* manifests as space, time and the five elements. Laws sustaining and governing the Universe, the intelligent order, is *Ishvara*'s manifestation. The physical and moral laws of the Universe are the "will of *Ishvara*".

Ishvara is the essence of everything that is perceived in this Universe. *Ishvara* manifests as the liquidity in liquids, heat in the fire, intelligence in the intelligent and strength of the strong. *Ishvara* is the Pure Consciousness, Awareness, immediate presence that is the core of every conscious being.

"There is nothing that exists apart from *Ishvara*. Just as waves arise, exist and merge back into the ocean, everything arises, exists and merges back in *Ishvara*."

Hinduism recognizes many forms of *Ishvara*, Lord (with attributes and qualities) as the creator, sustainer, as the giver of blessings, dispenser of *Karma phala* (results of action). Various aspects of *Ishvara*'s power and glory are deliberately superimposed on various forms, *deities, Ishta devatā* (personal God). (*note: read more on this topic in "Symbolism" Chapter 6, pages 287-290) A worshiper can have devotion towards a particular name and form, deity of his/her choice called – *Ishta devatā* (personal God).

To recap:

- *Brahman* is the eternal, unchanging, infinite, changeless underlying reality at macrocosm (cosmic) level, which is the divine ground of all matter, energy, time and space. *Brahman* is the non-dual reality due to which everything else exists, limitless source of existence and consciousness.

- *Ātmā, Ātman* is *Purursha* (Subject, Pure Consciousness, Awareness, changeless underlying reality at microcosm (individual) level).

- *Brahman* (Absolute Infinite Reality) with its creative power, *Māyā*, is known as *Ishvara*. Manifestation of impersonal underlying principle, *Brahman* into the Universe is *Ishvara.* The fabric of the Universe and the intelligent order of the Universe is manifestation of *Ishvara*.

- *Brahman* (Pure Consciousness, Awareness, *Ātmā*, *Purusha*) + *Māyā* (*Prakruti*) is the duality of the Universe, names and forms, objects and matter perceived by us.

Three *Guṇa* (3 qualities)

Brahman is the division-less Reality, infinite, changeless, without properties or qualities and thus beyond time and space. Creative power of *Brahman* is called *Māyā.* This *Māyā shakti* leads to time and space duality.

Everything manifest in the Universe because of the *Māyā shakti. Māyā* is endowed with 3 *guṇa*-s (*Sattva, Rajas, Tamas*). And thus everything is a manifestation of innumerable combination of the three *guṇa*.

- *Sattva* - the illuminating, pure or good quality, which leads to clarity and mental serenity
- *Rajas* - the quality of mobility and activity, which makes a person active and energetic, tense, willful
- *Tamas* - the dark and restraining quality, which obstructs and counteracts the tendencies of *Rajas* (activity) and *Sattva* (clarity and serenity).

A yogi by his/her constant and disciplined study of his/her own self (thoughts, words, actions, objects which the sense organs pursue), makes an effort to lead a life full of *sattva*. This yogi eradicates *tamas* and moves towards *rajas* and finally with efforts, moves towards *sattva*. From action-less, negativity (*tamas*) to selfish action (*rajas*) and from selfish action to selfless action, pure and good action (*sattva*) is the journey on the path of spiritual inquiry.

With *sattva* predominating, all actions and thoughts are from the clarity and serenity of the mind, they are illuminating, pure and of good quality.

Hatha yoga (postural *yoga – āsana* practice, *prāṇāyāma, kriyā, bandha, mudrā*), *Karma Yoga, Bhakti Yoga* (singing devotional chants, prayers), meditations *(Rāja Yoga)* provide purification of the mind.

A pure mind, a subtle and a refined mind is the prerequisite for self-inquiry and self-inquiry is a prerequisite for knowledge of the highest, *Ātmā*.

Layers of personality

In the *Katha Upanishad,* our personality (body, mind, senses) is compared to a vehicle for reaching the goal of self-realization. Just as a vehicle should be in a fit condition for travelling and successfully reaching the goal, our personality must be in a fit condition. For the sake of understanding, the Hindu scriptures divide our personality into different layers.

This layer wise division/analysis of the personality is explained by using *Pancha* (five) *Kosha* method or with the analysis of three bodies, *Sharīra trayam* method. The word *"sharīram"* means that which is subject to constant changes and decay.

***Pancha Kosha* (five *kosha*) and *Sharīra trayam* (three bodies)**

* Note: *(Annamaya, Prāṇamaya.....)* ending with "maya" in each of the five words means "composed of/made of".

"maya" in *Anna**maya**, Prāṇa**maya**......* is **NOT** the same as the word ***Māyā*** *(MAyA, Maayaa)**

- *Anna-maya kosha* - Gross, physical body *(Sthūla Sharīra)*. Physical sheath consisting of that which has come into existence and has grown by the essence of food.

- *Prāṇa-maya kosha*, *Mano-maya* and *Vijñāna-maya (Vignyāna-maya) kosha* - Subtle body *(Sūkshma Sharīra)* made up of *prāṇa* to keep it alive *(Prāṇa-maya)*. Also includes mind, thoughts, emotions, feelings *(Mano-maya)*, intellect, ego, discriminative capacity *(Vignyāna-maya)*.

- *Ānanda-maya kosha* - Causal body *(Kāraṇa Sharīra)* made up of sheath of ignorance *(avidyā)* or bliss, for example - deep sleep experience when body and mind are resolved.

One gets identified with any or all of these five *kosha*s at any given moment in life. Where does the body sheath end and the mind begins? Where does the mind sheath end and the intellect begins? These sheaths, *kosha* cannot be divided, they are interrelated. A *kosha* is a notion, not a visible layer, it is a limitation superimposed upon the limitless self (all-pervading divine consciousness). This notion or limitation arises due to the false identification with different aspects of one's personality.

1. *Anna-maya kosha,* Gross (physical) body - *Sthūla Sharīram*

The *Anna-maya kosha,* gross body, is made out of gross matter which is in the form of the five gross elements. *Ākāsha* or space, *Vāyu* or air, *Agni* or fire, *Jala* or waters, *Pruthvi* or the earth.

The body has earth, *Pruthvi* element (solid stuff), body has water, *Jala* element (gives shape to the body). Body has *Agni*, fire element (body temperature of 98.7), has *Vāyu* (breath) and the body has space, *Ākāsha* element (which occupies the body). The Hindu scriptures point out that the gross physical body is only a "temporary residence" used by the individual. The physical body is visible and tangible, perceived and experienced.

2. *Prāṇa-maya kosha*, *Mano-maya kosha* and *Vijñāna-maya (Vignyāna-maya) kosha*, Subtle body - *Sūkshma Sharīram*

The *Prāṇa-maya, Mano-maya* and *Vijñāna-maya (Vignyāna-maya) kosha* make the second body called *Sūkshma Sharīram* or Subtle body.

These three *kosha*s or subtle body is born out of subtle matter which consists of the subtle aspect of the five elements - subtle space, - subtle air, - subtle fire, - subtle water, - subtle earth

The Hindu scriptures point out that the subtle body (3 *kosha*) has nineteen components, each one being an instrument of transaction. A physical body (*Anna-maya kosha*, Gross body) requires instruments for conducting transactions. The nineteen instruments of *Prāṇa-maya, Mano-maya* and *Vignyāna-maya kosha*, subtle body are the tools for transacting with the world.

The five sense organs for gaining knowledge: *Pancha* (five) *Jñāna* (*Gñāna* - knowledge) *Indriyāṇi (organs)*. These are the five sense organs; these are not the physical parts which belong to the physical body, these are the subtle powers of perception.

For example, the eyeball belongs to the physical body but the organ eye - power of seeing belongs to the subtle body.

Similarly the ear lobe belongs to the gross, physical body but the power of hearing belongs to the subtle body.

- Sight - (eyes) for gathering the knowledge of colors and forms.
- Hearing - (ears) for gathering the knowledge of sounds.
- Smell - (nose) for gathering the knowledge of all kinds of smell.
- Taste - (tongue) for gathering the knowledge of all forms of taste.
- Touch - (skin) for gathering the knowledge of all varieties of touch.

Five organs of action: *Pancha* (five) *Karma* (action) *Indriyāṇi* (organs). Organs of knowledge (as enumerated in the previous paragraph), are for receiving input and stimuli. Organs of actions listed below, are meant for output or expressing our responses.

Organ of Speech, Organ of Hands, Organ of Legs, Organ of Evacuation, Organ of Procreation

Fivefold *Prāṇa*: *Pancha Prāṇa.* The energy generating system or fuel converting system is the *Prāṇa shakti,* supporting the organs of action. *Prāṇa shakti* lends energy. There are fivefold *Prāṇa* known as:

- Respiratory system - *Prāṇa* - inhalation and exhalation, absorb *Prāṇa* or oxygen and move carbon dioxide out.
- Evacuating system - *Apāna* - energy behind functioning of the evacuation system or waste removal. Any form of removal of waste from the body is because of *Apāna*

- Circulatory system - *Vyāna* - oxygen has to be circulated; nutrition that is generated in the stomach has to be carried to all parts of the body

- Digestive system - *Samānaḥ* - this converts eaten food into various nutrients such as - carbohydrates, proteins, fats, salts, minerals.

- *Udānaḥ* - means the reversing system, that which operates at the time of death when all bodily functions reverse and cease functioning.

Four-fold division of activities of the Mind:

- Mind or *Manaḥ*: stands for all forms of emotional faculty. Can be translated as the emotional faculty and also the doubting faculty. For example - should I do this or should I do that? To be or not to be?

- Intellect or *Buddhi*: Rational faculty or judging faculty or the discriminating faculty or the reasoning faculty

- Memory or *Chitta*: to receive and record experiences in the mind

- Ego or *Ahaṅkāra*: the faculty of self-reference, that which refers to myself, i-ness, reference to individuality is called *ahaṅkāra*.

The above 19 are the components of *(Prāṇa-maya, Mano-maya* and *Vignyāna-maya kosha) Sūkshma Sharīram* - Subtle body. All forms of transactions are done by the Subtle body with the help of the above enlisted 19 instruments. Some instruments are meant for input and some for output and some for both, for example, mouth).

Subtle body is evident and recognizable to one's own self and it is not available for others to perceive. I know what is in my mind, I know what are my feelings and thoughts and memory, but others are not able to see my mind or know my feelings or my memory. Because it is available only for me and not for others, it is called a Subtle body.

3. *Ānanda-maya kosha,* Causal body - *Kāraṇa Sharīram*

The material out of which Causal body, *Ānanda-maya kosha,* is made of is called causal matter, the subtlest form of matter. The subtlest form of matter is called *avidyā* - ignorance of the true self. Causal body, *Ānanda-maya kosha,* is un-evident and un- decipherable for anyone.

The potential form of the two bodies, Gross body and Subtle body, is called Causal body. Causal body serves as the receptacle or ground or source from which Gross body and Subtle body arise, and into which they ultimately resolve.

Things come into manifestation from un-manifest condition. When destroyed, they go back to un-manifest form. In scientific language, matter destroyed becomes energy. Energy is un-manifest matter. Energy again condenses into matter.

Stars explode to become energy, energy condenses to form stars. In the Universe, stars are constantly formed and destroyed. Stars are converted into energy and energy is reconverted into matter by the Law of Interconvertibility of matter and energy. As per the Law of Conservation of matter, matter can never be produced or destroyed.

Thus the components of *Ānanda-maya kosha,* Causal body -

Kāraṇa Sharīram is nothing but Gross body - *Sthūla Sharīram,* and Subtle body - *Sūkshma Sharīram,* when they are in subtle or potential form.

For example, a tree that you saw a few years ago was not the same as the tree that you see today. Before growing as a tree, is was in a potential form or un-manifest form as a seed. The tree cannot arise without a seed. In the same manner, the Causal body evolves into Gross body and Subtle body, just as the seed evolves into a tree.

During creation, out of Causal body will arise Gross body and Subtle body. During resolution, Gross body and Subtle body will go back to Causal body. Causal body will not be destroyed even during resolution of the Universe, it resolves only after liberation, *Moksha, Kaivalya.*

Why analyze five *kosha,* three bodies, and the nature of one's own self?

1. Five *kosha* or three bodies' method of analysis is to systematically illustrate various levels of body and mind, where a person creates a false identity and commits errors in understanding oneself.

   Anna-maya kosha - identification with the physical body (I am fat, I am tall, I am mortal..)

   prāṇa-maya kosha - identification with 5 vital *prāṇa* (I am hungry, I am thirsty…)

   Mano-maya kosha - identification with emotions and perceptions (I am angry, I am sad…)

   Vignyāna-maya kosha - identification with the intellect (I am a scientist, I am a student…)

Ānanda-maya kosha - identification with experiential, limited *Ānanda* (I am happy, I am ecstatic.....)

2. The final goal is NOT just to reach *Ānanda-maya kosha* and have a fleeting blissful experience! The ultimate goal is to understand the truth of all experiences arising at each *kosha* level and thereby transcend the *koshas. "Kosha"* word represents the ignorance which (as though) conceals one's true self as *Ātmā.*

3. With the help of the above discussion and analysis of the five *kosha* and three bodies, the spiritual seeker's attention is gradually drawn to the unchanging reality which underlines the changing world of all matter, including the body and the mind (matter).

4. The goal is to realize the truth of one's own nature as Divine, Self, *Ātmā.* The goal is to recognize the Reality, that which pervades and enlivens all five *kosha* and three bodies, and into which they all resolve.

Ātmā is the basis for all experience and is of the nature of *"sat chit ānanda"* – existence, consciousness and limitless. *Ātmā* is *Brahman,* the unchanging underlying Reality of all existence, including the Reality of ever changing body and mind (five *kosha*).

Diagrammatic representation summarizing topics covered in this chapter

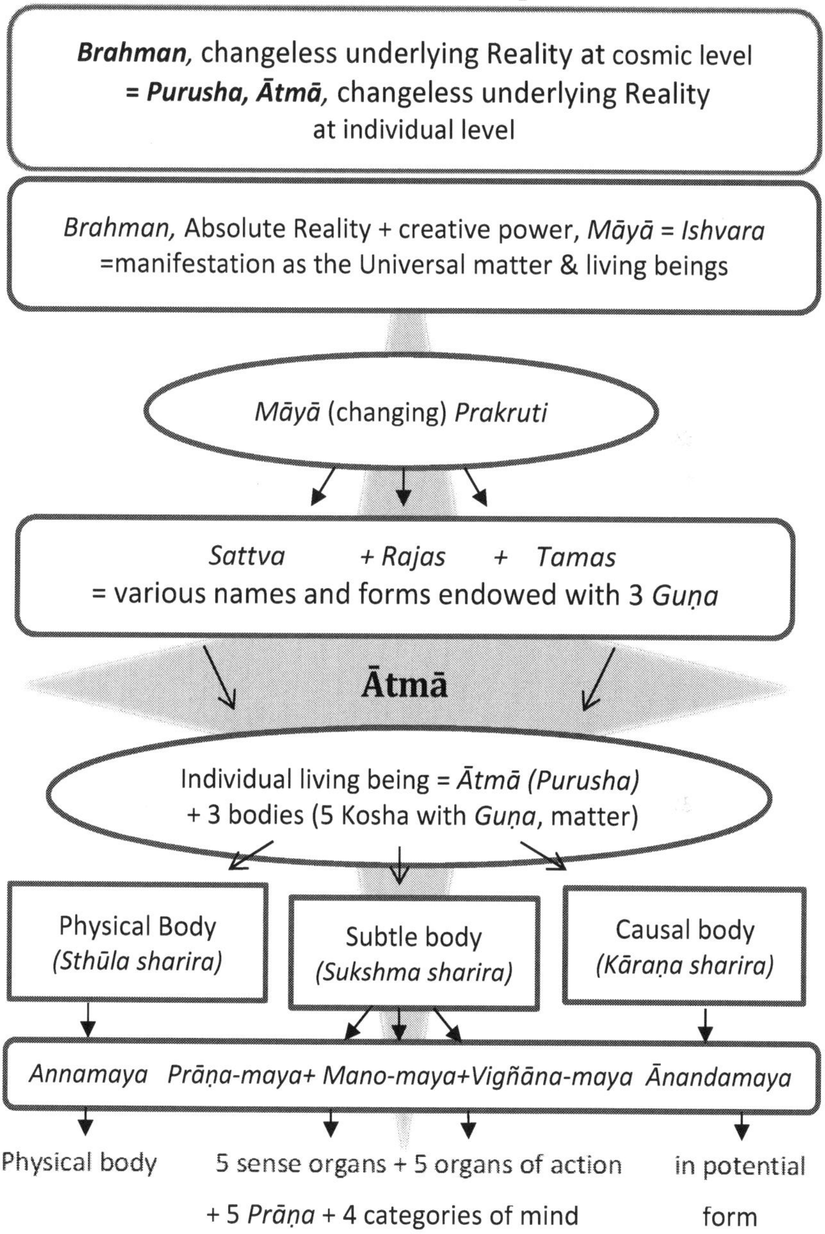

OM

"Life is a pilgrimage. The wise man does not rest by the roadside inns.

He marches direct to the illimitable domain of eternal bliss, his ultimate destination."

~ Swāmi Sivānanda

"Alert and vigilant living itself is a *'sādhanā'* (spiritual practice) in the true sense."

~ Swāmi Chinmayānanda

Chapter 6

Symbolism

Key to correct pronunciations for Symbolism chapter

a (short a) sounds like u in "sun" or "up",
ā (long a) sounds like aa in "father" or "car"
ṇ sounds like n in "under", **i** (short i) sounds like i in "sit"
ī (long i) sounds like i in "pizza", **u** (short u) sounds like u in "put"
ū (long ū) sounds like u in "rule"
jñ the consonant cluster can be pronounced as "nny" or "dny" or "gy", never like "j" in "age"
ś or **ṣ** can be pronounced as English sh in "shine"
c sounds like the ch in "church", not like k as in "car"
g is always a hard g as in "god", never a soft g as in "gym"
o sounds like the o in "opal", as in *loka* (world),
ṛ sounds like the r in "grind", as in *Kṛshṇa (Krishna).*

Important words without diacritical marks:

Moorti - t sounds like soft t in "pasta" - cerebral sound
Namaste - a sounds like u in "sun", **never** like aa in "charge"

Deva - d sounds like softer d sound, e sounds like e in "prey"

Gaṇesha, Vishṇu - ṇ sounds like the n in "under"

Devii - d sounds like softer d sound in "dart"
Lakshmii, Sitaa, Sarasvatii, Durgaa, Ambaa, Kaali, Paarvatii, Raadhaa,
Kṛishna - ṛ sounds like the r in "grind"

Poojaa, Yaaga (Yagna or *yagya), Homa*

Agni - a sounds like u in "up", gn sounds like gn in "ignite"

Swastika - a sounds like u in "sun" or "up"

Aayurveda - e sounds like e in "prey", d sounds like softer d
Japa - a sounds like u in "sun", *maalaa*

|| OM ||

What is the role of Symbolism?

Since ancient times, symbols in Indian civilization have been used as a powerful representation of the higher reality. The principle of "Absolute Reality", the Supreme, and the Divine has been understood with the support of symbols. The link between the inner and the outer worlds has been created and sustained through the language of symbols.

To understand and comprehend the Absolute Reality, where the sight cannot go, nor the mind, and where the usual means of understanding cannot be employed, symbolism helps us to connect and comprehend the Supreme Reality on our plane of existence. Symbolism here is the interpretation and the understanding of religious symbols, and applying the understanding to one's own life. Symbolism is employed to simplify human effort to expose the Divine, the universal principle and the ultimate truth. Symbolism plays an important role by helping to maintain the ancient culture and heritage.

What is the Absolute Reality?

In the *Vedas* and subsequently in the Bhagavad Gitā, Absolute Supreme Reality (referred to as *Brahman*), the Divine is the universal principle which includes everything that exists in this Universe and beyond. Absolute Supreme Reality is *sat chit ānanda.*

Sat is the Existence principle, *Chit* is the Pure Consciousness which imparts consciousness to all the inert objects, and *Ānanda* is the source of infinite joy, contentment, and limitless peace. From the non-dual Supreme Reality manifests a Universe of innumerable names and forms.

The Absolute Reality, the Supreme, the Divine is beyond all concepts. There is nothing that exists apart from the Supreme universal principle. Just as waves arise, exist and then merge back into the ocean; everything arises, exists and merges back in the Absolute Reality.

What do many different forms of deities signify?

Hindu scriptures state that the Absolute Supreme Reality is without qualities, without form, without any attributes whatsoever, non-dual and is beyond space and time. The Absolute Reality is unaffected by the beliefs or limitations of any finite being.

With this understanding of the Absolute Reality, how can one worship this Supreme that has no form, no attributes or qualities? Absolute Reality, *Brahman,* with its creative capacity *Māyā,* is *Ishvara. Ishvara,* the Lord is the universal principle which includes everything that exists in this universe and beyond.

Ishvara as the manifest Absolute Reality (*Brahman*) is the very material out of which the Universe is created. Since the whole Universe is *Ishvara*, a universal God, every form is *Ishvara*'s form. However, a worshiper desires to have a personal relationship with the Supreme. Without such a relationship, the emotional connection that lies at the heart of devotional practices cannot develop.

Hinduism recognizes many forms of *Ishvara* (Lord with attributes and qualities), as the creator, sustainer, as the giver of blessings, dispenser of *Karma phala* (results of action). Various aspects of *Ishvara*'s power and glory are deliberately superimposed on various forms for the purpose of visualization; these forms are the deities - *devatā*. A worshiper can have devotion towards a particular name and form, the deity of his/her choice, personal God, called - *ishta devatā*.

Hindu devotees do not worship the form. The devotees worship the Lord for whom a form is given.

Ishvara, the all-pervasive Lord of the cosmos abiding in all things everywhere, can be addressed by any one of many names, and worshipped through various forms and rituals. This depends on the context and the wish of the worshipper. For example, when starting any endeavor, the Lord is worshipped as *Gaṇesha; Ishvara*'s power to remove obstacles is superimposed on *Gaṇesha. Ishvara*'s power to sustain the Universe is superimposed on *Vishṇu.* When seeking wealth, *Ishvara* is worshipped as *Devī* (goddess) *Lakshmī*. When studying, Lord is worshipped as *Devī Sarasvatī.*

Whenever faith in goodness is endangered greatly, Lord incarnates to establish the power of goodness and faith. In the Bhagavad Gitā, Krishna is the incarnation of Lord *Vishṇu* and therefore Krishna's teaching to Arjuna is called "Song of the Lord"!

We cannot put limits on the names of the Lord. The names of the limitless (without attributes, without form, non-dual) Lord, *Ishvara,* are limitless. Hindus worship the Supreme Reality in different forms and with different names depending upon the languages, cultures, customs and practices of different regions of India.

The important point is to understand that having different names and forms for the *Ishvara* does not mean that there are innumerable Gods. As said earlier, there is nothing that exists apart from the Absolute Reality. Hindus worship limitless *Ishvara* in many forms and call *Ishvara* by many different names. There are said to be 330 million gods and goddesses in Hinduism. These 330 million gods and goddesses is a metaphor for innumerable ways one can imagine and depict some of the infinite qualities of the Infinite. These innumerable forms are not independent but they are different aspects of the Absolute Supreme Reality. **Hindus are not polytheists, Hindus do not believe in many Gods!**

What are these different forms represented in "*Mūrti*"?

In Hinduism, a *mūrti* (pronounced as *"moorti"*), or *murthi,* or *vigraha* or *pratimā* (this can be a symbol, picture or an image) typically refers to an image that expresses the Absolute Reality. The word *"mūrti"* literally means "embodiment". *Mūrti* is a representation of the divinity as *ishta devatā,* deity of worshiper's choice, made usually of stone, wood, or metal, which serves as a means through which divinity may be worshiped.

Hindus consider a *mūrti* worthy of serving as a focus of divine worship only after the divine is invoked in it for the purpose of offering worship. The depiction of the divinity must reflect the gestures and proportions outlined in religious traditions. The word *"mūrti"* **cannot** be substituted with or translated in English as statue or idol.

Hindus do not worship idols or statues!

Mūrti is a Sanskrit word which is meant to point to the Absolute Reality (*Brahman*). Absolute Reality is immanent, "existing or operating within; inherent" and transcendent, "existing apart from and not subject to the limitations of the material universe".

Mūrti or sacred symbols and pictures help a devotee to focus his/her mind upon higher, nobler qualities as depicted by the *mūrti*. Just as a flag of a country arouses thoughts of patriotism, in the same way, a devotee is inspired to embody the qualities represented in a *mūrti.* A *mūrti* of any deity on an altar, in a temple (temple can be at home or a community temple) is a means of communication with the Lord.

This is similar to our ability to communicate with others through the telephone. One does not talk to the telephone; rather the telephone is a way to interact with another person. Without the telephone, one could not have a conversation across long distances; and without the sanctified image in a temple, one cannot easily communicate with *Ishvara*, Lord.

Thus, a *mūrti* is considered to be more than a mere likeness of a deity, but rather a manifestation of the Divine itself. The *mūrti* is a way to communicate with the abstract, Lord, *Ishvara* as the creator, sustainer, and one responsible for the dissolution of the Universe.

If one looked carefully at the features of any *mūrti*, there is much that can be understood about what that particular form represents. The deep significance underlying each *mūrti* has to be clearly understood – not only because the symbolism has been alive for over thousands of years, but because the message is still significant today.

Multiple arms in a *mūrti* are an artistic way of suggesting that *Ishvara,* Lord is omnipotent, having unlimited power, all-mighty, supreme. The third eye represents unlimited knowledge. The venomous snake around the neck of Lord *Shiva* suggests fearlessness and the conquest of death. A trident in the hand represents justice and moral rule. Every feature of the *mūrti* is thus a meaningful statement about *Ishvara.*

The symbolism behind some of the commonly seen *mūrti*-s *(vigraha)* and few of the commonly used words, sounds and images are now explored:

Namaste

"Namaste" or *"namaskāra"* is the Indian way of greeting each other. Namaste and its common variants *"namaskāra"* or *"namaskāram"*, is a form of formal traditional greeting mentioned in the *Veda.*

In Sanskrit the word is *"namah + te = Namaste"* which means "I bow to you", my greetings, salutations or prostration to you. Namaste can be a casual or a formal greeting, a cultural convention or an act of worship.

Spiritual significance:

The reason why we say *"Namaste"* has a deeper spiritual significance. It recognizes that the life force, the Divinity, or the essence of who I am or my Reality as "Self, *Ātmā"*, is one and the same in all. Acknowledging this oneness with the meeting of the palms, we honor the divinity in the person we meet. When we honor the Divine as the Reality of another person, we are honoring the Divine as the Reality of everything and everyone around us. Thus *"Namaste"* symbolically points to the fact that there is nothing that exists apart from the Divine.

OM

Other names: *Praṇava (praṇava)* or *Omkāra*

OM symbol is of paramount importance in Hinduism. This symbol is a sacred syllable representing *Brahman*, as the impersonal Absolute – non dual, omnipotent, omnipresent, and the source of all manifest existence. A symbol becomes mandatory to help us realize the Absolute which is formless, free of attributes and infinite.

Praṇava is the Sanskrit name for OM. *Praṇava* literally means "that by which Lord is effectively praised". The Yoga Sutras by Patañjali Rishi declares in 1st *Pāda,* sutra 1.27- 1.28,

Praṇava - OM represents *Brahman*, Absolute Reality and one can attain *samādhi*, meditative absorption by its repetition.

The word OM can be expanded into 3 letters, a-u-m. This expansion is for symbolic reasons only. According to the rules of Sanskrit grammar, it is entirely incorrect for the word OM to be written or pronounced as "aum". The symbolism of a-u-m can be interpreted in several ways. Om represents both the un-manifest and manifest aspects of *Brahman*. a-u-m can represent the Lord, *Ishvara* (manifestation of the Absolute Reality) as the creator, sustainer, and resolver – *Brahmā, Vishṇu* and *Shiva* respectively. OM is a mantra or prayer in itself.

These letters can represent three states of experience as per the *Māndukya Upanishad*; "a" is for the waking state, "u" for the dream state and "m" for the deep sleep state. On one hand, OM projects that which is abstract and inexpressible and on the other hand, it makes the Absolute Reality more tangible and comprehensive.

OM is the one eternal syllable for all that exists. The past, the present, and the future are all included in this one sound, and all that exists beyond time is also implied in it.

The gap or silence between repetitions of OM sound represents the underlying Reality from which everything arises and into which everything resolves. It is the basic, primordial sound and contains all other sounds. OM encompasses all potentialities and possibilities; it is everything that was, is, or will be.

Gaṇesha (Lord of the *Gaṇa* – people)

Lord *Gaṇesha* is always prayed to first when starting any endeavor. Lord *Gaṇesha* is the most revered form of *Ishvara*. *Gaṇesha* is the remover of all obstacles. A few other names for *Gaṇesha* are – *Gaṇapati* (leader), *Vināyaka* (one who is endowed with all the features of a leader), *Gajānana* (one with elephant face), also known as *Vighnahartā* (the obstacle remover).

As the master of *Riddhi* (prosperity) and *Siddhi* (spiritual power), he is remembered and offered prayers at the beginning of all other prayers, special ceremonies and rituals.

Symbolism:

Elephant head symbolizes sharp intelligence and brilliant thinking. Large ears and small mouth symbolize listening more and talking less. Focused eyes indicate sharp vision and concentration. The trunk symbolizes immense strength, efficiency and adaptability. Partial tusk on one side signifies intelligence and full tusk on the other side represents faith. The big belly (*Gaṇapati* often referred to as *Lambodara* – one with big belly) signifies one who is able to digest all life experiences without losing control.

The mouse sitting by *Gaṇesha*'s feet represents our mind with desires. Unless our mind/desires are under control, they can cause havoc in our lives, just like the mouse which can bring big disasters by gnawing and nibbling! *Gaṇesha* is the one who has mastered the mind and has desires under control. Multiple arms represent *Gaṇesha* to be all powerful and all mighty. Various weapons represent various means to cut of negative tendencies, bonds of attachments and passions.

One hand is in *"abhaya mudrā",* mudra for blessing and protection for devotees. Sweets *(modak)* in one hand signify the faith, *shraddhā,* that hard work and devotion will bring joy, satisfaction and contentment to a devotee.

Lord *Shiva*

Other names include *Shankara, Neelkantha, Mahesh*. Other forms include *Natarāja, Shiva Linga.*

Lord *Shiva* is one of the three main aspects of *Ishvara*; (the other 2 are *Brahmāji* and *Vishṇu*). *Shiva* means auspiciousness. Lord *Shiva* represents the principle of dissolution. Everything in the Universe with a name and a form goes through dissolution. *Shiva* is the cause for making the dissolution possible, dissolution which is essential for creation. Lord *Shiva* is the embodiment of *tapas* – austerities, *vairāgya* – detachment and *vidyā* – knowledge. Lord *Shiva* is often shown in a meditative posture, symbol of utter simplicity and austerity.

Symbolism: The third eye represents vision beyond space and time. Tiger skin represents slain ego and control over all senses. The snake around the neck represents power over all things "poisonous". Trident in one hand shows that the Lord is beyond three *guṇa* – *sattva*, *rajas* and *tamas*, beyond 3 states of consciousness (waking, dream and deep sleep) and beyond past, present and future. The small drum, *damaru*, represents the cosmic rhythm by which the universe maintains its dynamic harmony and balance. The river *Gangā* emerging from his locks represents the eternal wisdom or knowledge flowing towards Earth. The crescent moon symbolizes complete control over time and control over mind. *Nandi*, the bull signifies *dharma*. Lord *Shiva*'s third eye is symbolic of his omniscience, insight, and enlightenment.

Shiva Linga: In Sanskrit, *Linga* means a 'mark' or a symbol, which points to an inference. Thus the *Shiva Linga* is a symbol of Lord *Shiva*. It represents *"nirguṇa Brahman"* or the attribute- less Supreme Self or the formless *Shiva*. The *Linga* is an ellipsoid (elongated sphere) and is a symbol of Creation. There is an indescribable power, *"shakti"* represented in the *Linga,* which induces concentration of the mind and helps focus one's attention.

Shiva in the form of ***Natarāja*** (dancing Lord *Shiva*) represents the cosmic laws of the dynamic Universe – Universe that is constantly in motion and balance. The form of *Natarāja* is a unified and dynamic composition expressing the rhythm and harmony of life.

Lord *Shiva* as *Natarāja* is seen dancing by lifting his left leg and balancing over a demon named *apasmara*, who personifies illusion and ignorance (symbolizes ignorance, *avidyā,* of the essence of one's true Self) over whom *Shiva* triumphs. His matted locks are whirling as he dances within an arch of flames which represent the endless cycle of birth and death.

The significance of *Natarāja*'s dance:

This cosmic dance of *Shiva* is called "*Ānandatāndava*" meaning the Dance of Bliss, and symbolizes the cosmic cycles of creation and destruction, as well as the rhythm of birth and death.

The famous physicist Fritzof Capra in his article "The Dance of Shiva: The Hindu View of Matter in the Light of Modern Physics," and later in the "The Tao of Physics" beautifully relates *Natarāja*'s dance with modern physics.

Mr. Capra says that "every subatomic particle not only performs an energy dance, but also IS an energy dance; a pulsating process of creation and destruction...without end. For the modern physicists, *Shiva*'s dance is the dance of subatomic matter. As in Hindu mythology, it is a continual dance of creation and destruction involving the whole cosmos; the basis of all existence and of all natural phenomena."

Devī Durgā

Other names include *Kālī, Bhavānī, Ambā, Pārvatī*

The word *Durgā* literally means formidable. As *Kālī mātā* (mother *Kālī*) the *devī* (goddess), represents the fierce and terrifying aspect of the Lord, a form to eradicate negative forces.

As *Pārvatī* and *Ambā Mā* (mother), she is a loving mother to those who are pious and devout. Goddess *Pārvatī* (*Durgā*) is the consort, *Shakti* of Lord *Shiva* (as *Shiva* and *Shakti, Purusha* and *Prakruti*), and is non-separate from *Shiva*. She is a part of the trinity of goddesses *Sarasvatī, Lakshmī* and *Durgā*.

All the three forms help the trinity of *Brahmāji*, *Vishṇu* and *Shiva* to create, maintain and regenerate (recycle) the Universe respectively.

Symbolism:

Various weapons represent different powers and capabilities that can be used to eradicate negative tendencies. The tiger or the lion represents uncontrolled animalistic tendencies of the mind such as delusion, anger, lust, greed, vanity, jealousy. The *Devī*'s vehicle, the tamed Tiger represents a disciplined mind which is a wonderful vehicle on the path of spiritual journey.

The lotus represents purity and fullness. Though seen in various ferocious forms (one who destroys *Mahishāsura* demon and other demons through her form of *Kālī*), goddess *Durgā* is a symbol of purity and fullness. *Durgā* holds *"abhaya mudrā"* to assure victory in the battle over the negative tendencies and demons, the demons that are within our minds in the form of delusions and impurities of the mind.

Lord *Vishṇu*

Other names include *Nārāyaṇa.* Lord *Vishṇu*'s incarnations on Earth include *avatāra* as *Rāma, Krishṇa, Bālāji.*

Lord *Vishṇu* is one of the three aspects of *Ishvara*, as the sustainer of the Universe. The other two in the trinity are *Brahmā* and *Shiva*. As the material cause and the intelligent cause, Lord *Vishṇu* pervades everything.

The word *"Vishṇu"* as derived from the Sanskrit verbal root *"vish"*" means one who pervades, permeates everything and is free from the limitations of time, space and objects. Lord *Vishṇu* pervades the entire Universe including all animate and inanimate objects, and beings. Lord *Vishṇu*'s consort is *devī Lakshmī*, the sustainer of the Universe is supported by the goddess of wealth.

Symbolism:

Lord *Vishṇu*'s skin is always shown blue in color, which has been associated with the Infinite since immeasurable space and deep ocean appear blue in color. Weapons in his hand are for preservation of good. Lotus in one hand represents perfection, compassion and manifestation of good qualities and beauty in us. *Gadā* – mace in his hand represents *Vishṇu* as the one who wields power. The conch shell is a symbol of the sound OM.

Lord *Vishṇu*'s vehicle is *Garuda,* eagle like large divine mythical bird.

Lord *Vishṇu* is often depicted as resting on *Sheshanāga* or *Ādishesha* who is the king of all *nāga* (serpent deities) and one of the primal beings of creation. Rishi Patañjali is considered to be an incarnation of the great *Sheshanāga*.

Devī Lakshmī

Other names include *Kamalā, Ambujā, Mahā Laxmī, Sitā* (Lord *Rāma*'s wife) are *Rādhā* (*Krishna*'s companion) are considered forms of *devī Lakshmī.*

Goddess *Lakshmī* is often depicted sitting or standing on a lotus flower. Sometimes the goddess is shown seated with Lord *Vishṇu* who is reclining on the great serpent *Ādishesha*.

Goddess *Lakshmī* is the consort of Lord *Vishṇu,* who is the sustainer of the Universe, preserving aspect of the Supreme.

Lakshmī devī is the form of Lord as the provider of all material things required to sustain and is therefore worshipped as the goddess of wealth, power and prosperity. She is also the goddess of beauty, harmony and balance.

Symbolism:

The lotus on which the *devī* is seated on or standing upon represents spiritual foundation as the base of all material things. The lotus stems held in her hands represent fully blossomed spirituality. At times, a pot is shown in her hand or coins are shown flowing from her hand, which signifies that *Lakshmī* blesses her devotees with abundance forever.

Wealth in this context does not mean only monetary wealth. It includes for example, the nobler values of life, the power of the mind and the intellect, moral and ethical values, all these constitute spiritual wealth. These are the types of wealth to be acquired before one's initiation into spiritual learning and knowledge.

There is a story about the emergence of the *Lakshmī devī* from the ocean. This emergence from the ocean symbolizes the emergence of *sāttvic* (filled with *sattva*) tendencies in the mind after developing good, ethical and noble values in life.

Devī Sarasvatī

Other names include *Shāradā, Vagīshwarī*

Devī Sarasvatī is the goddess of spiritual knowledge and wisdom. She is a part of the trinity of *Sarasvatī, Lakshmī* and *Durgā.* She is the consort of Lord *Brahmāji,* the creator of the Universe, who needs all the knowledge for creation.

Sarasvatī is the goddess, form of *Ishvara* by whose grace one attains knowledge and wisdom. *Sarasvatī* is the goddess of speech and music, one who shines through our intellect and is invoked before beginning all studies.

Symbolism:

Goddess *Sarasvatī* is depicted seated on a white lotus flower, holding a *Veeṇā* instrument and wearing white clothes, with a white swan nearby. Her white clothes symbolize purity, since knowledge has to be pure without confusion and misunderstanding. The *Veeṇā* (musical instrument) in her hand symbolizes joy and harmony which arises with wisdom.

The white swan represents discriminating intellect and a peacock nearby is the symbol of beauty, harmony and perfection. The pure white lotus symbolizes the Pure Consciousness as the foundation for all knowledge and wisdom. The *Devī* holds *"Veda"*, scriptures in one hand and beads for *"japa"* in other hand.

During the famous festival of *Nava rātri* – festival of nine nights, *Durgā devī* is invoked for the first three nights. Goddess *Durgā* removes obstacles and negative tendencies inherent with in us.

Goddess *Lakshmī* is worshipped the next three nights to bring about wealth and prosperity – wealth of good, noble and ethical values along with the material prosperity required for sustenance.

Sarasvatī devī is worshipped for the last three nights to help us make progress with knowledge and focused intellect on the path of spiritual wisdom.

Hanumāna - Ānjaneya

Other names for *Hanumāna* include *Ānjaneya, Māruti, Pawan- suta, Rāma-dūta*

Symbolism:

Hanumāna is the embodiment of service *(sevā),* devotions *(bhakti)* and surrender. His face, tail and hair show the body of a monkey. His qualities are divine. He is endowed with tremendous physical and mental strength. *Hanumāna* shows sublime devotion towards Lord *Rāma* and *Sitā*.

Lord *Rāma* is an incarnation of Lord *Vishṇu,* depicting an ideal human, playing the role of an obedient son, and also a committed husband to *Sitā devī,* a true friend and a fair, compassionate, righteous king. *Hanumāna, Ānjaneya* (son of *Anjani devī*) is shown carrying a mountain in his hand, which shows tremendous devotion to carry out tasks given by his master, Lord *Rāma.*

Hanumāna is worshipped by all, especially those who are engaged in yogic practices as he is the embodiment of calm and controlled mind, a mind that is ready to discover inner hidden potential.

Hanumāna chālisā, composed by the saint named *Tulasidāsa,* has forty verses giving the description of *Hanumāna* and his qualities and deeds, and are sung by devotees. These verses remind us of physical, mental, emotional and spiritual strengths.

Through the description of *Hanumāna*'s qualities, these verses guide us towards knowledge through humility and devotion. These verses show us the importance of qualities like fearlessness, selflessness which arise after surrendering the ego at the feet of *Ishvara*.

Lord *Kṛṣṇa (Krishṇa)*

Other names include *Kishan, Kanhaiyā, Nand Lāla, Kānhā*

Various forms of Lord *Krishṇa* are seen from the innumerable mythological stories about *Shri Krishṇa,* such as: often shown standing with *Rādhā,* imparting Bhagavad Gitā to Arjuna, seen as baby *Krishṇa* eating butter, young *Krishṇa* as a cowherd, *Krishṇa* lifting a mountain to protect village people, *Krishṇa* conquering fierce *Kaliyā nāga* and many other forms.

Symbolism:

In Sanskrit, the word *Kṛshṇa* means dark, indicating supreme consciousness. Lord *Vishṇu*'s *avatāra* as *Krishṇa* is shown ever smiling, lotus eyed, with a garland of flowers around his neck. His skin color, blue, is the color of the infinite which represents omnipotent, omniscient, all pervading Self.

Lord *Krishṇa*'s flute represents matter which by itself cannot create music; however the flute comes alive when Lord *Krishṇa* plays music through it. Similarly the human body by itself is inert and insentient. The human body however becomes alive and sentient when the Infinite Consciousness expresses itself by providing sentiency and life to the inert matter, physical body. The peacock feather represents beauty in nature. The cow represents service or giving and is worshipped as a mother.

Rādhā – The beautiful lady who is often seen standing next to Lord *Krishṇa*, represents a state of yearning and intense, unconditional love. The love of *Rādhā* and *Krishṇa* is symbolic of the eternal love between a devotee and the divine. *Rādhā*'s yearning for *Shri Krishṇa* is the devotee's longing for spiritual awakening.

Temples:

Devālaya, Mandira

Hindu temples come in different styles. They are built using different construction methods and are adapted to different deities and regional beliefs. Hindu temples are found in South Asia particularly India and Nepal, in Southeast Asian countries such as Cambodia, Vietnam, the island of Bali in Indonesia and also Malaysia.

All Hindu temples share certain core ideas, symbolism and themes. The symbolism and structure of Hindu temples is rooted in Vedic traditions. The spiritual principles symbolically represented in Hindu temples are explained in the ancient Sanskrit texts, *Vedas* and *Upanishads.* Their structural rules are described in various ancient Sanskrit treatises including *Vāstu shāstra* which is an ancient text about architecture and construction.

It is not mandatory for a Hindu person to visit a temple. Since all Hindu homes usually have a small shrine or "*pujā* room" for daily prayers, devotees have the choice to visit temples only on auspicious occasions or during various religious festivals. Temple priests known as *"pujāri"* or *"purohita"* are salaried workers, hired by the temple authorities to perform daily rituals, as opposed to the ascetics known as *"swāmi/swāmini"* who are teachers of scriptural study and spirituality.

Temples are designed to represent *Ishvara,* Divinity's presence in our hearts. A traditional metaphor depicts our body as a temple and our heart as an altar at the center of the temple where the Divinity resides. The temple's outer wall represents our body's outer layer; temple's four gateways represent our eyes, ears, nose and mouth. Entering the inner hall, sanctum sanctorum called *"garbhagriha"*, represents withdrawing attention from the world outside and meditating on the *Ishvara*'s Divine presence within.

What is *Pujā* and *Yāga*?

Hinduism as a religion caters to all types of people. Devotees believe in either the Lord, *Ishvara*, with a form or the Lord, *Ishvara*, without a form.

In the Bhagavad Gitā, Lord Krishna proclaims:

"Patram pushpam phalam toyam, yo me bhaktyā prayacchati
tad aham bhakty-upahritam, ashnāmi prayatātmanah"

"He who offers Me with love and devotion - a leaf, a flower,
fruit or water, I will accept it wholeheartedly"

Ritualistic worships can be elaborate, spanning over several hours, with the chanting of *mantras*, offering *prasādam* (consecrated food) and *ārati* (songs sung in praise of the deity when lamps, light from wicks soaked in *ghee* (purified butter) or camphor are being offered). Or it can be as simple as offering a single leaf of *tulasi* (the holy basil). While ritualistic worships satisfy some people, others are satisfied chanting Lord's name or meditating on the formless Lord. Needless to say, any form of worship reflecting on *Ishvara,* requires a pure and steadfast mind.

***Pujā* worship:** *Pujā* is a special way of worshipping *Ishvara,* Lord.

There are numerous forms of worship among Hindus, of which *pujā* is one of the more popular forms of worship. It combines all three types of worship – mental, physical and verbal. In a complete process of worship, actions are done on the plane of the body, chanting of the *mantra*s is done on the plane of speech and devotional attitude is on the plane of the mind.

Pujā as a form of worship can be performed at home on a daily basis, as well as on any special occasion or festival. On special occasions one may invite a priest, a *pujāri* to perform *pujā* on one's behalf, but for daily worship one can perform *pujā* oneself. *Pujā* is also done in temples by the priests.

Whether the *pujā* is performed at home or in a temple, the essential steps are the same. The *pujā* can be done in its more elaborate form like the sixty-four-step *pujā* or in its simplest form which is the sixteen-step *pujā. Shodashopachāra* a sixteen-step *pujā* is one of the most complete forms of worship. *Shodasha* means sixteen and *upachāra* means offerings given with love and devotion.

The main purpose of this type of *pujā* is two-fold. Primarily, it is to uplift the five senses of the worshiper, and by doing so elevate him to a higher level of awareness that will promote good thoughts and actions.

Secondarily, it draws upon the Indian traditions of honoring a guest. For example, when a guest comes to our house; we welcome the guest; offer him/her a seat, offer food and other things and eventually bid the guest a farewell. In the *pujā,* ritual or worship, the Lord is welcomed as a guest and the entire process is in the form of a prayer.

One has to perform the *pujā* with a clean body and mind creating an environment into which one invites *Ishvara* in the form of a deity, *devatā.*

The sixteen steps of *pujā* are:

Dhyāna – Meditating on the deity that is being invoked.

Āvāhana – Inviting the deity into the altar.

Āasana – Giving the deity a seat.

Pādya – Washing the deity's feet with clean water.

Arghya – Offering the deity water to rinse hands and mouth.

Āchamana – Offering the deity water to drink.

Snāna – Bathing the deity with various auspicious items.

Vastra – Dressing the deity with clean clothes.

Yagnopaveeta – Offering the deity a clean sacred thread.

Gandha – Applying fresh sandalwood paste on the deity.

Pushpa – Offering fresh flowers while chanting the deity's names.

Dhoopa – Spreading incense smoke throughout the altar.

Deepa – Moving a lamp to illuminate freshly adorned deity.

Naivedya – Offering food to the deity.

Tāmbula – Offering the deity a refreshing mix of betel nut and leaves as mouth freshener.

Pradakshinā & Namaskāra – Circumambulating the altar and bidding farewell to the deity.

Among these sixteen services, five hold more importance than the rest. Together these five services are referred to as the *pancha upachāra*. Collectively, these five services engage the five senses.

Gandha – Touch. Sandalwood paste cools the skin and is a natural insect repellant.

Pushpa – Hearing. The recitation of the deity's names that accompanies each flower engages the ears.

Dhoopa – Smell. Incense envelops the entire temple with a refreshing fragrance for the nose.

Deepa – Sight. The lamp illuminates the deity and brings out the beauty of the form to the eyes.

Naivedya – Taste. Food that has been offered to the deity is eaten. Food entices the taste buds.

Thus in *pujā:*

1. one invokes *Ishvara*'s presence in the form of a deity, *devatā*

2. treats *devatā* as an honored guest

3. offers worship

4. seeks *Ishvara*'s blessings with reverence.

All the ingredients used during a *pujā* (also during *yagña, homa* or other rituals), for example: ghee, rice grains, turmeric powder, beetle nut, beetle leaves, mango leaves, sesame seeds, hold spiritual significance. These are used in daily life and most of the ingredients are essential items of an Indian diet. Because of their basic life-sustaining qualities and their medicinal and holistic properties, these various ingredients are revered as a potent symbol of auspiciousness, prosperity and fertility and are used extensively in Hindu religious rites and rituals.

Homa, Havana, *Yajña (yagna), Yāga* – Holy Fire rituals:

There are numerous *Homa,* the holy fire rituals described in the Hindu core scriptures, the sacred texts, the four *Veda.*

The meaning of the word *yāga, yajña,* "act of worship or devotion" is derived from the Sanskrit verb "*yaj*", which means to worship. One prays to an aspect of the Lord through the medium of divine "*agni*", into which oblations are poured. Everything that is offered into the fire is believed to reach the particular aspect of the Lord, deity or deities, *devatā.*

The *Yajur-Veda* contains the knowledge of the principles and methods of performing *homa.* The *Sāma-Veda* focuses on the musical chanting patterns of the mantras that deal with more subtle forms of *homa.*

Spiritual significance of *yāga:*

The heat endowed in *yāga,* is a source of immense energy. The idea is that just as the *"agni",* fire melts or sublimates all the gross substances poured into it, we too should burn out all our vices, ill-tendencies, lethargy, dullness and despair and energize our personality with the warmth of new zeal energy, awareness and hope.

Scientific aspects of *yāga:*

Ancient texts are full of legends wherein ancient sages performed *yāga* and the demons *(asurā)* tried to destroy them. Whether these are just folklores, myths, legends or history is a debate, but there is no denying the fact that *yāga* was related to slaying negativity since the Vedic times. Let's explore how and why…

1. *Yāga* involves energy from heat, light and sound. In performing *yāga,* these three energies, namely, the heat from *yāga*'s fire, the light of the fire and the sound of the chanting of the *Vedic mantra,* are blended together to achieve physical, psychological and spiritual benefits.

2. Chanting of Sanskrit, the power of sound vibrations has been long since acknowledged in the field of science. It is said the Sanskrit terms are believed to provide a therapeutic benefit when pronounced and heard. The rich phonetics of Sanskrit strikes the palate at multiple reflex points. The tongue positions of pronunciations stimulate energy in numerous meridians that awaken dormant parts of the brain and enhance the circulation and flow of energy throughout our body.

3. The Hindu fire ritual – *yāga, homa, yagña* or called *havana* is a healing process. *Homa* creates a pure, nutritional and medicinal atmosphere. It is said that this renews the brain cells, revitalizes the skin, purifies blood and prevents growth of organisms capable of causing diseases. Thus *homa* heals the atmosphere and the healed atmosphere heals a devotee.

Symbolism of commonly used forms and objects:

Swastika

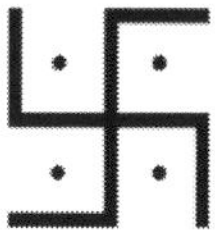

Swastika is a Sanskrit word, which comprises of - *su* meaning “good,” *asti* meaning “to be” and *ka*, a suffix. It is translated as “good being,” “fortune”. Word “*swastika*” literally means – “it is well” or “conducive to wellbeing.” For Hindus, the *swastika* is a symbol of auspiciousness, prosperity and good fortune. It also represents the sun and the cycle of life. The four bent arms stand for the four human aims, called *purushārtha*, righteousness is *dharma*; wealth is *artha*; desire or pleasure is *kāma*; and liberation is *moksha*.

This is a potent emblem of *Sanātana Dharma* (now called Hindu religion), the eternal truth. Hindus use the *swastika* to mark the opening pages of accounting books, thresholds, doors and offerings. No ceremony or sacrifice is considered complete without it, for *swastika* is believed to have the power to ward off misfortune and negative forces.

In the Buddhist tradition, the *swastika* symbolizes the feet or footprints of the Buddha. It is often used to mark the beginning of texts. All Jain temples and holy books contain the *swastika* and ceremonies typically begin and end with creating a *swastika* mark several times with rice around the altar.

In China and Japan, the *swastika* has been used to represent abundance, prosperity and long life. It was used by the Ancient Greeks, Celts, and Anglo- Saxons and the oldest examples of *swastika* have been found in Eastern Europe, from the Baltic to the Balkans.

In many Western countries, the *swastika* has been highly stigmatized because of its use in, and association with Nazism. Most Europeans and Americans still perceive any *swastika* as a Nazi or neo-Nazi symbol, despite differences in its color and the direction in which it points.

Before the Nazis misappropriated the *swastika* symbol from the ancient world, various cultures throughout Asia, Europe and the Americas had been uniform in assigning positive and favorable meaning to the symbol. For the most part, since ancient times, cultures have used the *swastika* sign in their religious practices to symbolize life, the sun, good fortune and prosperity.

Padma (Lotus)

The lotus flower is the symbol of purity. Lotus flower remains pure and clean even when it grows in muddy water. It is a symbol of the Universe rising from the naval of *Vishṇu* (*Ishvara* as sustainer of the Universe) and is the seat of *Brahmā* (*Ishvara* as the creator of the Universe).

Shankha (Conch)

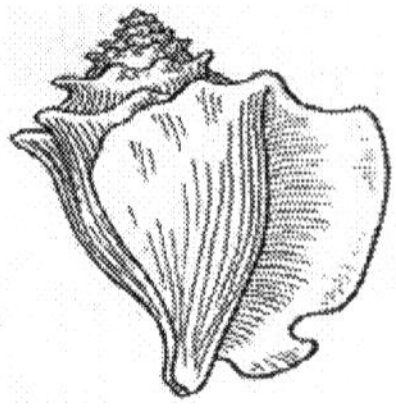

The conch is a symbol of pure sound, represents the primeval sound. The sound that emanates when a *shankha* is blown is the sound OM. *Shankha* thus symbolizes the origin of the Universe from a single source. Lord *Vishṇu* is seen holding conch, symbolizing *Nāda Brahma – Ishvara* in the form of sound.

Deepa (Lamp) 

Light is a symbol of knowledge. Lamps are traditionally made up of clay and the wick is made of cotton. The liquid used is either oil or ghee. The light from these lamps symbolizes removal of darkness and ushering of the rays of knowledge (Self-knowledge) which remove the darkness of ignorance, *avidyā* (ignorance about the true Self, the reality of who we are as *sat chit ānanda Ātmā*).

Sūrya (Sun)

The Sun is the symbol for light. Being the source of light and energy, the Sun is a symbol of creation. The famous *Gāyatrī mantr*a is a prayer to the Lord in the form of Sun, and not to the star Sun, a big ball of burning gas. *Gāyatrī mantra* is a prayer to *Ishvara* in the form of the Sun, to grant the worshipper with light of wisdom, as bright as the Sun.

Tilaka (red dot, sandalwood paste) **_Vibhūti, Bhasma_**

Tilaka is the mark of red powder or sandalwood paste applied to the forehead. Applying *tilaka* symbolizes the retention of the memory of the *Ishvara*, contemplating upon the Reality throughout one's daily activities.

Vibhūti or *Bhasma* is applied to the forehead by some devotees. Symbolism of *vibhūti* – everything in the Universe is transient, everything goes back to ashes and arises from the ashes and thus *vibhūti* represents Lord *Shiva* as time.

It reminds us to turn our minds towards the unchanging Infinite, away from ever changing names and forms in this world.

Nārikela (Coconut)

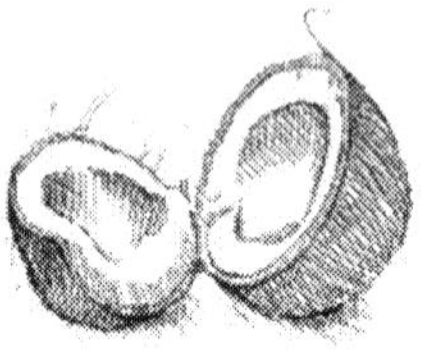

Offering of the coconut suggests transcending the outward layers of body, mind and intellect and realizing the truth of Self within. Offering coconut in a temple or to a *Guru* symbolizes surrendering attachments born out of body, mind and intellect.

Pūnrṇa Kumbha (auspicious pot)

A *"Pūrṇa kumbha"* is a pot filled with water and topped with fresh mango leaves and coconut and is used to begin a *pujā* or any ritual. This pot symbolizes Mother Earth, water symbolizes life source, coconut is the divine Consciousness and mango leaves symbolize life, entire *"Pūrṇa kumbha"* symbolizes goddess *Lakshmī* and good fortune.

Rangoli (decorated symbols on the floor)

Rangoli, also known as *Kolam, Alpana* (or other region specific names) is an art form that uses symbols of auspiciousness from India. Design patterns are created on the floor in front of the house, at the altar in a temple, or in courtyards in order to bring prosperity. They are made with materials such as dry flour, colored rice, sand or flower petals. These designs are usually made on daily basis or during any auspicious occasion or ritual or for Indian festivals.

A *Kolam* (from southern part of India) is a geometrical line drawing composed of curved loops, drawn around a grid pattern of dots. While a *Rangoli* designs can be fixed or free-flowing artistic designs. Every morning many Hindu women draw *Rangoli, kolam* on the ground with white rice flour.

Decoration is not the main purpose of this creative expression of art and designs. In olden days, these were drawn using coarse rice flour, so the ants would not have to go too far for a meal. The rice powder also invited birds and other small creatures, thus acknowledging other beings in everyday life, a daily tribute to harmonious co-existence.

Rangoli is a sign of invitation welcoming all, especially *Lakshmī devī,* the goddess of prosperity and wealth.

Japa mālā and number 108

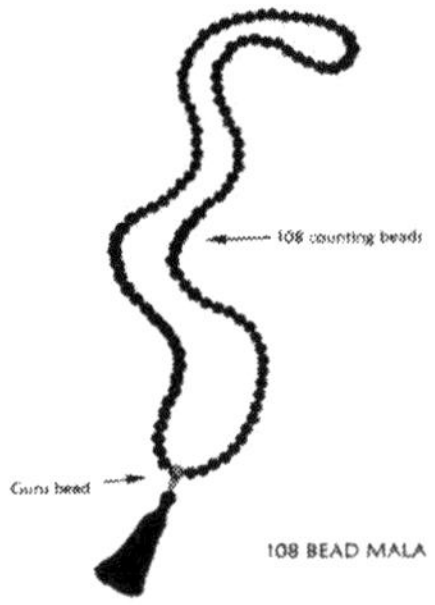

Japa mālā is usually 108 beads long.

108 is a number that symbolically represents completeness. *Rudrāksha* seed *mālā* are associated with Lord *Shiva* and *tulasi* beads with the forms of Lord *Vishṇu*, various other crystal beads or sandalwood beads are also used for *japa mālā*.

A few of the many interesting theories as to why *japa* is done 108 times are as follows:

- In ancient India, Vedic seers had calculated and concluded that the distance (which modern scientific measurements have reconfirmed) between the Earth and the Moon is approximately 108 times the diameter of the Moon.

- 108 times is important as it is the product of 12 zodiac signs and 9 *navagraha,* planets.

- According to certain *Āyurveda* traditions, there are 108 *marma* points throughout the body. A *marma* point is defined as an anatomical site where flesh, veins, arteries, tendons, bones and joints meet. Each point has its own intelligence, which co-ordinate with the mind and body.

OM

जितात्मन: प्रशान्तस्य परमात्मा समाहित: |
शीतोष्णसुखदु:खेषु तथा मानापमानयो: ||७||

Jitātmanaḥ praśhāntasya paramātmā samāhitaḥ|
śhītoṣhṇa-sukha-duḥkheṣhu tathā mānāpamānayoḥ||

"The Yogi who has conquered the mind, rises above the dualities of cold and heat, joy and sorrow, honor and dishonor.
Such a Yogi remains peaceful and steadfast in a state of composure."

~ The Bhagavad Gitā, chapter 6, verse 7

"When the mind is still, Truth gets the chance to be heard in the purity of the silence."

~ Sri Aurobindo

"You are not the mind. If you know you are not the mind, then what difference does it make if it's busy or quiet? You are not the mind."

~ Sri Nisargadatta Mahārāj

Chapter 7

Pronunciations of Hatha Yoga Terms

Key to correct pronunciations

Pay very careful attention to: "**a**" and "**ā**"
"**a**" - sounds like u in "up" or "cup"
"**ā**" - sounds like aa in "car" or "far"

Meaning can be very different for words with "a" or "ā" sound
For example:
"mala" (impurity/waste) and ***"mālā"*** (string)
"bala" (strength) and ***"bāla"*** (child)
"maya" (composed of/made of) and ***"māyā"*** (power)

Other important pronunciations:

ṇ sounds like n in "ant"
gn sounds like gn in "ignite"
g is hard g as in "god", **not** soft g as in "gym"
ś or **ṣ** may both be pronounced as English sh in "shine"
c sounds like ch in "church", **not** like c in "car"
o sounds like o in "opal", as in *loka* (world)
ṛ sounds like r in "grind", as in *Kṛshṇa (Krishna)*
ñ sounds like ñ in "jalapeño"

Āsana names are - prefixes + word *"āsana, Asana, aasana"*
For example:

Taada (mountain) + *aasana* = ***Tādāsana*** *(Taadaasana)*

Trikoṇa (triangle) + *āsana* = ***Trikoṇāsana*** (ṇ like n in "ant")

Vīrabhadra + *aasana* = ***Vīrabhadrāsana*** *(Viirabhadraasana)*

Pronunciations

Frequently used terms in Hatha Yoga practice

Three transliteration schemes:

IAST (diacritical marks), for example - ***ahiṃsā***
HK (ASCII) or ITRANS – ***ahiMsA***
Roman alphabets – ***ahimsaa***

English Names	Sanskrit Names	Meaning
Patañjali's Yoga Sutras	ashtānga, ashtAnga, ashtaanga	ashta = eight, anga = limbs
1st limb	Yama (not Yaama, nor Yaamaa)	self-restraint
—	ahiṃsā, ahiMsA, ahimsaa	non-violence, non- injury
—	satya	truth
—	asteya	non-stealing
—	aprigraha	renouncing
—	brahmacharya	chastity, study of the Veda
2nd limb	Niyama (not Niyaamaa)	precept, rule, law
—	śaucha, shaucha	purity of mind
—	santosha	content
—	tapas	penance, austerity
—	svādhyāya, svAdhyAya, svaadhyaaya	to study, study of the Veda, self-study

English Names	Sanskrit Names	Meaning
—	Īśvara Praṇidhāna, Ishvara praNidhAna, Praṇidhaana (or praṇidhaanam)	prayer or contemplation on Ishvara (Supreme)
3rd limb	āsana, Asana, aasana	posture
4th limb	prāṇāyāma, prANAyAma, praaṇa + aayaama	regulating breath
5th limb	pratyāhāra, pratyAhAra, pratyaahaara	withdrawal (five senses from external objects)
6th limb	dhāraṇā, dhAraNA, dhaaraṇaa	concentration
7th limb	dhyāna, dhyAna, dhyaana	meditation, contemplation
8th limb	samādhi, samAdhi, samaadhi	intense absorption

Āyurveda terms	Dosha ("d" like soft d̲, similar to dental sound "the")	
Ā or ā is a̲a̲ in "fa̲r"	vāta, vAta, vaata (soft "t" - dental sound in "pasta")	vaata = airy element, space + air
t̲t̲ soft dental sound	pit̲t̲a	pitta = fiery fire + water
a̲ like u̲ in "up"	kapha, Kafa	kapha = watery water + earth
Waste	mala, Ama	mala = waste, Ama = indigested
Digestive fire	jathara agni ("gn" as in "ignite", **not** aajni or ajni)	jathara = stomach, agni = fire

English Names	Sanskrit Names	Meaning
Centers (wheels) of energy	Chakra ("Ch" as in China and not Ch as in Chicago, **never** "Shakra")	Chakra = Wheel
Root Chakra	mūlādhāra, mUlAdhAra, moolaadhaara	moola = root, origin + aadhaara = support, base
Sacral	svādhisthāna, svAdhishthAna, svaadhishthaana	one's own place
Naval center	maṇipūra, maNipUra, manipoora	naval
Heart	anāhata, anAhata, anaahata	unstruck, intact
Throat	vishuddha,	very pure, clear
Third eye	ājñā, AgnyA, aagnyaa (**gn** as in "**ign**ite") (**ñ** as in "jalape<u>ñ</u>o")	aagñaa (aagnyaa) = command, order
Crown	sahsrāra, sahasrAra, sahasraara	sahsra = thousand, ara= spokes, petals

Sheaths	Kosha	Layers

<u>a</u> in "maya" sounds like <u>u</u> in "up"

Food	anna-maya	anna = food, maya = composed of
Vital force	prāṇa-maya, pRAṆa-maya, praaṇa-maya	praaNa = vital force + maya
Mind	mano-maya	manas = mind, maya = made of
Intellect	vijñāna-maya, vigyaana-maya or vignyaana-maya (gn, **not** j-n) (**ñ** as in jalape**ñ**o")	vignyaana = intellect, maya = made of

English Names	Sanskrit Names	Meaning
Experiential bliss	ānanda-maya, Ananda-maya, aananda-maya	aananda = blissful experience, maya = made of
Breathing techniques	Prāṇāyāma, PrAṇAyAma, PraaṆaayaama	pRaaNa + aayaam = regulation of pṛāṇa
OM	pṛaṇava, pRaNava	pRaNava = OM
Bellows	bhastrikā, bhastrikA, bhastrikaa	bhastraa = bellows
Victorious breath	ujjayi	ujjayati = be victorious, acquire by conquest
Forehead shining	kapālbhāti , kapAlbhAti, kapaalbhaati	kapaala = forehead, bhaati = shine
Alternate nostril	nādi shodhanā, nAdi shodhanA, naadi shodhanaa	shodhanaa = cleansing
Humming bee	bhṛamarī, bhRamarI, bhramarii	bhRamarii = humming bee
Cooling breath	shitalī, shItalI, shiitalii	shiitala = cold, shiitakara = causing coolness
Inhalation	pūraka, pUraka, pooraka	pooraka = filling
Exhalation	rechaka	rechaka = emptying the lungs
Retention	kumbhaka (**not** kumbhaakaa)	kumbhaka = stopping breath
Three locks	Tri Bandha	tri = three, bandha = lock
Root lock	mūla, mUla, moola	moola = root

English Names	Sanskrit Names	Meaning
Abdominal lock	uḍḍiyaṇa, uDDiyaNa, uddiyaṇa	uddayaNa = flying, soaring
Chin lock	jālandhara, jAlandhara, jaalandhara	jaala = web, dhara = holding
Gaze	Nava dṛshti, dRshti, drishti	nava = nine, drishti = gaze,
Thumb	aṅgustha-madhye	angushtha = thumb, madhye = middle of
Tip of nose	nāsāgre, nAsAgre, naasaagre	naasaa = nose, agre =tip
Hand	hastāgre, hastAgre, hastaagre	hasta = palms of the hand, agre = tip
Sideways (left or right)	pārśva, pArshva, paarshva	paarshva = side
Upward	ūrdhva, Urdhva, oordhva	oordhva = upward, above, rising
Naval	nābhichakre, nAbhi-chakre, naabhi-chakre	naabhi = naval, chakra = circle, entral circle
Toes	pādayoragre, pAdayor-agre, paadayor-agre	paada = feet, agre = tip of
Third eye, ājñā (aagyaa, aagnyaa) chakra	bhrūmadhye, bhrU-madhye, bhroo-madhye	bhroo = eyebrows, madhye = middle of, third eye
Sun Salutations	Sūrya Namaskāra, SUrya NamaskAra, Soorya namaskaara	soorya=sun, namaskaara= salutations
Lunge	ashva sanchālanāsana, ashva sanchAlanAsana (sanchaalanaasana)	ashva = horse, sanchaalana = rider - lunge

English Names	Sanskrit Names	Meaning
Plank	chaturanga dandāsana, chaturanga dandAsana (dandaasana)	chatur = four, anga = body, danda āsana = Plank
Knees chest chin	ashtānga pṛaṇāma, ashtAnga pranNAma, ashtaanga praṇaama	ashta = eight, anga =limbs, pranNaama = salutation
Cobra	bhujangāsana , bhujangAsana, bhujangaasana	bhujanga = cobra snake
Downward facing dog	adho mukha śvānāsana, Adho mukha shvAnAsana (shvaana-asana) - **not** shvanaa	adho = downward, mukha = facing, shvaana = dog
Upward facing dog	ūrdhva mukha śvānāsana, Urdhva mukha shvAnAsana, oordhva mukha shvaanaasan	Urdhva mukha = upward facing, shvaana = dog
Standing forward fold	uttanāsana, uttanAsana, uttanaasana	uttan = intense, stretch or extend or fold
Mountain pose	tādāsana, tAdAsana, taadaasana - always taada, **never** tadaa	taada = mountain + aasana
starting pose of equanimity	samasthitiḥ, samasthitiH, samasthitihi	sama = even, equal, sthiti = position

	Standing āsana	
Warrior poses	Virabhadrāsana 1, 2, 3, VIraBHadrAsana, Viirabhadraasana	Viirabhadra = mighty warrior's name
Intense side stretch, Pyramid pose	pārśvottānāsana, pArshvottanAsana, paarshvottanaasana	paarshva = side, uttan+ aasana = intense forward fold

English Names	Sanskrit Names	Meaning
Triangle	trikoṇāsana, trikonNAsana, trikonaasana	tri = three, koṆa = angle
Revolved triangle	parivṛtta trikoṇāsana, parivRitta trikoNAsana (trikonaasana)	parivRitta = twisted, trikoNa = triangle
Three legged dog	tri pāda adho mukha śvānāsana, tri pAda (paada) adho mukha shvAnAsana (shvaanaasana)	tri = three, paada = leg, shvaana = dog
Crescent lunge	Āñjaneyāsana, AnjaneyAsana, Aanjaneyaasana	Āñjaneya = Lord Hanumaana
Twist in crescent lunge	parivṛitta Āñjaneyāsana, paRivRitta AnjaneyAsana (aanjneyaasana)	parivRita = revolved, Āñjaneya = Lord Hanumaana
Split	Hanumānāsana, HanumAnAsana, Hanumaana+aasana	Lord Hanumaana āsana
Half-split	ardha Hanumānāsana, ardha HanumAnAsana (Hanumaanaasana)	ardha = half, Hanumāna aasana
Chair pose	utkatāsana, utkatAsana, utkataasana	utkata = powerful
Twisted chair	parivṛitta utkatāsana, paRivRitta utkatAsana (utkataasana)	parivrita = twisted, utkata = powerful
Reverse warrior	viparita Virabhadrāsana, viparIta VIraBhadrAsana, vipariita Viirabhadraasana	vipariita = reversed,

English Names	Sanskrit Names	Meaning
Extended side angle	pārśvakoṇāsana, pArshva-koNAsana, paarshva-konaasana	paarshva = extended, koNa= side angle
Half moon	ardha chandrāsana, ardha chandrAsana, ardha chandraasana	ardha = half, Chandra = moon
Wild thing (flipped dog)	chamtkārāsana, chamatkArAsana, chamatkaaraasan (ch as in change)	chamatkaara = amazing
Hands to big toes	pādanguśthāsana, pAdangushthAsana, paadangushthaasana	paada = foot, angushtha = big toe
Hands under feet	pādahastāsana, pAdahastAsana, paadahastaasana	paada = foot, hasta = hand
	Seated āsana	
Boat pose	paripūrṇa nāvāsana, paripUrNa nAvAsana, paripoorna naavaasana OR naukāsana, naukAsana, naukaasana	paripoorNa = complete, nāva or naukā = boat
Upward (east) facing plank	pūrvottanāsana, pUrva+uttan+Asana, poorvottanaasana	poorva = east, uttanaasana = intense forward fold
Seated forward bend	paśchimotanāsana, paschima+uttan+Asana, pashchimottanaasana	pashchim = west
Head to knee forward bend	jānu śirṣāsana, jAnu shIrshAsana, Jaanu shiirshaasana	jaanu = knee, shiirsha = head

English Names	Sanskrit Names	Meaning
Bound angle pose	baddha koṇāsana, baddha koNAsana, baddh koṇaasana	baddha = bound, koNa = angle
Wide-angled seated forward bend	upavishta koṇāsana, upavishta koNAsana (konaasana)	upavishta = sitting, koNa = angle
Big double toe	ubhaya padāngushthāsana, padāngushthAsana (padaangushthaasan)	ubhaya = both, pada +angushtha = big toe
Cat stretch	mārjāryāsana, mArjAryAsana, maarjaaryaasana	maarjaari = cat
Cow face pose	gomukhāsana, gomukhAsana, gomukhaasana	gomukha = cow faced
Camel pose	uśtrāsana, ustrAsana, ushtraasana	ushtra = camel
Lotus pose	padmāsana, padmAsana, padmaasana	padma = lotus
Hero pose	virāsana, vIrAsana, viiraasana	viira = brave, hero
Pigeon pose	kapotāsana, eka pāda rājakapotāsana, eka pAda rAjakapotaAsana, eka paada raaja kapotaasana	kapota = pigeon, eka = one, paada = leg, rājā = king
Thunderbolt pose	vajrāsana, vajrAsana, vajraasana	vajra = thunderbolt
Squatting pose	malāsana, malAsana, malaasana	mala = impurities, waste, mala+aasana

English Names	Sanskrit Names	Meaning
Garland pose	mālāsana, mAlAsana, maalaasana	maalaa = garland maalaa + aasana
Seated spinal twist	ardha matsyendrāsana, ardha matsyendrAsana, matsyendraasana	ardha = half, matsya = fish, matsyendra = yogi, a saint
Seated twist	bharadvājāsana, bharadvAjAsana, bharadvaajaasana	bharadvaaja = name of a Rishi, also a lark
Sage's pose	marichyāsana, marichyAsana, marichyaasana	marichi = name of a Rishi
Seated yoga seal	yogamudrā, yogmudrA, yogamudraa	mudraa = hand position
	Balances	
Tree pose	vṛkśāsana, vRkshAsana, vrkshaasana	vRksha = tree
Lord Natarāja - dancers pose	Natarājāsana, NatarAjAsana, Nataraajaasana	Nataraaja = Lord Shiva
Eagle pose	garudāsana, garudAsana, garudaasana	garuda = eagle
Standing half split	ūrdhva pṛasārita eka pādāsana, Urdhva pRasArita eka pAdAsana, oordhva prasaarita eka paadaasana	Urdhva = upward, prasaarita = streached
Peacock pose	ardha pincha mayūrāsana, pincha mayUrAsana, pincha mayooraasana	ardha = half, pincha mayoora = peacock

English Names	Sanskrit Names	Meaning
Crane pose	bakāsana, bakAsana, bakaasana	baka = crane
Crow pose	kākāsana, kAkAsana, kaakaasana	kaaka = crow
Supported headstand	sālamba śirṣāsana, sAlamba shIrshAsana, saalamba shiirshaasana	sa = with,aalamba =support, shiirsha= head
Headstand	śirṣāsana, shIrshAsana, shiirshaasana	shiirsha= head

	Prone and reclining āsana	
Sphinx pose	sālamba bujangāsana, sAlamba bhujangAsana, saalamba bhujangaasana	sa = with, aalamba =support, bhujanga =cobra
Frog pose	bhekāsana (maṇdūkāsana), bhekAsana (maNdUkAsana), bhekaasana (maNdookaasana)	bheka = frog, maNdooka = frog
Locust pose	śalabhāsana, shalabhAsana, shalabhaasana	shalabha = locust
Bow pose	dhanurāsana, dhanurAsana, dhanuraasana	dhanush = bow, dhanuraakaara = bow shaped
Lord Vishnu's pose, side reclining leg lift	Anantāsana, anatAsana, anantaasana	Ananta = Infinite, endless

English Names	Sanskrit Names	Meaning
Abdominal twist	jathara parivartanāsana, parivartanAsana, parivartanaasana	jathara = stomach, parivartana = turn around
Reclining bound angle pose	supta baddha koṇāsana, supta baddha KoNAsana, konaasana	sputa = reclining, baddha = bound, koNa= angle
Wind release pose	pawanmuktāsana, pawan muktAsana, muktaasana	pawan = wind, mukta =release
Knees to chest pose	apānāsana, apAnAsana, apaanaasana	apaana = one of the five Praṇa
Happy baby pose	ānanda-bālāsana, Ananda-bAlAsana, aananda-baalaasana	ānanda = happy, baala = baby
Bridge pose	setu bandha sarvāngāsana, sarvAngAsana, sarvaangaasana	setu = bridge, sarva = every, anga = limbs of the body
Plough pose	halāsana, halAsana, halaasana	hala = plough
Shoulder stand - without support	sālamba sarvangāsana, sAlamba sarvAngAsana, saalamba sarvaangaasana	saalamba = without support, sarva = every, anga = limb
Fish pose	matsyāsana, matsyAsana, matsyaasana	matsya = fish
Corpse pose	śavāsana, shavAsana, shavaasana	shava (śava) = corpse, aasana =

For more on Pronunciations: www.yogatomasterthemind.com

Om Tat Sat

Other Resources for In-depth Study

Please visit: **www.yogatomasterthemind.com**

Patañjali's Yoga Sutras

The Yoga Sutras of Patañjali - by Sri Swami Satchidananda
http://www.arshabodha.org/yogasutra.html
http://swamij.com/yoga-sutras-intro.htm
Patañjali's Yoga Sutras - by A.K. Aruna

The Bhagavad Gitā

The teaching of the Bhagavad Gita - by Swami Dayananda
The Holy Geeta – by Swami Chinmayananda
http://www.arshabodha.org/gita2011.html
http://www.arshabodha.org/bhagavadgita.html

Mantra chanting

Mantra Yoga and Primal Sound - by David Frawley
http://www.arshabodha.org/chanting.html
http://swamij.com/index-yoga-meditation-mantra.htm

To learn Sanskrit

http://avg-sanskrit.org/introduction-to-sanskrit/
http://www.samskritabharatiusa.org/
http://www.arshabodha.org/IntroductorySanskrit.html
http://learnsanskritonline.com/
http://www.sanskritsounds.com/about-sanskrit/46/index.html

Meditation and Vedānta

Introduction to Vedanta - by Swami Dayananda
Meditation-A Journey of Exploration - Swami Tadatmananda
Vedantic Meditation, Vedic yoga - by David Frawley
http://www.arshabodha.org/teachings.html
http://www.arshavm.org/
http://www.arshavidya.org/home.html

Pronunciations of Yoga terminology

The Language of Yoga – by Nicolai Bachman
http://www.tilakpyle.com/sanskrit.htm

About the Author

Born and raised in India, Anjani Gharpure received Business and Law degrees and has been a resident of USA since 1990. She has completed her MBA in Finance. Instead of entering the corporate workplace, Anjani decided to volunteer for various non-profit organizations. Deep interest in the study of the scriptures, under the guidance of world renowned scholars of Advaita Vedānta, helped Anjani delve deeper into Vedānta and study of Yoga – Yoga philosophy in particular.

Having had the privilege to study texts which impart invaluable spiritual wisdom, from the teachers established in long standing lineage of teaching tradition – *guru shishya parmparā*, Anjani decided to first teach at local Yoga teacher trainings. From the initial Yoga certification program onwards, Anjani has been actively involved in teaching Yoga philosophy at each and every certification program she has attended, including Yoga for Children, Therapeutic Yoga, and Yoga for Cancer patients.

As it was not possible to reach out to innumerable Yoga teacher-training-programs in person, Anjani decided to compile this guidebook to address the need for an easy-to-use handbook on the authentic teachings of Yoga philosophy, as taught by the traditional scholars of Vedānta.

Three important questions compelled Anjani to undertake the project of creating a concise handbook on various topics of philosophy of Yoga:

1- Yoga is marketed mostly as a physical practice and mistaken for an exercise regimen, focusing only on the fitness and wellness of the body. How does an average person get access to the very important authentic spiritual teaching of Yoga on fitness and wellness of the mind?

2- What about the future generations? Without proper training and appropriate teachings of Yoga philosophy, what version of Yoga will be passed on to our future generations?

3- What is the methodology used for teaching Yoga philosophy to Yoga teacher trainees? Are there any standardized textbooks that are followed by all seeking Yoga teacher certification? And in absence of any methodology or standardized text books, how does a Yoga teacher trainee meet the certification requirement of 40 to 60 hours study of Yoga philosophy?

"Yoga to Master the Mind" is a handbook presenting the basics of all relevant topics of Yoga philosophy in a short concise format, through the lens of Vedānta, as taught by the sages of ancient India.

This guidebook is for Yoga teacher trainees, Yoga instructors, Yoga practitioners and enthusiasts to understand the spiritual teachings of Yoga.

OM

Please visit:

www.yogatomasterthemind.com

॥ ॐ श्री गुरुभ्यो नमः हरिः ॐ ॥

Om Shri Gurubhyo Namaḥ Hariḥ Om ll

"My reverential salutations unto all my teachers (*guru*)."
"Hariḥ Om."

Printed in Great Britain
by Amazon

50229412R00208